"A provocative starting point for a discussion that has long needed to take place in church planting circles. In this book, Sean and his compatriots have raised a series of issues related to gentrification and re-gentrification of urban center neighborhoods, while skewering simplistic and romanticized notions of planting churches in places where they could do as much harm as any good they might do."

Al Barth
Global Network Coordinator
Redeemer City to City

"The topic of gentrification has become a bit of a hot-button issue. Some see it as a solution to urban revitalization, while others believe it causes real harm to real people. In his latest book, Sean Benesh (and his co-conspirators) give the church an extremely helpful resource that not only sorts out the complexities of the issue, but also provides real, practical steps of engagement for those with a passion for loving cities in all the right ways. I highly recommend this resource for anyone who desires to see a true reflection of the Kingdom birthed in the city they live in."

Brad Brisco
Author of *Missional Essentials* and *The Missional Quest*

"Is one supposed to smile widely while reading an intellectually thorough, investigative, and missiological volume like this one? Possibly not, but I found its multifaceted approach, refusal to label complex concepts simplistically, and present-future outlook truly delightful. A wonderful contribution to the study of urban ministry."

Linda Bergquist
Author *The Wholehearted Church Planter* and *Church Turned Inside Out*

"Restoration, renewal, and reconciliation are the building blocks of city life lived in community. This book is a must-read for city practitioners, including the Church, who desire not only to restore old buildings or renew the spirit of entrepreneurship, but also to reconcile longstanding cultural and generational differences to build healthy communities. Who then is responsible for the transformation of the human spirit, as well as for the multiple facets in the gentrification process? Is it each individual, organization (both for-profit and non-profit), or city government?"

Earnestine Cellestine
Vice President of Academic Affairs
North Portland Bible College

"One part theology, one part sociology, and one part missiology, this work on urban ministry is a necessary tool in the kitbag of any church planter who is serious about urban ministry. Whereas the majority of books about planting map the geographical borders of the targeted zone, this book also explores the zone within, and focuses on where those two borders meet. An invaluable study."

Peyton Jones
Founder, New Breed Church Planting
Managing Editor, *Church Planter Magazine*
Author of *Church Zero*

"This book is a must-read for every single person who cares about the city in any way. The complex topic of gentrification absolutely needed to be researched and handled in this honest, in-depth way by concerned and committed Christians who love the cities. I often struggle to do the topic of gentrification justice in urban classes because of the multi-layered complexities of its nature. This book will be a resource I will use personally and point students to again and again. With pleasure!"

Kendi Howells Douglas
Professor of Cross-Cultural Ministries
Great Lakes Christian College

"Do you love the city? The United Nations predicts that by 2050 one-half of the world's population will be squatters or urban poor slum-dwellers. In his skillfully crafted book, Sean Benesh and his selected contributors help us understand the dynamics of the changing urban landscape and force us to consider appropriate ministry responses. We are all called to serve in our own contexts, and for most of us, that means the city."

Doug Priest
Executive Director
CMF International

"I have struggled with the challenges of gentrification first-hand in the multicultural urban neighborhood where we lived and founded Urban Neighbours Of Hope. After about a decade, our neighborhood in Kelvin Grove, Springvale, Melbourne, went from being considered one of the worst streets to one of the most sought-after in the area. Real transformation was happening. Public drug use and violence disappeared. A sense of village emerged where residents began to trust and value each other's diverse cultures, foods, and gifts. However, there were also unintended consequences. The price of rents, for example, doubled, and the local leaders who came to faith and helped make this transformation possible could not afford to stay there. Our friends and neighbours were again dispersed to cheaper neighbourhoods around the city while other, more well-healed folks, reaped the neighbourhood's newly celebrated benefits. This is the first book that I know of that tackles this phenomenon from a Christian perspective. As such this is a crucial read for any Christian who wants to love their neighbours and neighbourhood enough to seek holistic change. I am grateful for Sean and his assembled activists-thinkers for engaging this important challenge to the neighborhood transformation processes and wish I had this book 20 years ago!"

Ash Barker
Convener, International Society for Urban Mission (newurbanworld.org)
Author of *Slum Life Rising* and *Make Poverty Personal*

"Despite the undeniable fact of the urbanization of our planet, the church of Jesus Christ still seems resistant to transform itself for the sake of her mission. Sean has thought deeply about the sociological implications of urbanization, and from that proposes an unexpected yet helpful missiological response. Beyond a simple suburban or urban strategy preference of ministry application, this book will drive its readers to an introspective analysis of the urban church, the Kingdom of God, and ultimately how Christ's followers might behave if the King got His way."

Jeff Christopherson
Vice-President, Canada, Northeast US
North American Mission Board
Author of *The Kingdom Matrix*

Vespas, Cafes, Singlespeed Bikes, and Urban Hipsters

Vespas, Cafes, Singlespeed Bikes, and Urban Hipsters

Gentrification, Urban Mission, and Church Planting

SEAN BENESH

Editor

Urban Loft Publishers | Portland, Oregon

Vespas, Cafes, Singlespeed Bikes, and Urban Hipsters
Gentrification, Urban Mission, and Church Planting

Urban Loft Publishers
2034 NE 40th Avenue #414
Portland, OR 97212
www.theurbanloft.org

ISBN-13: 978-1492846345
ISBN-10: 1492846341

Made in the U.S.A.

To those engaged in urban mission.

Contents

PART II: CHURCH PLANTING AND GENTRIFICATION

PART III: RESPONDING TO GENTRIFICATION

Contributors

Dave Arnold

Dave Arnold is an author (*Pilgrims of the Alley*), blogger, speaker, minister, and an advocate for refugees and immigrants. He's worked with refugee ministry for the last eight years, including five with World Relief in Chicago. He is currently working with immigrants from the Middle East in Dearborn, MI. Dave is married to Angie and they have one son, Luke, who is three years old. To learn more, go to www.reflectionsfromthealley.org.

Cole Brown

Cole Brown is founding and lead pastor of Emmaus Church, a multi-ethnic church in Portland, Oregon, where he lives with his wife and two children. He is author of *Lies My Pastor Told Me* and *Lies Hip Hop Told Me* and blogs at www.colebrownpdx.com.

Michael Carpenter

Michael Carpenter is a church planter (www.churchargenta.org) and small business owner (www.mugscafe.org) in the Argenta Arts District of North Little Rock, Arkansas. He and his wife Amanda have been married since 2003 and have two children—Austin and Max. Michael is an entrepreneur, a lover of coffee, and a missiologist. He leads the way in engaging culture with the gospel though proclamation and service. Michael hold a BA in Christian Ministries from Williams Baptist College and a MA in Global Leadership from Fuller Theological Seminary.

Michael Crane

Michael Crane (MDiv, ThM, PhD) has lived in global cities in Southeast Asia for most of his life. He is currently teaching urban missiology at a seminary and working with Christian leaders who desire to bring transformative change to their cities. Michael and his family also spend time helping refugees who come through their city.

Caleb Crider

Caleb and is co-author of *Tradecraft: For The Church On Mission*. Caleb and his family lived in Spain for six years. He currently resides in Richmond, Virginia, with his wife, two children, a dog, and some chickens. Caleb works for the International Mission Board of the Southern Baptist Convention. He believes that all Christians everywhere should think and act like missionaries.

Jon Hall

The grandson of a Pentecostal preacher, a mechanic and a peanut farmer, Jon's roots are in the rural towns of Central California. A big chunk of his life was spent as a child of the suburban master-planned neighborhoods of Southern California, eventually moving to the urban setting of San Diego, which he now considers his true home.

Jon's favorite t-shirt is the one that says "I Draw Pictures All Day," a self-inflicted jab at his 25 years in the creative services world of design, branding, and marketing. He's served on church board and staff positions, helped establish a neighborhood-based missional-monastic community in Golden Hill outside downtown San Diego called NieuCommunities and considers himself a student of place, neighborhood and the arts. He's a husband, father to three young ladies, a rescued dog and owns/operates two local businesses in his neighborhood. And oh yeah, he's currently learning the ukulele.

Jon Huckins

Jon Huckins is on staff with NieuCommunities. He is also the co-founder and CEO of The Global Immersion Project, which cultivates everyday peacemakers through immersion in global conflict. Jon has a Master's from Fuller Theological Seminary and writes for *RELEVANT Magazine, Sojourners, Red Letter Christians* and numerous other publications. He has written two books, *Teaching Through the Art of Storytelling* and *Thin Places*. Jon sits on his neighborhood council, helps manage the local famers market and spends as much time as possible with his wife, Jan, and two daughters, Ruby and Rosie.

Orvic Pada

Orvic Pada is a sociologist whose urban-immersion experiences range include major urban centers in the Philippines, Brazil, and California. He currently conducts research on urban transformation, and is an adjunct professor at Biola

University, Chapman University, and California State University Fullerton. His research interests are in urban studies, globalization and development, multiculturalism in faith-based groups, race and ethnicity, and gender.

Brandon Rhodes

Brandon Rhodes (D.Min) is a freelance writer and lay scholar exploring God's reign with Springwater, a neighborhood church in Lents, Oregon. He serves as Grassroots Storyteller and Field Guide for the Parish Collective, a motley network of churches and Christian practitioners rooted in neighborhoods and linked across cities. Brandon is currently completing a book manuscript on the past, present, and future effects of cars and cheap oil on American Christianity. His writings have appeared in *The Intentional Christian Community Handbook, Christianity Today, Conspire Magazine, PRISM Magazine,* JesusRadicals.com, *The Englewood Review of Books,* and more.

Glenn Smith

Glenn Smith is the executive director of Christian Direction in Montréal, Quebec, and professor of Urban Missiology at the Institut de théologie pour la francophonie in Montréal affiliated with Université Laval and the Université chrétienne du nord d'Haïti in Limbé, Haïti. He is also adjunct professor of Mission at the Montréal School of Theology at McGill University.

Preface

Gentrification. It's probably one of the most polarizing words that is spoken today. Depending on where one lives this word can find its way into everyday conversation where it is as normative as talking about the weather, politics, or favorite local sports teams. Yet for a large swath of North American society this term is as foreign as trying to understand cricket matches in Mumbai. I have been on both sides of the fence and both sides of the above scenario.

I still remember when I first heard of gentrification. It was in one of those settings—a room full of doctoral students—where I was squeamish about revealing that I had no idea what the word even meant as everyone else in the room batted it around like a volleyball. Since that day I have been on a personal quest to not only understand and study gentrification, but to seek to uncover the missiological implications for existing churches in these kinds of transitioning neighborhoods as well as the role that new church plants can (or should) play in these same neighborhoods. This book stems from this quest.

Of all of the books I have written this has by far been the most difficult and the most time-consuming. Usually when I delve into a writing project I am on a strict writing schedule and plow through until I am complete. Writing this Preface comes on the heels of me sending off to my publisher the manuscript for another book, *The Urbanity of the Bible.* Before typesetting it had come to 315 pages, not including the bibliography or front matter. That took six months to write despite its academic nature (675 footnotes). This book has been simmering, percolating, and slow-roasting for over two years now.

Every time I would start down a particular line of thought about gentrification I would inevitably uncover more layers, perspectives, nuances, and disciplines with which to view the topic at hand. I would then pause my writing to attempt to gain a better grasp on these various perspectives ... because there are many. You see, gentrification is more than simply about succession of different population segments, socioeconomic groupings, and ethnicities in neighborhoods. There are multiple macro and micro actors and movements involved ranging from global to local economics, systemic racism, mobility and transportation, globalization, urbanization, immigration, changing cultural preferences, real estate speculation and development, architecture, education, and that is only the tip of the proverbial iceberg.

My hope in this book is to humbly and simply broach the topic and extract specific essentials from the conversation that are most relevant for the church and urban mission. Due to the volatile nature of the topic I am confident I will write something that offends someone as at times I try to articulate my position and where I stand on certain points of the gentrification debates. I also am fully aware of my own leanings, biases, worldview, upbringing, inclinations, and perspective which make me even more inclined to tread lightly, with fear and humility, into this controversial topic.

More specifically, I am white. I am middle class. It could be argued that I am a dreaded gentrifier as I pedal my singlespeed bicycle from coffee shop to brew pub. I grew up in small-town Iowa in a predominantly white town except for the Native American settlement on the edge of town. In other words, I did not grow up as a member of an ethnic minority watching my neighborhood bottom out and become blighted due to neglect. I have never lived through the process of neighborhood succession and displacement by being priced out of my home due to an influx of people more affluent than me. I admit that I have cultural blindspots when addressing this topic because of my ethnicity and upbringing. I am not neither apologizing nor indulging in *white guilt*, but simply admitting that I approach the topic from the only vantage point I know ... my own.

I am also acutely aware of the theological dividing lines on this issue that are played out in print, social media, and the blogosphere between the Neo-Reformed and the Neo-Anabaptists. Given the current negativity and mudslinging associated with these different theological frameworks, I have purposely made this book not about one side or the other. In fact, I have intentionally invited *both* sides to contribute to this book—those who humbly hold to a Reformed orthodoxy, and those who are Anabaptist in orthodoxy. What I aim for in this book is a helpful and informative *orthopraxy*. That does not diminish my own theological leanings nor the need to cast everything in light of theology, which I have attempted to do, but rather to let you the reader know that this is not about one side or the other. Surprisingly to most, both sides take different approaches and postures in living out urban mission in gentrifying neighborhoods which is needed. I applaud and affirm.

Lastly, I fully recognize that the topics and the various voices heard within this book do not reflect all of the actors and participants in the gentrification process. My hope is that in successive editions we can expand the African-American and Hispanic perspectives as well as include the perspectives of others who are willing or unwilling participants in neighborhood succession.

In light of everything that I have just shared here, one of the realities that surfaces is the presence of tension. My goal is not to dispel it nor write it away, but instead to humbly ask that you abide in it as you wrestle with gentrification and how to embrace the *missio Dei* in these neighborhoods and districts that are in need of both Gospel demonstration and Gospel proclamation.

Acknowledgements

I'd like to thank each of the contributors who made this book what it is. Your contributions are invaluable and I could not have done this without you! Thanks as always to Frank Stirk for his work in crafting and shaping this manuscript.

Introduction

The large coffee shop windows offered Darren a glimpse into two worlds simultaneously. As if he was straddling the threshold between two parallel dimensions, his seat by the window offered him an opportunity to read, journal, and reflect on what he was observing inside the coffee shop and then the street scene outside. Six months ago Darren jumped into the deep end of the pool and moved into this inner-city urban neighborhood which we will call Goldfield after graduating from a seminary on the east coast.

Along with his wife of four years and their five-month-old daughter, Darren felt compelled to plant a new church somewhere. But where? During his time in seminary Darren became enraptured with the changing dynamics of the city and the transformations taking place in cities across the country, especially in his home town of Cincinnati. The Cincinnati of his adulthood has changed significantly from the Cincinnati of his childhood. No longer did he think of the downtown and inner city as places to be avoided or to quickly exit after a sports event. Now seeing the changes taking place there he fell in love with it. He loved the incoming transformations, the repurposing of historic buildings—including the new restaurants, coffee shops, brew pubs, and loft conversions.

While in seminary Darren felt his generalized calling to pastoral ministries and missions become more and more focused on church planting. He ended up taking classes on church planting, but that only soured him on the idea of becoming a church planter. His professor was a Baby Boomer who espoused the ideals of planting attractional churches in the suburbs. Darren read lots and heard more about church planters and the churches they planted like Bill Hybels and Willow Creek, and Rick Warren and Saddleback Church, and many more. While he was humbled and encouraged to hear of their faithfulness and how God had used them, he had no desire to start a church in the type of suburb that he had grown up in. It wasn't his frontier. So he turned his attention to urban ministry.

What he learned in the urban ministry courses he took was the polar opposite of what he had heard in his church planting classes. The only similarities between the two were the faithfulness of the pastors and church planters who took risks, trusted God, and believed wildly in his power. Most of the topics addressed revolved around homeless ministry, dealing with drug addictions, community development, welfare, crime, and all other things typically associated with the late-twentieth-century inner city. But something simply didn't click. Darren still felt the same sort of disconnect. When he would visit his parents in Cincinnati and go into the city he saw something different from what was being taught in his classes. He watched the city being revitalized and the tide of out-migration slow and stop. When Darren would visit other cities back east ... Boston, Manhattan, Brooklyn or Portland, Maine ... he noted that their urban cores were becoming increasingly desirable to him. The images of the typical inner cities of his childhood were quickly being abandoned in favor of something new and better.

Through conversations with his denomination, Darren and his wife began exploring options of not only which city to move to, but also which neighborhood to dive into. Through much prayer, conversations with denominational church planting leaders and his wife, visiting several cities, and much online research they had narrowed down their focus to three different neighborhoods in two cities. They prayerfully visited each one, but there was something about Goldfield that captured their hearts and imagination. With the backing of hundreds of prayer partners and with most of their funding raised they moved.

Goldfield as a neighborhood is turning the corner in terms of revitalization. Its worst days as a high-crime urban neighborhood are over. It's now on the front end of a trajectory that will change its identity over the ensuing decades. As a result there are still pockets where Darren and his family were able to buy an affordable small walk-up apartment. It is a third story unit in a building built in the late 1800s when the neighborhood comprised almost exclusively German immigrants. The cornerstones on many of its building tell the story of the place whether they be churches, meeting halls, or businesses. Back in the day, German immigrants would land in Goldfield (before it was called Goldfield) and live there for a couple of generations as their ethnic enclave grew. It was a tight-knit community where everyone knew everyone much like you would find in a small town, except that this was a large city.

But then things began to change. The 1920s and 1930s were the high-water mark for this German neighborhood as expansion towards the sunbelt states and new jobs caused many families to move west. Add to the mix the aging nature of its buildings. The neighborhood began showing signs of distress. Families moved out, and buildings didn't always get the repairs they needed. The rise of suburbia also meant that many younger families opted to move out of the city for greener pastures and a yard. On the heels of the out-migration of ethnic Germans came the in-migration of African-Americans from the South who had moved north looking for manufacturing jobs. The neighborhood continued to transform from almost exclusively white to almost exclusively black.

By the 1980s Goldfield was a shell of its former self as buildings deteriorated even more. Landlords and owners no longer cared about maintaining their properties. The building stock was in shambles and unsafe. Some of the buildings would simply collapse due to age and neglect. Once part of a four story apartment building simply caved in killing 13 people ... all African-Americans. This only stirred up the angst of the current populace. They felt neglected ... which they were. Frustration turned to violence along with the proliferation of an informal economy that included drugs and prostitution. Riots were not uncommon as more and more of the basic services were simply cut off. Buildings burned, people were shot and stabbed, and fire and ambulance services were at best slow to respond. Schools fell behind in performance ratings as children had more on their minds than basic arithmetic or learning about the rise of ancient Greece.

Darren was aware of these dynamics when he moved into Goldfield. He had learned much from Wikipedia and other websites, but he wasn't prepared for what life would *really* be like. Beginning in the mid-90s Goldfield had shown signs of change and transformation. Actually, many would argue that the genesis of these changes started in the late 70s and early 80s when a group of local artists began moving into several abandoned building. As the 90s wore on this artist colony not only grew in size, but also in popularity as they brought signs of change to a declining neighborhood. Some of these artists banded together to start a non-profit that taught art to neighborhood kids after school. Many of the locals grew to love and appreciate their efforts of positively contributing to life in the hood. It wasn't *us* versus *them* ... it was simply *us* ... black, white, it didn't matter, because they all called Goldfield home.

However, these artists, not by any intention on their part, actually grew in size and expanded their reach. They were running several art galleries that garnered positive reviews in the local culture section of the metro newspaper and in various magazines. One of the friends of the artists who moved in started a high-end French bistro next to one of the art galleries which was also next to a black soul food restaurant. It was lively and fun. The newcomers loved the dynamics of the neighborhood and the established neighborhood loved to see the positive changes. However, what started off as a trickle eventually turned into a torrent. Goldfield's proximity to the city's central business district and decades of sprawling suburbanization made this a desirable neighborhood. It was a prime location for a new in-migration and the work that these artists started soon began to take over block by block.

And so Goldfield became "*the* place." High-end restaurants began opening and old, defunct factories began to be converted into swank residential lofts by developers and speculators hoping to beat the rush to the next housing boom. And they did. By the time Darren and his family moved into Goldfield in the early 2000s the neighborhood had already changed dramatically, but it was far from complete. It had gone from 93 percent African-American to now about 60 percent. The rest were the newcomers and most of them were ethnic whites. The tensions and the angst felt the community had felt in the 70s and 80s did not dissipate, but had only shifted.

From Darren's vantage point at Shift Coffee, the scenes both inside and outside through the big windows represented a snapshot of the current state of affairs in Goldfield. On the inside, all of the patrons are white and middle class, and included a large number of creative-types who were trying to get established in their respective industries. This is a pretty typical scene in a neighborhood that is still mostly black. However, the scene outside told a different story. The brick four- to six story buildings on both sides of the street were showing signs of transition. From coffee shop to brew pub to the barber that still caters to the black community to the pawn shop to the art gallery, this is typical in Goldfield. A block down where there was once a vacant lot known as a place to buy crack, the foundation is being dug for a new five story apartment building. This new addition to the neighborhood will offer no parking for cars but instead ample indoor secured bicycle parking that caters to a specific demographic ... the young creative class ... who are predominantly white.

When Darren and his young family moved into Goldfield they had every intention of starting a church for this creative class. The imagery and appeal of the prospectus they put together for raising funds looked like a continuous ad for Chrome bags, clothing, and shoes. Even their church name and logo were strategically crafted with the young hipster in mind. When they met with potential financial partners they hyped the whole inner-city thing and the need to reach those who were moving back into these neighborhoods ... the new power-brokers and cultural creatives shaping the city. However, just six months later Darren was again feeling uneasy.

What about the majority population that is black? How could I have simply and blindly looked over them? Darren wrote in his journal that morning. Those questions haunted him as he penned them. He was almost too embarrassed to write those words. In a moment of honesty he felt ashamed. God is all about justice, mercy, equity, and the care for the marginalized but yet everything about Darren's new church catered to and focused on the creative class who by and large are white and affluent. With that Darren packed up his computer and journal and walked out of the coffee shop. With a knot in his stomach he slowly made his way home unsure of what to do next ...

Introduction

PART I
LAYING THE FOUNDATION
FOR GENTRIFICATION

Gentrification is one of those misunderstood words. Depending on the source it can either be touted as destructive or helpful or somewhere in between. The trajectory of Part 1 is to dispel some of these misunderstandings, assumptions, and myths about gentrification. Whether you are well-versed on the topic or tentatively sticking your proverbial toes in the water, Part 1 will lay much of the groundwork and foundation for the book. In this section we will look at some examples of gentrification as well as at those who are being displaced by the process. Defining gentrification is also paramount as the chapter addressing definitions weaves through numerous variances of the process and where the differences arise. We will continue to strive to flesh out what it looks like on the ground here in Portland through a case study involving conflicts surrounding race, economics, and bicycles.

We also must be honest in our admission that for those who are deemed gentrifiers there are many aspects of gentrification that many find appealing. There has to be a reason (and several at that) as to why the middle class have moved back and are moving back into the central city in droves. We will explore that together and begin sorting through the positive and negative elements of the process. In the discourse on gentrification, while this book is far from exhaustive on the topic, there are several chapters in this section that widen the scope, tackling it from a global point of view outside of North America as well as digging deeper into issues of race and religion in gentrifying neighborhoods.

It is assumed that the readership of this book will be urban ministry practitioners, pastors, church planters, denominational leaders, and professors of urban ministry, urban mission, and urban church planting. Throughout the book we attempted to make sure that it is not too technical or academic, but still weighty enough for the classroom (and coffee shop). At times we dive deep into some of the more technical aspects of gentrification, while at other times stepping back to flesh out these concepts with stories, examples, and case studies. Part 1 reflects this healthy tension. Again, this book is written for the church by the church.

Chapter 1

The Tale of Two Neighborhoods
Sean Benesh

The scene up on Alberta Street in NE Portland was dizzying in terms of sensory overload. I walked my singlespeed bike through the dense crowd that filled the streets as dusk turned to darkness. If one wanted to find a vibrant urban scene (Portland-style) then this was it. City block after city block, the street, blocked off from vehicular traffic, was filled with vendors, dancers, musicians, food carts, and pedestrians mingling and flowing in and out of cafes and restaurants that lined the streets. Wafting through the air was a mixture of smells of various ethnic and eclectic foods, beer, cigarettes, and marijuana. There seemed to be a common storyline to those who were there that evening. Most were young, tattooed, urban hipsters ... hip, trendy, and white at that. Sprinkled in among the burgeoning crowd of thousands were a few African-Americans. In some ways remnants of what used to identify this part of the city. Welcome to inner-city Portland.

Just a week before this event I had coffee with one of the directors of a local non-profit that focuses on bicycling advocacy and education. They also run a bike shop up on Alberta Street. I listened intently as she unfolded the story of what this neighborhood was like back in the mid-90s. Alberta Street, where the giant street party took place, was once mostly boarded-up and a poster child of urban blight. Fast forward to today, and it is lined with cafes, coffee shops, restaurants, chic fashion boutiques, micro-breweries, art galleries, and other odd assortments. Portland State University professor Karen Gibson writes of this transition in an article entitled "Bleeding Albina,"[1] "In the 1990s, for the first time in 50 years, the population of Albina grew. The pattern of racial transition was reversed, as Whites reclaimed the housing they had left decades earlier, enticed by the Victorian housing stock, affordable prices, and reinvestment efforts the city had been making."[2] The Alberta Arts District has quickly become one of our favorite parts of the city to spend time in as we lived only blocks away when we first moved to Portland. It's always buzzing with activity and cultural energy. According to the ever-popular Wikipedia, "Since the 'Urban Renewal' in the Northeast area, Alberta Street is the heart of an arts, restaurant, and shopping district approximately 20 blocks long. The area around Alberta is becoming very popular with yuppies as well as hipsters, bohemians, hippies and other groups associated with the counterculture."[3]

It was a disorienting transition from Vancouver, BC, Canada, to Portland, Oregon. We moved from a neighborhood that was marked by immigration, condensed multiculturalism, new urbanism, transit-oriented development, and high-density. In many ways we were in the minority but now we find ourselves in the majority. All of a sudden we realized just how much we fit in here. The bike tire tattoo above my right ankle I got years ago as a hiking and mountain biking guide now is normative and if anything, I may need more tattoos to fit in. Portland most certainly lives up to its reputation as a bike-friendly city. "Portland has become *the* place for bikes."[4]

One of the first things we noticed were all of the two-wheeled pedal-powered commuters on the road. It was mesmerizing and intoxicating. I had found a home and felt like a six-year-old in a Lego store. While I brought a couple of mountain bikes with me when we moved, one of the first things I did was go out and get a singlespeed urban bike ... just like many of the bikes I see racing up and down the streets minute by minute from dawn until dusk (and after). Portland-based author Jeff Mapes says of this phenomenon, "Portland residents use the bike for transportation more than any other large city in

---

1 Albina is a larger area in NE Portland that encompasses numerous neighborhoods that made up this historic African-American community.

2 Gibson, "Bleeding Albina," 20.

3 Wikimedia Foundation Inc., "Alberta Street, Portland, Oregon."

4 Heying, *Brew to Bikes*, 108.

America, and the city has gained an international reputation for encouraging bicycling."5 Years ago I thought I was on to something when I began riding singlespeed mountain bikes in the desert foothills of the Santa Catalina Mountains in Tucson only to realize that they are incredibly popular and the preferred steel horse of the urban hipster cowboy (or cowgirl).

For the first six months in Portland we lived across from a tree-filled park. On the second night after moving into the neighborhood I stepped outside onto the front porch and heard the distinct sound of electric guitar distortion in the distance. I followed the sound until I came across a spontaneous concert in the middle of the park on one of the covered basketball courts. I ran back home to get the rest of the family. We sat in the cool evening grass with about forty other onlookers while we watched and listened to the band, some kind of alternative punk bland, play before an audience of earthy neo-hippie types. By the assortment of bicycles that dotted the hillside it appeared that most had biked to the park. It was a surreal scene for me as I was attempting to grasp the scope of the transition we just made from a city like Vancouver to Portland. From heterogeneous to mostly homogeneous. It is truly a city of paradoxes. In my first week in Portland I saw a giant man in a kilt, another guy sunbathing in a busy park while wearing a speedo, and an array of Vespa scooters. Welcome to Portland.

Neighborhood after neighborhood across central city Portland the storyline remains constant with varying degrees of differentiation distinguishing one district from the other. Districts, streets, and neighborhoods like Hawthorne, Belmont, Mississippi, Alberta, the Pearl, and Nob Hill are all incredibly desirous places not only to socialize and shop, but to live. Housing and rent prices are reflective of this reality. Not too long ago it was almost impossible to obtain bank financing to buy or renovate a home in Albina in NE and North Portland. Segregation was rampant and a painful reminder of the city's ugly past. As Gibson notes, "Segregation is a tool of social and economic control that operates by confining Black citizens to a designated section of the city."6 Whereas once these places were identified as urban blight, and white flight ensued in some

---

5 Mapes, *Pedaling Revolution*, 142-143.

6 "Bleeding Albina," 4.

neighborhoods, it seems as though the trends, transitions, and rebirth of various neighborhoods signal another new era in the long history of these areas.

Welcome to gentrification and urban revitalization. Professor and author Richard Lloyd calls these kinds of communities *neo-bohemian* and identifies the emerging artistic energy of this Creative Class that is fueling these metamorphic shifts not only in Portland, but other cities across the U.S. and Canada. Lloyd comments, "The 'revitalization' of core city districts through the leveraging of artistic energies produces a mixed bounty, fruitfully countering the low-road, tourism-directed policies that had dominated revitalization strategies in an earlier period, and enriching the cultural landscape, but also abetting the neoliberal tendencies toward cutthroat interurban competition and the promotion of gentrification."[7]

Immediately upon moving to Portland I knew that I had to do what was necessary to become an "insider." I began working through my "I'm a Portlander" check list; ride a singlespeed bike (check), have at least one visible tattoo (check), own a Mac (check), ride a scooter (check), maintain a blog (check), hang out at coffee shops or pubs (check) … I was "in." Not only that but I soon learned that as a family we had to begin transitioning and adapting as well which wasn't too difficult since we went through a similar process when we moved to Vancouver. On the boys' first day of school we drove them only to realize that in our neighborhood many parents either walked or biked their kids to and from school. Soon our older two boys were longboarding to school while I would bike alongside our youngest. Again, all part of becoming embedded and rooted in the neighborhood. In Vancouver we lived without a car and either walked or took transit everywhere. Now? I find myself biking or riding my scooter all over the place. We had found a home.

My daily activity involves exploring our NE and North Portland neighborhood on bike and venturing into SE. After biking the boys to school I head up to one of the many coffee shops that can be found in the Alberta Arts District or on North Williams. There are more coffee shops and cafes than most any other business, it seems. As I pedal my bike down these streets I see pedestrians on the sidewalks, other cyclists beginning their commute to work (or the coffee shop), and an array of bicycles parked and locked up outside coffee

---

7 Lloyd, *Neo-Bohemia*, xii.

shops as caffeine-deprived urbanites get their jump-start for the day. Believe it or not, but there are so many great coffee shops that some days I have a hard time deciding which one to settle in at. I have it narrowed down to several in the area to keep things "simple" … Heart Coffee, Extracto Coffeehouse, Caffe Vita, or Ristretto.

Today's journey finds me at the Extracto Coffeehouse on Killingsworth as it has become a favorite of ours. Great coffee, ample seating, big windows, and it also houses the roastery so at times you can watch them roast the many large bags of exotic green beans that are stacked up in the back of the shop. The patrons and baristas are just as much part of the scene as the coffee. Wave after wave of mostly young urban hipsters make their way in and out of Extracto. Some grab their coffee to go while most find a table, unload their notebook computers, and hang out a while. The ownership encourages this hanging-out since they offer wifi and a free refill for coffees that are "for here."

The room is decorated with an assortment of mismatched furniture and colors that I remember my grandparents had when I was little, but it all fits somehow and is funky and cool. The same can be said of the patrons. While many are truly urban hipsters, that label actually applies to many different kinds of people. College students, young families, older families, married, unmarried, straight, gay, and so forth. "Hipsters are hipsters. They come in many shapes, sizes, and degrees of hipness, but you know them when you see them."[8] We all collect in this vibrant Third Place as we're drawn not only to the coffee shop but also to this neighborhood. There certainly is an overarching storyline or meta-narrative that binds us together. As a follower of Jesus I observe this storyline hovering over the neighborhood, and I wonder to myself, while sitting here today, where I along with God's plan to redeem this place and these people, fit in.

Now for the "Other Side"

A few weeks after arriving in Portland I found myself on my scooter zipping across the city to meet up with a friend who is involved in community development in the low-density sprawl of outer SE Portland. I left my chic

---

8 McCracken, *Hipster Christianity*, 51.

neighborhood which houses a growing population of urban hipsters on singlespeed bicycles and Vespas to head out to explore new terrain. Within a thirty-minute ride, while still within the city limits of Portland proper, it was as if I was transported to a different country. Gone were the abundance of coffee shops and the vibrant street scene marked by walkability and bikeability. Instead I found low-density sprawl that resembled developers and planners simply "vomiting" out ugly houses and strip malls at random. I arrived at the area two hours early for my meeting in hopes of settling into a coffee shop in order to check emails, read, and so forth. However, that turned out to be rather problematic. I rode around for twenty to thirty minutes trying to find something even resembling a coffee shop before I settled on a Starbucks drive-through that had only outdoor seating. But at least it had wifi.

As I sat there and watched the scene unfolding before me there was no denying that this indeed was a completely different world. For the first time I saw an abundance of minorities whether Asian or Hispanic. I could also tell that the area was socio-economically depressed by observing the quality and the architecture of the houses and businesses as well as the few pedestrians who happened to be out. Also, those on bicycles didn't ride chic Italian singlespeed bikes, but instead rode the kinds of bikes one finds on the cheap at Walmart or at garage sales. No Vespas or other scooters either. Welcome to the other side of gentrification.

When the time came I made my way over to meet with my friend, Clark Blakeman of Second Stories.[9] He had invited me to a community-wide meeting between apartment owners, local police, business leaders, community developers, and pastors.

Recently an article in one of Portland's alternative newspapers, the *Willamette Weekly*, featured life out on the outer fringe titled "The Other Portland." The story starts off:

> In case you didn't get the invite, Portland is an endless party in a shining urban utopia where everyone has a $1,000 bicycle, eats locally sourced gourmet dishes from food carts and is blindingly, self-consciously white. It's Paris in the 1920s, but with iPhones. Portland is not just a noun, it's an adjective for good government and livability, smart planning and the next

9 Visit www.secondstories.org to learn more.

hip thing. Well, wake up. There's another Portland you should know about, one unknown even to many longtime locals. It's an expanse of the city without a single Zipcar spot or independent microbrewery, where you'll see more pajama bottoms than skinny jeans. It's a landscape of chain link and surface parking that, by contrast, makes 82nd Avenue look positively gentrified. It's a cookie-cutter residential sprawl so devoid of landmarks, public spaces and commercial centers that some residents simply call is "The Numbers."[10]

I was pleasantly surprised to find that this very meeting was featured in the article. What was the nature of the meeting? This part of the city was and is a hotbed for crime and unsavory conditions. The newspaper article revealed that, "The intersection of Southeast 162nd Avenue and Burnside is consistently among the top three locations for police service calls in the Portland metro area."[11] Rather than waiting for someday when real estate prices would indeed be so bad through disinvestment that gentrification would begin to "turn around" the neighborhood, they decided to work collaboratively to see their neighborhood transformed without displacement or the ill effects of gentrification.

You see, the neighborhood I live in is hip and trendy and thoroughly gentrified, but at what price? "As real estate developers gentrify these neighborhoods, displaced tenants move to places they can afford—slums, in many cases."[12] What happened to those who left, were forced out, or priced out of my neighborhood? They now live in such places as outer SE Portland. Gentrification comes with a price and a personal cost. "In Portland, the Black community was destabilized by a systematic process of private sector disinvestment and public sector neglect."[13] There are clear winners and losers.

Those gathered at the meeting wanted to see their neighborhood transformed without the displacement that gentrification causes. They were seeking a more "socially just urban renaissance" that seeks, according to Lees, Slater, and Wyly, "to counter the negative aspects of gentrification; this requires the active support of local and national governments and committed political

---

10 Pein, "The Other Portland," 13.

11 Ibid., 16.

12 Phillips, *City Lights*, 48.

13 "Bleeding Albina," 6.

action by working-class communities and organizations."[14] Gentrification needs to go beyond simply new housing stock and amenities. As sociologist Sharon Zukin comments, "Cool boutiques and farmers' markets convince us that we are helping to keep the balance by living local, but with land values rising and our strong desire to consume, we are pushing the neighborhood over the edge."[15]

In many ways the neighborhood in outer SE Portland reminded me of where we lived in Metro Vancouver. Although this is thoroughly low-density compared to our more high-density former neighborhood, there were commonalities in regards to immigration, proximity outside of the central businesses district, as well as a lack of architectural richness.[16] Whereas Edmonds Town Centre in Burnaby had a growing number of high-rise residential towers that was altering the socio-economic landscape, it was the gentrification process that was changing things there. Before gentrification hit full force in Edmonds it was anchored by an ugly strip mall surrounded by a sea of surface parking and a proliferation of low-rent apartments. Outer SE Portland is still in "pre-gentrification" mode which is why it is still attracting immigrants and minorities looking for more affordable housing. Unfortunately this is also where crime is on a growth curve.

What are we to do with the phenomenon known as gentrification that is taking place in every city across North America and even globally? How are we to think about it? For those of us who are followers of Jesus, what should our stance and approach be in this process? How do we address it biblically and theologically? Along with those questions new ones are birthed as we ask out loud what God thinks of this. How would God respond? How would God have us respond? Is there a way to experience, live through, embrace, or reject gentrification that aligns with God's overall plans, purposes, blueprints, and templates for both urban people and urban places? Along with exploring gentrification conceptually and theologically, what should a hands-on approach look like? How are we to minister in neighborhoods marked by gentrification whether they are early on in the process or midway through the transformation?

---

14 Lees et al, *Gentrification*, xxiv.

15 Zukin, *Naked City*, 122.

16 This is more reflective before gentrification set it unless one deems the new towers to be unappealing.

On the other hand, what should the response and posture among Christians be in those neighborhoods that are on the receiving end of displacement from gentrification in other parts of the city? Lots of questions and a lot of ideas to chew on and work through.

The two neighborhoods detailed in this chapter were both affected by the same phenomenon: gentrification. One is on the sending side and the other is on the receiving end. One neighborhood is on a growth trajectory in terms of economic revitalization while the other continues to spiral downward. One has hope and the other is simply trying to survive. Most often when we read or talk of gentrification we address the former rather than the latter. We're drawn to the newly transitioned chic neighborhoods with a burgeoning population of urban hipsters and Richard Florida's Creative Class.[17] Too often we neglect to address what happens on the other side of gentrification. The losers of urban revitalization, if you will.

How has the church responded? In terms of church planting what shaping effect does this phenomenon have? What is the geography of church planting? Are church planters drawn to gentrified neighborhoods or conversely, are they instead drawn to areas blighted from the fallout of gentrification? As the world goes urban these are certainly questions we need to address in our approach to the city, not just here in North America but globally as well. I'm an advocate of the fact that a city's built environment and overall urbanism truly have a shaping effect on how we live out the *missio Dei* in the city. We are all more or less armchair missiologists studying our given context in hopes of living out and proclaiming the Good News of the Kingdom of God in word and deed. The city shapes us and we shape the city. In terms of urban gentrification this is certainly a prevailing shaping force that we must address with sensitivity, humility, and a willingness to be open and to learn. We're dealing with lives marked by transition whether it be people moving into urban neighborhoods or those who've given up and are relocating to more affordable housing or to be closer to friends who had left the neighborhood ahead of them.

As followers of Jesus, whether urban ministry practitioners, pastors, church planters, and-or residents, how are we even to view gentrification? As positive or

---

17 A good primer on the subject is *The Rise of the Creative Class* by Richard Florida. I also begin addressing the subject of church planting among the Creative Class in *Metrospiritual: The Geography of Church Planting*.

negative? There are elements both good and bad that we cannot deny. Those who deride gentrification fail to consider the impact of the reinvigorated economic vitality that comes with the process. Some of the other positive benefits are social mixing, job creation, a stronger tax base, improved housing stock, and poverty dilution. On the other hand, in the same movement we watch as the social fabric risks being torn apart. "There are long-standing claims that gentrification leads to displacement, as working-class and minority residents are steadily priced out of gentrified areas."[18] We live in that tension. As a friend recently posted on my blog:

> Hey Sean—the whole gentrification thing is definitely becoming more of an issue in the neighborhoods around downtown Tucson and U of A. I am so conflicted on this—like you, I long for a reinvigorated downtown, increased density, TOD. The UA is also now a big player in pushing off-campus student housing towers as a response to neighborhoods that have long complained about partying students, run-down rentals, and mini-dorms. The hard part is that many of the neighborhoods have such a NIMBY-reflex against the UA that many oppose these dense student housing (500 to 700 students) options and see them as ruining the funky neighborhood character. I love both the funky hood I live in and am also excited to see the newest hip restaurants and coffee shops downtown. I have a feeling it's going to be contentious slog for the next 5+ years as everyone adjusts to the new street-car and private investment dollars it will bring.[19]

We may desire it and yet abhor its negative elements, but we need to be cognizant of both sides. Lees, Slater, and Wyly dedicate a chapter in their book on gentrification to this very notion. They articulate and display research that favors, compares, and contrasts both sides. They conclude the chapter by stating:

> Gentrification is promoted positively by policy makers who ignore the less desirable effects of the process. Their promotion of gentrification as a way to socially mix, balance, and stabilize neighborhoods has connections with the ideologies of pioneer gentrifiers who seek/sought both residence in the inner city and sociocultural diversity. Many of these pioneer gentrifiers were women (including lesbians) and gay men. These 'marginal' groups chose to live in the inner city to avoid the institutionalized heterosexuality and

---

18 *Gentrification*, 217.

19 Colby, December 21, 2011 (10:23 a.m.), commented on Sean Benesh, "Excerpt From View From the Urban Loft," *The Urban Loft*, December 21, 2011. Blog post is no longer active.

nuclear family units of the suburbs. The inner city for them was an emancipatory space. By way of contrast, many more authors view gentrification to be a negative process, one that causes direct or indirect displacement, and that purifies and sanitizes the central city. Some see it to be a visceral and revanchist process of capital appropriation.[20]

In a book of this scope there are numerous layers and approaches to addressing gentrification ranging from urban economics, urban planning, public policy, real estate, architecture, transportation planning, immigration, employment, local church ministry, church planting, urban ministry, and so on. My desire is to expose the reader to a varied approach by addressing gentrification from a biblical, theological, and thoroughly Christian response. That does indeed tie into all the layers or approaches just mentioned. However, the difference is I'm casting it in a framework that desires to see holistic community transformation in the city that most certainly includes the spiritual dimension. As followers of Jesus our approach to gentrification includes an overarching spiritual or Kingdom meta-narrative. It is more than addressing the blessings and curses of urban revitalization; it is to help move the neighborhood and city to be more reflective of the Kingdom of God. To do so we cannot turn a blind eye to the spiritual forces in a city. As Robert Linthicum notes:

> The discontent that needs to be fostered in a neighborhood or city to motivate the people enough to seek their community's transformation must not only center on the problem "out there." It must also center on the enemy within the community midst and within each of us. We are a part of the problem. True community reformulation cannot occur until we admit the evil within us, confess our own complicity and our ancestors complicity in contributing to our bondage or marginalization, and throw ourselves upon the mercy and forgiveness of God. "Secular community organization rarely reaches this community-transforming place because it has difficulty turning to God for forgiveness for the people's sinful contribution to their own disenfranchisement. To turn to God would be to cease being a secular organization; it would mean admitting to the spiritual dimensions of a community's and a city's bondage."[21]

---

20 *Gentrification*, 234.

21 Linthicum, *City of God City of Satan*, 224.

We're to do more than simply walk with people through the transition called gentrification, but we're to key them in on the reality of the Kingdom. This Kingdom indeed has a King.

Last night as I was preparing to go to bed I heard the distinct sound of a gunshot followed by another ten seconds later. A few days prior I had been scouring the Internet reading local news reports of the numerous shootings in the last twelve months that had occurred in my part of the city. Just three days ago armed gunmen burst into a house only blocks away looking for marijuana. Several days before that a man was fatally shot in the chest mere blocks from the coffee shop where I spend a lot of time. I am weekly reminded that gentrification as a process puts two worlds onto a collision course. In this case an historic African-American neighborhood is being uprooted by the influx of urban hipsters and middle-class whites. Can they co-exist? Does the reality of violence deter others from moving in, or can we assume that things will simply be "cleaned up" over time? It is precisely this point of tension that I am most interested in exploring by means of this book, and especially how the followers of Jesus who love the city and call it home can best respond to it.

Chapter 2

Defining Gentrification
Sean Benesh

Gentrification is one of those hotly debated topics and conversations that can elicit a wide variety of responses. On top of that, as I've seen happen many times, the conversation can stir up strong emotions and passions. It all depends on one's definition of gentrification as well as their vantage point. A few months ago I posted an entry on my blog entitled "When Gentrification Is A Good Thing."[1] That post prompted a good and healthy dialogue. What was clear from the conversation, though, is that for many the words "gentrification" and "good" are never, and should never, be mixed. Gentrification is bad. But is it really?

Not too long ago a friend here in Portland told me a story of when he was at a party with a bunch of people and the topic of gentrification came up. He was shocked that the collective response was an angry outburst about the evils of gentrification. It was as if it ranked up there right next to the other great global social evils ... genocide, war, famine, AIDS. The great irony of the evening was that this was a group of young white twenty-somethings at a house in a hip and trendy inner-city district in Portland. Gentrification is "evil" if it is "over there," but cool when it is "here." There's not much of an outcry when we find out our favorite coffee shop, yoga study, or artisan start-up had moved into its current space after the ethnic deli that had been in business for over forty years had been priced out of business.

---

1 Benesh, "When Gentrification is a Good Thing." Blog post is no longer active.

I've had the opportunity of watching gentrification take place in three different cities that are at different stages on the gentrification, redevelopment, and urban regeneration spectrum. From a southwest desert city (Tucson) to an international city in Canada (Vancouver), and now currently in Portland. Each city has neighborhoods that are going through gentrification, but interestingly they all look different even though they carry similar attributes. In addition, our classic demarcations of who the "typical" gentrifiers are do actually vary from city to city and nation to nation. Not all gentrifiers are skinny-jeans-wearing young white hipsters on singlespeed bikes who listen to indie bands and smoke clove cigarettes. What we found in Vancouver was that gentrifiers can even be affluent Mainland Chinese who are new immigrants to the city. Hardly the stereotypical bohemian gentrifier that we think of in places like Williamsburg in Brooklyn, Wicker Park in Chicago, Mission District in San Francisco, or Mississippi Avenue in Portland.

Before we venture further it would be helpful to pause and define the term, as well as explore the parameters and the different kinds of gentrification. It is simply not all the same all the time; nor does it look or act the same in every setting. This is an enormous task to tackle in one brief chapter, so I will simply take a cursory glance at each topic. My goal is not to present an exhaustive look at these various topics, but instead to address them for the purposes of this book so there's a shared or common knowledge base we're collectively working from.

Defining Gentrification

"The term 'gentrification' was first coined by the British sociologist Ruth Glass in 1964, although it is rumored that she used the term 'gentrified' in an unpublished study of housing in North Kensington in 1959."[2] In the brief history of the term it is important to note that the definition is indeed in flux. It has evolved and continues to evolve. While at first its focus was more along the lines of residential rehabilitation, as cities de-industrialized the term has also encompassed more of a re-imagining of what they could be. Rather than simply the middle-class reclaiming old Victorian homes or brownstones, there are new

---

2 Lees et al, *Gentrification*, 4.

spaces created from scratch in the central cities, specifically for the middle-class. We will get into those specifics later in the chapter.

So what is gentrification? Lees, Slater, and Wyly define it as "the transformation of a working-class or vacant area of the central city into middle-class residential and/or commercial use."[3] I would add to that definition that affected neighborhoods usually house members of lower-income ethnic minorities who work in the service industry. Urban ministry veteran Wayne Gordon writes, "Gentrification is practically understood as the process by which middle-income professionals buy and restore homes in depressed communities."[4] The ever-snarky *Urban Dictionary* defines gentrification as:

> When "urban renewal" of lower class neighbourhoods with condos attracts yuppie tenants, driving up rents and driving out long time, lower income residents. It often begins with influxes of local artists looking for a cheap place to live, giving the neighbourhood a bohemian flair. This hip reputation attracts yuppies who want to live in such an atmosphere, driving out the lower income artists and lower income residents, often ethnic/racial minorities, changing the social character of the neighbourhood.[5]

Gentrification is not always uniformly normative in each neighborhood, city, or nation. Along with that, as cities mature, sprawl, and densify the gentrification process is not solely limited to the central cities anymore. My goal in taking the gentrification conversation global means that some of the presumed assumptions simply do not fit in all of the usual boxes. Just today I was talking with an urban studies professor at a state university who specializes in community development. When the conversation of gentrification came up in regards to the global city, in developing countries in particular, he plainly stated, "You know, gentrification in developing countries is simply called 'slum removal' and is not healthy."

In his book, *Urban Christianity and Global Order*, Andrew Davey writes about the changing nature of the city.

---

3 Ibid., xv.

4 Gordon, "Gentrification," 39.

5 Urban Dictionary LLC, "Gentrification."

Some cities will find their centers attracting new populations through deliberate policies, the evolution of cultural sectors, or commercial developments. This may include warehouse and loft conversions to residential accommodation, the expansion of higher education, or the promotion of an entertainment or club quarter. Such developments raise poignant questions about the alienation of residual pockets of older communities. (Gentrification often happens alongside areas of social housing, which results in the city core being dominated by young single professionals and minority ethnics communities.[6]

Types of Gentrification

That brings us to the topic of the different types or kinds of gentrification. As I've previously mentioned, not all gentrification looks, acts, and feels the same. It is a misnomer to assume that gentrification is always easily spotted, especially in cities and neighborhoods where the players and projects involved look vastly different from one another. Let me explain.

As I have shared and written about on numerous occasions, including above, the neighborhood we lived in while in Canada displayed a unique expression of gentrification compared to the classic norms that we associate with the process. Notably absent are any old Victorian homes or classic majestic brownstones. Quite the opposite, as much of the neighborhood's housing stock includes nondescript apartments and multi-family homes called "Vancouver Specials." "The Special is the outcome of a particularly lean-spirited impulse in the provision of infill housing during the 1960s and 1970s. Unusual in its tersely expressed structural frame, the Special maximized site coverage and provided inexpensive habitable space on a standard city lot. The consequence of affordability resulted in immense popularity with small-scale builders and immigrant buyers, proliferating across nearly the entire spectrum of the city's residential neighbourhoods."[7] For a photographic "journey" through these homes visit the Vancouver Special website.[8]

---

6 Davey, *Urban Christianity and Global Order*, 19-20.

7 Macdonald, "The Vancouver Special Redux."

8 http://www.vancouverspecial.com.

Through Greater Vancouver's Livable Region Strategic Plan, Edmonds was categorized as a town centre due to its densification and infrastructure investment. As a hub for transit-oriented development the neighborhood began the gentrification process. However, as we'll see later in this chapter, this didn't fit the norm for gentrification in that it consisted of numerous fifteen- to twenty-four story residential towers being constructed. Along with that, the neighborhood actually became *more* ethnically and socio-economically diverse. Just yesterday I happened to meet two tourists from Vancouver. One of them, having grown up in Burnaby, lamented about the changing nature of the city due to a massive influx of ethnic Chinese and other immigrants. She literally said, "I feel like we (meaning ethnic whites) were pushed out." Again, gentrification is a larger process than initially realized. Let's explore some of the variations.

Classic Gentrification

We'll start off with what we normally think of when it comes to gentrification. An article in *The Atlantic Cities* entitled "Are These the Fastest-Gentrifying Neighborhoods in the U.S.?" reveals the most common perception of gentrification, namely, white people moving into central cities and ethnic minorities moving out. Based upon that statistical marker, the article revealed the zip codes of those areas experiencing the highest transition. The article is an analysis of an article by Michael J. Petrill that showed up on the *Thomas B. Fordham Institute* website. Petrill states, "For the past several years I've been obsessed with the issue of gentrification. Mostly that's because of a book I've been writing about diverse public schools. What's clear is that gentrification—for all of its downsides—is providing a once-in-a-generation opportunity to integrate some of our schools—at least if we don't let it go to waste."[9]

In the tongue-and-cheek website, *Stuff White People Like*, gentrification showed up #73 on the list.

In general, white people love situations where they can't lose. While this does account for the majority of their situations, perhaps the safest bet a white person can make is to buy a house in an up-and-coming neighborhood.

---

9 Petrill, "The fastest-gentrifying neighborhoods in the United States."

White people like to live in these neighborhoods because they get credibility and respect from other white people for living in a more "authentic" neighborhood where they are exposed to "true culture" every day. So whenever their friends mention their home in the suburbs or richer urban area, these people can say "oh, it's so boring out there, so fake. In our neighborhood, things are just more real." This superiority is important as white people jockey for position in their circle of friends.

They are like a modern day Lewis and Clark, except instead of searching for the ocean, they are searching for old properties to renovate.

In a few years, if more white people start moving in, these initial trailblazers will sell their property for triple what they paid and move into an ultramodern home.

Credibility or money, they can't lose!

When one of these white people tell you where they live, you should say "whoa, it's pretty rough down there. I don't think I could live there." This will make them feel even better about their credibility and status as neighborhood pioneers.[10]

Classical Gentrification can thus be described as "the restoration of run-down urban areas by the middle class (resulting in the displacement of low-income residents)."[11]   It is usually what comes to mind when one thinks about gentrification and its typical characteristics. I hesitate to use the word *classical* since it communicates something old or historic. As we'll explore throughout this chapter, gentrification as a concept and reality is in constant flux, evolution, and mutation. Let me attempt to paint the picture of what *classical gentrification* looks like here in Portland.

Recently I taught a seminary course called "The Mission of the Urban Church." It was and is my contention that the term *urban* is in serious need of revamping and redefining, especially when it is linked to *mission* or *ministry*. In many cities across the United States and Canada, *urban* in no longer associated with degraded inner city neighborhoods which house high percentages of lower-

---

10 Lander, "Gentrification."

11 WordNet, "Gentrification."

income people, immigrants, and ethnic minorities. The reality in some cities is that this is still a normative reality. However, in places like Portland, *urban* is now synonymous with *cool, hip, hipster, trendy,* and *desirable.* I detailed much of this in Chapter 1.

In deciding where to hold the class we opted for Mt. Zion Baptist Church. The building's cornerstone reveals that it was built by German immigrants in 1914. However, for over the past thirty to forty years it has transitioned into an African-America church that mirrors the transition in the neighborhood from ethnic whites to ethnic blacks. Since cities are constantly changing and reinventing themselves, the neighborhood has begun morphing once again. Andrew Davey writes, "Populations can change in less than a generation as waves of migration come and go. Elsewhere spatial, social and political changes can shift populations through relocation and regeneration schemes as the built environment is renewed or areas are gentrified. Cities are rarely benign territory."[12]

Whereas the area surrounding the church in inner NE Portland once consisted of neighborhoods full of affordable low-income housing, the recent influx of middle-class whites has skyrocketed housing prices. Not only that, but along came many new businesses catering to these new consumers of goods, services, and culture. Holding the seminary course at that particular church was critical because we could walk and bicycle the streets and neighborhood talking about all of these changes and tensions that are arising as a result. I've watched house after house get a good facelift and renovation. I have heard from many people that as recent as the mid-90s not many would dare venture into these neighborhoods. A professor friend told me about being shot at across the street from the church in Irving Park. Much has changed. This is what we think of when we talk about *classic gentrification.*

In *Gentrification* by Lees et al, they highlight Clay's (1979) Stage Model of Gentrification from his book *Neighborhood Renewal: Middle-Class Resettlement and Incumbent Upgrading in American Neighborhoods.* His model which I summarize here is worth repeating as it details the process of *classical gentrification*:

---

12 Davey, *Crossover City*, 26.

Stage 1 – A small group of risk-oblivious people move in and renovate properties for their own use. Little public attention is given to renovation at this stage, and little displacement occurs because newcomers often take housing that is vacant or part of the normal market turnover in what is often an extremely soft market. Sweat equity and private capital are used almost exclusively since conventional mortgage funds are unavailable.

Stage 2 – A few more people of the same type of people move in and fix up houses for their own use. Subtle promotional activities are begun, often by a few perceptive realtors. Small-scale speculators may renovate a few houses in visible locations for resale or rental. Some displacement occurs as vacant housing becomes scarce.

Stage 3 – At this stage major media or official interest is directed to the neighborhood. The pioneers may continue to be important in shaping the process, but they are not the only important ones. Physical improvements become even more visible because of their volume and because of the general improvement they make to the whole area. Prices begin to escalate rapidly. Displacement continues ... The newer middle-class residents begin to organize their own groups or change the character of the pioneers' organization. The organized community turns outward to promote the neighborhood to other middle-class people and to make demands for public resources. Tensions between old residents and the gentry begin to emerge.

Stage 4 – A large number of properties are gentrified, and the middle-class continues to come. What is significant about the new residents is that more are from the business and managerial middle class than from the professional middle class ... Small, specialized retail and professional services or commercial activities begin to emerge, especially if the neighborhood is located near the downtown or a major institution. Rapid price and rent spirals are set off. Displacement now affects not only renters but some home owners as well.[13]

Those stages represent the progression and characteristics of *classical gentrification*. In the area surrounding Mt. Zion Baptist Church these stages are abundantly evident. Last night I was given a walking tour around several blocks by an African-American friend who lives in the Boise neighborhood in inner NE Portland. This is only about a half mile from the church and was the focal point for disinvestment and neighborhood neglect. As an urban studies major in college, she masterfully wove us the story of the changing neighborhood from

---

13 *Gentrification*, 31-33.

the young white couple who moved in across the street and who are expecting their first baby, to the crack dealers a few houses down who helped capture the purse thief who broke into her house. In an odd way, these neighborhood "guardians" (the drug dealers) made sure that no one messed with or harmed this single mom with two children. In our walk she talked about the "signs of hope" that showed the neighborhood was turning around, albeit with the tension that gentrification brings.

Gordon aptly states, "We know that gentrification is coming to our neighborhood when we see billboards that say, 'We buy ugly houses,' when there is new interest in vacant land and abandoned buildings, when a new business such as Starbucks starts up, and grocery stores move in and begin to operate."[14] But who are the gentrifiers?

One of the points that Clay brings up and Lees et al highlight, is that many of the first-wave gentrifiers were part of the gay community. We've seen this reality in cities like San Francisco as well as here locally in Portland. An example comes to mind of a couple we know who were part of this first wave of gentrifiers in NE Portland seeking refuge as part of the gay community. They were aware of this reality and trend and moved into inner NE Portland back in the mid-90s. The neighborhood they moved into was in the midst of cultural turmoil. By all accounts it was a ghetto. But this white middle-class couple eschewed the safety and sterility of the suburbs and moved in. They bought the house on the cheap and over the years masterfully renovated it.

Their premise of moving into the neighborhood was to escape the W.A.S.P.y suburbs. (W.A.S.P. stands for White Anglo-Saxon Protestants.) The city became a refuge for them and they'd rather risk life and limb by moving into a war zone than to live in the suburbs which house a higher density of evangelical Christians.

New-Build Gentrification

"New build residential developments, nevertheless, stand in stark contrast to the renovated Victorian and Georgian landscapes of classic gentrification."[15]

---

14 Gordon, "Gentrification," 40.

15 *Gentrification*, 139.

What this reveals is that gentrification is not always easy to spot. In regards to new-build gentrification, Linda Bletterman writes,

> In a world in which cities increasingly have to compete for residents, investment and visitors, governments are looking out for some new strategies to attract them. The attraction and retention of middle- and upper-income households through the manipulation of the built environment has become an explicit or implicit urban policy aim for local governments. Governments are initiating or stimulating restructuring and new-build development projects, in order to achieve further social and economical urban policy objectives. Several authors and scientists have argued that these new-build developments, restructuring projects and flagship regeneration projects (of for example urban waterfronts, wasteland and Brownfield sites) can be accounted for as the post-1990s new type of gentrification; namely the "third wave." This change in the definition and the meaning of gentrification lies intrinsic to the problem statement of this thesis.
>
> The question rises whether these developments can be accounted for as being gentrification? And do the residents of new-build developments have the same characteristics, motivations and preferences as the gentrifiers?[16]

What this continues to reveal is that gentrification, while sharing some baseline characteristics, looks markedly different in its various aberrations.

I love taking out-of-town visitors into Portland's downtown core to the Pearl district. What is immediately noticeable is that it is an urban playground and cultural consumption district for the middle class. Whether one lives in the Pearl, or travels in from other neighborhoods, the district is desirable, hip, trendy, and safe. Since cities are not static, but instead in continuous flux and transition, then it should be noted that the Pearl used to be a rough-and-tumble warehouse and industrial district. As recent as twenty-five years ago it was in disrepair and neglect. In a recent conversation with a friend who grew up in Portland, he told me that when he was a teen his mother would tell him not to go north of Burnside into NW Portland because it wasn't safe. Now? A trip to Jamison Square on a sunny summer day reveals hundreds of people, mostly families, playing in the fountain surrounded by condos, coffee shops, and restaurants. What happened? Is this still considered gentrification?

---

16 Bletterman, "Who are the gentrifiers in new-build gentrification?"

Another example from urban Portland highlights the importance of identifying various types of gentrification. South Waterfront, just on the southern edge of Portland's CBD, is a large development project. Some may call this *brownfield gentrification* in that there was nothing there except a few buildings used for light industry. Now the neighborhood boasts of numerous high-rise residential mixed-use towers anchored by the lower campus and research facilities of OHSU (Oregon Health and Science University). South Waterfront makes the claim of having the highest number of LEED-certified buildings in a neighborhood in the United States. Architecturally it has more in common with Vancouver, BC than Portland, but some contend that is in fact a type of gentrification. "When luxury condos are built on reclaimed industrial land, does it count as gentrification? These are not old houses, and there is no displacement of a lower-income community."[17]

Some of the arguments for this being a form of gentrification are: It causes displacement (albeit indirect and/or sociocultural), in-movers are the urban new middle classes, a gentrified landscape/aesthetic is produced, and capital is reinvested in disinvested urban areas.[18] While neighborhoods and districts like the Pearl and South Waterfront did not cause direct displacement, the belief is that this occurs in surrounding neighborhoods while also creating "exclusionary displacement" because lower-income groups are not able to move in. Displacement is more indirect as *new-build gentrification* elevates housing prices in adjacent neighborhoods which can also price people and businesses out as well.

Event-Based Urban Regeneration

Another point of consideration in the gentrification conversation is *event-based urban regeneration*. In his book *Events and Urban Regeneration: The Strategic Use of Events to Revitalise Cities*, Andrew Smith, Senior Lecturer in the School of Architecture and the Built Environment at the University of Westminster, UK, writes, "Major events are staged for many reasons. They are opportunities for socialising, celebrations of achievement, markers of time and vehicles for

---

17 *Gentrification*, 138.

18 Ibid., 140.

political posturing. In the contemporary era, events have become platforms to sell a variety of products, including the host city itself. Major events are also increasingly associated with urban regeneration."[19] The reason I am adding this topic into the gentrification conversation is because the forces behind utilizing events as a vehicle for urban regeneration can lead to gentrification whether *classical, new-build, or super-gentrification.*

While living in Vancouver, we saw this take place up close before, during, and after the 2010 Winter Olympics. Much of it centered around False Creek in the downtown core. "The regeneration of former industrial sites in Vancouver has been assisted by staging multiple events. The (northern) shores of Vancouver's False Creek were redeveloped to stage Expo '86; the 2010 Winter Olympic Games were used to extend the regeneration project to the southeastern side of the Creek."[20] What was jumpstarted by Expo '86 took another leap forward with the advent of the 2010 Winter Olympics. These events were used to spur on development and regeneration of not only the False Creek area, but also the Downtown Eastside which houses a large homeless population.

This regeneration project in Vancouver has multiplied the effects of *new-build gentrification*, which, by offering the prospect of affordable housing for those who are on low income and marginalized, is seen by many as simply a political, greedy ploy to line the pockets of the investors. In other words, the city added new buildings, most notably the Olympic Village, which makes the jewel of the downtown sparkle even more. The premise of the Olympic Village was that afterwards it would be converted into private dwellings with a robust selection of affordable housing. Slowly but surely, after the Olympics the number of affordable housing units continued to decline as costs added up.

Could this be viewed as a form of gentrification? Based upon the last section, *new-build gentrification*, one would concur that this is precisely what has and is taking place. With the False Creek area even more pristine, growing, and desirable, not only has housing values continued to climb, but it prices out those who cannot afford to live there. It's become a district for the urban middle and upper classes. As with *new-build gentrification*, the surrounding areas are also

---

19 Smith, *Events and Urban Regeneration*, 1.

20 Ibid., 109.

buttressed in their housing prices. While historically the Downtown Eastside is the poorest part of the city, with the poorest postal code in Canada, through regeneration projects this continues to change. Whether it's event-based regeneration like the Winter Olympics or redevelopment projects like the Woodward's Building, the effect is the same ... gentrification. Poverty diffusion and escalating housing prices are some of the resultant effects of these types of projects.

Smith address the topic of regeneration in his book, which goes beyond simply the built environment of the city. "The term regeneration implies that efforts are being made to recover the position that a city once held. The term derives from the notion of rebirth and this suggests that regeneration involves more than simply restoring or replenishing cities."[21] Interestingly, Smith goes on to draw parallels between the regeneration of a city's built environment and the biblical concept of regeneration or transformation. "Regeneration also has a religious meaning; a sphere where to be 'born again' has great significance."[22] He then adds, "Biblical derivations imply that people can be transformed and this is relevant to contemporary urban regeneration, which now includes attention to social objectives."[23]

This highlights the dissonance as well as the opportunity that urban regeneration can bring about. Along with that, urban regeneration is not merely physical, there are social (and I'd add spiritual) elements as well. The city's built environment has a direct impact and bearing on the urban citizen's worldview. A regeneration project can stir the waters, so to speak, which in turn can open the doors for a deeper transformation. Viv Grigg asks, "Global processes among urban missions strategies and theologians have provoked the question, '*What is the relationships of the Spirit of Christ to the transformation of a postmodern city?*'"[24]

---

21 Ibid., 8.

22 Ibid.

23 Ibid.

24 Grigg, *The Spirit of Christ and the Postmodern City*, 4.

Super-Gentrification

The last variation of gentrification that I will highlight is super-gentrification. Lees, Wyly, and Slater define it as:

In the term 'super-gentrification', the prefix 'super' is used to demonstrate that this is not only a higher level of gentrification, but also one superimposed on an already gentrified neighborhood; one that has global connections—social, economic, and cultural; and one that involves a higher financial or economic investment in the neighborhood than previous waves of gentrification, and as such requires a qualitatively different level of economic resource. The suffix 'gentrification' is used as a metaphor for social change; here as new, more elite, more globally connected gentry is moving into the neighborhood.[25]

The scope of this super-gentrification is happening only in a few select neighborhoods in top-tiered global cities like London and New York.[26]

An example would be in Barnsbury in North London. Sarah Cassidy observes the difference between "normal gentrifiers" and the new globally-elite super-gentrifiers, "But whereas traditional gentrification was carried out by people who had a strong sense of community identity and wanted to mix with their less well-off neighbours, the new 'super-gentrifiers' did not tend to associate with people who were different to them."[27] Dr. Lees is quoted in this same article, and in *Gentrification*, she, Slater, and Wyly discuss this group of gentrifiers.

Certain neighborhoods have become the focus of intense investment and conspicuous consumption by a new generation of super-rich "financiers" fed by fortunes made in the global finance and corporate service industries. Importantly, super-gentrification is different from re-gentrification, which may well happen to other neighborhoods, because super-gentrification is only likely to happen in neighborhoods in global cities that are easily commutable to global financial headquarters such as the City of London—the "Golden Square Mile"—or Wall Street—or in cities such as San Francisco with very particular

---

25 *Gentrification*, 149.

26 Ibid.

27 Cassidy, "'Super-gentrifers' ruin integration."

circumstances, in this case the impact of Silicon Valley and IT (information technology) companies.

This breaks from the norm of gentrification and highlights the need to not be too narrow about what we deem as gentrification. This super or hyper form of gentrification makes neighborhoods that had already been gentrified become even more gentrified, if that were possible. Instead of the middle class moving in, with artisans as the pioneer gentrifiers, this brand of gentrification has the gentrifiers being part of the global elite. The neighborhoods themselves are enclaves for this demographic which is evidenced by housing values as well as the types of support businesses and services that crop up.

My intention here is to highlight this form of gentrification knowing that most church planters and urban missionaries won't (or don't) venture into these kinds of neighborhoods. In the conversation between urban mission and gentrification, most often the default setting is to work with, live among, and minister to the lower-income, ethnic minorities, and marginalized populations. Books like *A Heart for the Community,* edited by John Fuder and Noel Castellanos, and *Crossover City*, edited by Andrew Davey, speak to that end. These are the groups who most often feel the brunt of the negative effects of gentrification. When it comes to *super-gentrification*, it'll take a significantly new and different kind of church planter or urban missionary. More than likely he or she will need to be an insider whether working in the global finance markets or the IT world. We certainly need a whole new generation of missionaries of this sort along with those who minister and live in *classical gentrification* neighborhoods.

Missiologically-speaking, the way one goes about church planting in a hipster-enclave gentrifying neighborhood in North Portland will be significantly different than a setting like Barnsbury. We can no longer make sweeping generalizations about gentrification as a one-size-fits-all phenomenon. Each form, variation, or mutation of gentrification brings about different opportunities as well as challenges. The motivation behind studying gentrification is at the heart missiological, rather than as some dry academic exercise. If we hold onto the reality that all who are in Christ are literally missionaries (sent ones) then it is imperative to study the ever-changing context of the global city.

Chapter 3

Gentrification, Bicycling, and Race on North Williams
Part 1: Racism and Gentrification
Sean Benesh

North Williams is a road that straddles the border between inner North and
NE Portland (called Albina). For a good portion of the 20th century this part of
Portland was primarily an African-American community. As the 21st century
moves forward gentrification has been reshaping the neighborhoods on both
sides of the road with the influx of middle-class whites and new artisan
businesses. Once a stereotypical inner-city neighborhood that was considered
"blighted" by local officials, it is now thoroughly stereotypical in its
gentrification ... or so it appears. However, there are numerous dynamics at hand
in this community that make it far from the stereotypical (or *classical*)
gentrification process. Namely, with Portland's unique artisan economy and
culture mixed in with the city being called "America's Bicycle Capital" there has
emerged a dynamic form of gentrification and conflict over something as
seemingly benign as ... the bicycle.

There is nothing stereotypical about urban decay in America's inner-city
neighborhoods that entails racism, economic exclusion, disinvestment, redlining,
and numerous other social ills being either forced upon or simply allowed in
these neighborhoods. Conversely, there is nothing stereotypical about the
gentrification process because there are unique dynamics at hand whether it be
in Brooklyn, Wicker Park in Chicago, Cincinnati's Over the Rhine
neighborhood, or the Downtown Eastside in Vancouver. What makes Portland a

unique case study in the dynamics of gentrification is that the flashpoint of controversy in this African-American community revolves around the bicycle. Not only that, but also a road—North Williams Avenue.

This is a case study[1] detailing the changes that have taken place along North Williams and the neighborhoods that border it. I will address these changes on both the macro as well as the micro scale because the transformative processes that have reoriented this section of inner-city Portland are part of larger national and global changes in culture, population migrations, and the flow of capital. In other words, to better understand why this area was disinvested, ghettoized, and then gentrified, is to take note of the larger picture that helps the reader understand not only why inner North and NE Portland is gentrifying, but as to why there is conflict. While I do not specifically address the church nor church planting in this case study apart from some final observations, my hope is that the case study will highlight and help you to think through the implications for urban ministry and church planting.

The Changing Story of North Williams

North Williams reflects the changing dynamics of gentrification in N/NE Portland. This afternoon finds me along this road in one of Portland's finest coffee shops, Ristretto Roasters. This is certainly the type of place to watch hipsters in their natural habitat. Sitting in this coffee shop for a few hours is a good way to identify who lives in this changing neighborhood. However, if the casual observer were to be transported directly into this coffee shop, whether in the morning during the week or at midday on the weekend, the assumption would be that, based upon the characteristics, attributes, and fashion of the clientele, that this is a white and very hip neighborhood. Seeing this demographic streaming in and out all day would lead the casual observer to this seemingly obvious conclusion. However, a different reality exists just outside the doors of the HUB building where Ristretto is located.

Like many who visit Ristretto or the numerous other business in the HUB building like Tasty n Sons, Sweatpea Bicycles, EaT: An Oyster Bar, or the yoga

---

1 A portion of this case study can also be found in the chapter on gentrification, "Gentrification: Race, Economics, and Housing" in my book *The Urbanity of the Bible*. Eugene: Wipf and Stock. I opted to use a portion of the same content in each book since I was writing them at the same time.

studio to name a few, I arrive by bicycle. With ample bicycle parking in the form of bike corrals on the street or covered bike parking under the patio, this building is certainly a hub for bicycle enthusiasts. In a typical Portland manner, many cyclists ride fixie singlespeed bikes. The fixie rider, as Magnuson quips, is "a person of mystery to most people in cycling, and because of this, everybody thinks fixies are cool."[2] However, the businesses in this building are only part of all of the other surrounding businesses that cater to bicycling hipsters in the area. Across the street from the HUB building is a new location for Portland's beloved Kenny & Zuke's Deli, Hopworks Bike Bar, and even the Portland location for the United Bicycle Institute which offers classes, training and certification for bicycle mechanics and frame builders. Again, to the casual observer, based upon the business types that cater to a particular socio-economic grouping, the presence of predominantly white customers, whether drinking coffee, partaking in yoga, or at one of the eateries, would lead one to suspect that this is a white hipster neighborhood.

But to walk out of Ristretto in any direction reveals a different reality. Across from the HUB building is also Life Change Christian Center, a predominantly black church that was started in the 1950s. Journeying away from North Williams Avenue and into the neighborhood a different picture and reality of life in inner North and NE Portland begins to emerge. The north side of the HUB building, where I park my bicycle at the bike corral is across from several homes of African-American families. To continue to walk and bike away from North Williams reveals more and more to the observer that this neighborhood is not as white and as hipster as the patrons of Ristretto would suggest. A few blocks further along are several other historic African-American churches and North Portland Bible College, a school that was started in the 1980s to train pastors and members of the numerous black churches in this part of the city.

This is a neighborhood in significant transition. The scene along North Williams reflects the changes taking place in this part of the city. The neighborhood in fact has gone through several in- and out-migrations of people of different ethnicities. My frequent bicycle rides through the neighborhood have showcased these changes. Many of the church buildings that house African

---

2 Magnuson, *Bike Tribes*, 185.

American congregations display the historic transitions taking place. A look at the cornerstones of these church buildings reveals that many of them were started and built by European immigrants, including Dutch and German, a century ago. However, as the 20th century progressed the neighborhoods around North Williams changed.

Gibson states, "Although the population [of the neighborhood] is very small (never comprising more than 7 percent of the city and 1 percent of the state), Portland provides an interesting case study of a Black community that found itself suddenly in the path of urban redevelopment for 'higher and better use' after years of disinvestment."[3] This is a significant insight because while there are commonalities between disinvestment and forced ghettos and the gentrification that ensues decades later, what makes Portland unique is partly due to its relatively small African-American population. However, the same forces behind segregation that impacted Portland were the same in other cities with a more notable African-American presence in terms of size. "While the scale of segregation has been very small relative to large cities in the Midwest and Northeast, the consequences for residents are similar."[4] By the 1940s half of Portland's black community was confined to the North Williams Avenue corridor.

While there were forces of homophily at play in the geographic settlement for not only the African-American community but other ethnicities as well, to the degree that many cities have or had a "Little Italy" or a "German Town" or a "China Town," the difference is that for the black community it was most often forced. This forced segregation took numerous shapes and forms. In other words, the forces that created these pockets of disinvestment and decay, whether in housing stock or a languishing local economy, were and are the same forces at work in gentrification. Unfortunately, as the layers that make up the process of gentrification are peeled back, there emerges the fulcrum of race and poverty struggles in urban America.

If only viewed on a superficial level, gentrification as the process of the middle class (i.e., white collar, creative class) moving back into central city neighborhoods such as along North Williams, there would be no cause for

---

3 Gibson, "Bleeding Albina," 3.

4 Ibid., 4.

alarm. However, the movement of middle-class whites reinvesting in central city neighborhoods brings other collateral effects such as the displacement of low-income renters and a loss of identity and community for longtime residents. This seems to be the epicenter of the controversy over gentrification in that there are multiple actors and moving parts feeding into these transitions both before and during gentrification. But how did we get there?

Using Brooklyn as an example, Sharon Zukin comments , "For most of the twentieth century Brooklyn had a sorry reputation as a place where artists and writers were born but were eager to escape from."[5] Cities and neighborhoods like Brooklyn, North Portland, or North Omaha are at the center of the gentrification debates. Many of these cities and neighborhoods were once places where people sought to get away from when these areas bottomed-out economically and housing was devalued. Brooklyn serves as a microcosm of gentrification in regards to race issues. The neighborhood has gone through wave after wave of change and transformation, but yet it was and is not uniform nor comprehensive. As *Atlantic Cities* writer Sarah Goodyear observes, "Depending on who you talk to, the borough of Brooklyn is a great urban success story, a painful hipster cliché, or a provincial backwater. It's actually all of those things, and many more. Brooklyn is a huge place, 71 square miles encompassing old-school blue-collar neighborhoods like Bay Ridge, trendy enclaves like Williamsburg, and decidedly ungentrified sections like East New York, which has some of the highest crime rates in all of New York City. Some 2.5 million people live in Brooklyn, and they are anything but homogenous."[6] Cycles of health, decay, blight, renewal, and gentrification are not happening uniformly even in places like Brooklyn.

The question that needs to be asked and addressed is, why or how did these neighborhoods become primarily low-income decaying ethnic neighborhoods in the first place? How did these neighborhoods, like inner North / NE Portland, transition from blue-collar Norwegian or German neighborhoods to mostly lower income African-American communities? William Flanagan begins uncovering the layers of race and gentrification: "The population movement that has had the greatest impact on residential segregation in the second half of the

---

5 Zukin, *Naked City,* 39.

6 Goodyear, "The Trendification of Brooklyn and the Perils of a Successful Urban Brand."

twentieth century has been the suburbanization of the white metropolitan population. It produced a pattern in which African American and other minority populations were concentrated in inner cities ringed by largely white, middle-class suburbs."[7] This is reflective of the storyline in Albina, but why did this movement and population reshuffling begin in the first place? How much of population dispersal was and is race-related? As we will see below, there are multiple factors for residential clustering for varying ethnicities; some of it is normative and "natural," but in other cases, especially for the plight of African-Americans, the process was more about containment and control by outsiders.

Jeb Brugmann succinctly addresses the plight of African-Americans in the mid-1900s. "Battle by battle, the aspirations that black migrants brought to the city were impeded and steered into their own ghetto-cities. By the 1950s these cities had matured into worlds of their own, creating a parallel urban universe and quietly seeding one of the first urban revolutions of the twentieth century."[8] Because of race, the black community was at a disadvantage as political bosses, business interests, urban planner, and at times the local police, fought black progress.[9] As a result these mostly black inner cities (South Bronx, Chicago's "Black Belt," Inner N/NE Portland, etc.) were neglected and disinvested in which, after bottoming-out, created the ripe conditions for reinvestment and the resultant gentrification process. Through purposeful neglect, redlining, economic and social exclusion these neighborhoods were simply left to free fall. Harvard sociologist William Julius Wilson contends that, "There is no doubt that the disproportionate concentration of poverty among African-Americans is one of the legacies of racial segregation."[10]

Racial segregation and limited economic access and opportunities created despair among the people of these blighted and neglected neighborhoods. The result was the proliferation of an "informal economy" which only made conditions worse. This led to such economic activities as the drug trade and prostitution. "Neighborhoods plagued by high levels of joblessness, insufficient

---

7 Flanagan, *Urban Sociology*, 291.

8 Brugmann, *Welcome to the Urban Revolution*, 63.

9 Ibid., 64.

10 Wilson, "From Institutional to Jobless Ghettos," 123.

economic opportunities, and high residential mobility are unable to control the volatile drug market and the violent crimes related to it."[11] It is easy for outsiders to be dismissive of drugs and crimes in inner-city neighborhoods by laying the blame solely on the residents. This is what Flanagan gets at when he writes about the "culture of poverty" in that poverty, crime, and other such things is a way of life—that in some ways it is a conscious choice of the people in these ghettos. But is it really a choice? Were there other factors involved? To look at it another way would be to address the "structure of poverty" where economic forces and racism were the catalytic drivers that created and accelerated poverty. This is what Hal Joseph Recino alludes to: "The violence and drugs in the city are, in part, byproducts of the structures of racism. Powerful leaders of white society have limited the structure of opportunity for people of color, forcing the people of the barrio and ghetto to find other ways to survive. For many, the drug economy provides one form of survival—perhaps for a while—in its violent world of death."[12]

If Flanagan and Recino are correct, then this reveals a darker side behind the poverty, place and gentrification that is at work along North Williams. People in impoverished neighborhoods were (and are) not just simply choosing this lifestyle; instead the "structure of poverty" has restrained and constrained them, leaving them with limited options to do otherwise.

The root of the problem was and is racism. Racism is more than simply disliking people of different ethnicities. In fact it can create a whole litany of social ills that affect millions of lives. As Recino boldly asserts, "A walk down any inner-city street tells the story of the results of the international drug business: hopelessness, hunger, economic marginalization, racism, and xenophobia haunt the inner cities of North America."[13] Because of their ethnicity, the African-American populace in the inner cities were systematically and permanently excluded from the market economy which in turn diminished their share of the economic benefits. In other words, not only were blacks spatially segregated by cultural pressures and economic limitations, they were also more or less cut off from access to the market economy. Wilson "argues that the changed structure of

---

11 Ibid., 124.

12 Recino, "Racism and Drugs in the City," 98.

13 Ibid., 101.

the US economy is more responsible for the plight of poor Blacks today than is racism."[14] But is that changed structure a form of racism?

For most ethnicities and cultural groupings there is the reality of homophily, mentioned earlier. This "desire to be with those who are similar to us is a consistent finding in studies of residential preferences. When choosing housing, individuals more often prefer potential neighbours who share a common racial or ethnic background or recent immigrant perspective."[15] This explains some of the reasons why people, particularly new immigrants, locate where they do in cities. Looking across the urban landscapes of America we can easily point out Italian neighborhoods, German neighborhoods, Puerto Rican neighborhoods, Polish neighborhoods, and so on. The point of differentiation with African-Americans is that not only were blacks oftentimes coerced into such collections, but outside pressures, policies and limitations prevented them from ever leaving. As a result, neighborhood after neighborhood which housed African-Americans continued to spiral downward through disinvestment and neglect. "Confronted with high costs and institutionalized neglect, the black districts deteriorated over a mater of decades. Their city was never upgraded or renewed, and its asset value declined, creating a structural impoverishment that still dogs American society."[16]

"In 1959, less than one-third of the poverty population in the United States lived in metropolitan central cities. By 1991, the central cities included close to half of the nation's poor. Many of the most rapid increases in concentrated poverty have occurred in African-American neighborhoods."[17] Ironically, though, these very blighted neighborhoods were soon to become the envy of outsiders and began to entice middle-class whites. In the 1970s "small pockets of the old inner city showed signs of reversal: in some places, government-driven urban renewal programs had created new offices, malls, or upscale residential developments for middle-class, mostly white households."[18] These same

---

14 LeGates and Stout, *The City Reader*, 117.

15 Hiller, *Urban Canada*, 286.

16 *Welcome to the Urban Revolution*, 63.

17 "From Institutional to Jobless Ghettos," 121.

18 Lees et al, *Gentrification*, 43.

neighborhoods that had undergone reduced policing, redlining by the banks, and economic disinvestment, now all of a sudden had new capital flowing back in to create a better environment for middle-class whites. Simultaneous to this, and a driver for some of this change, was an evolving lifestyle preference among the middle class which also began influencing locational preferences.[19]

So what we have now are inner-city neighborhoods like what we find along North Williams that have gone through decades of neglect and abandonment. Culturally and economically cut off, the spiral continued downward in both the culture and structure of poverty. Internal and external forces were exerted on these neighborhoods which only exasperated these conditions. While for many, notions of urban renaissance and revitalization projects are welcomed and appreciated, they fail to see the forces that lie beneath the surface. "The sunny view of 'revitalization' and renaissance' ignored the harsh realities of poverty, displacement, and chronic shortages of affordable housing."[20] This reveals both the positive and negative elements of the gentrification process. I recall a recent conversation with a friend who has lived in North Portland for the past 40 years. As an African-American woman, she certainly admits enjoying the positive elements that gentrification is bringing to her neighborhood, especially the reinvigorated economic outlook. But at the same time, she says, this does not cancel out some of the dubious policies and practices that allowed this same neighborhood to decline to the point that it did in the first place.

So who is moving into North Williams?

19 Ibid.

20 Ibid., 44.

Chapter 4

Gentrification, Bicycling, and Race on North Williams
Part 2: Economics and the Creative Class
Sean Benesh

Portland, like many other American cities, has seen an uptick in people moving back into the central city. This is especially prominent and noticeable in the neighborhoods along North Williams Avenue. One of the reasons why it is a highly visible transition is because of the differing ethnicities. For example, Boise Neighborhood where Ristretto Roasters is located, was 84 percent black in 1970. Through neighborhood change brought on in the gentrification process saw this number drop to 50 percent by 2000.[1] Why the changes, especially given the reputation of neighborhoods with purported gang violence and depleted economic resources? Richard Florida notes the growing allure of urban central cities and the reverse-migration of people moving back in:

> Several forces have combined to bring people and economic activity back to urban areas. First, crime is down and cities are safer. Second, cities have become the prime location for the creative lifestyle and the new amenities that go with it. Third, cities are benefiting from powerful demographic shifts. With fewer people living as married couples and more staying single longer, urban areas serve as lifestyle centers and as mating markets for single people. Fourth, cities have reemerged as centers of creativity and incubators of innovation. High-tech companies and other creative endeavors continue to sprout in urban neighborhoods that we once written off, in cities from

---

1 Gibson, "Bleeding Albina," 8.

New York to Chicago to Boston. Fifth, the current round of urban revitalization is giving rise to serious tensions between established neighborhood residents and newer, more affluent people moving in. Finally, in one of the most ironic twists in recent memory, both sprawling cities and traditional suburbs are seeking to emulate elements of urban life.[2]

The significance of this in relation to our conversation at hand is that those who are moving in along North Williams are often associated with bohemians, artisans, hipsters, and the creative class. As time passes, what has become abundantly clear is that cities are pulling out all the stops to attract and retain these neo-bohemians. "Cities around the world are in competition with one another to attract and serve knowledge workers in the new economy and professional and managerial classes through entertainment districts and the arts, loft and luxury condominium developments in downtown core, and high-tech industrial parks on the exurban fringe."[3] The irony is that bohemians were once a marginalized class in European cities and yet now they are the poster-children of hip and trendy urban districts in the U.S. How did that happen?

In his book *Neo-Bohemia*, Richard Lloyd explains, "In Paris in the nineteenth century, the term 'bohemia' evolved into both an ethnic designation, including the remnants of this defunct state scattered throughout Europe, and a more general epithet synonymous with gypsy and beggar."[4] These Bohemians began scattering throughout European cities and were considered a seedy lot. Over time "Bohemian" became increasingly synonymous not only with a certain ethnicity, but with more or less a lifestyle grouping. In the *Westminster Review* in 1862, we read of these emerging urbanites. "The term 'Bohemian' has come to be very commonly accepted in our day as the description of a certain kind of literary gipsy, no matter in what language he speaks, or what city he inhabits ... A Bohemian is simply an artist or littérateur who, consciously or unconsciously, secedes from conventionality in life and in art."[5]

Giacomo Puccini's opera *La bohème* is about a group of bohemians living in the Latin Quarter in Paris in the 1840s. The opera premiered on February 1,

---

2 Florida, *The Rise of the Creative Class*, 287-290.

3 Hiller, *Urban Canada*, 212.

4 Lloyd, *Neo-Bohemia*, 52.

5 Harper, "Bohemian."

1896, and became wildly successful. With flamboyant costumes, the opera romanticized and endeared bohemians to the wider population. In tracing the historic development of hipsters, Brett McCracken writes, "The bohemians—immortalized a century later in Puccini's *La bohème*—were mostly poor writers and artists who congregated in various enclaves of Europe's most fashionable cities, often participants in underground literary and journalistic projects that commented on the heightened political tensions of the period."[6] Bohemians were no longer simply people from the former nation of Bohemia, but represented artists, writers, and, more or less what we think of in terms of cultural creatives.

"In the United States, bohemia materialized most prominently at the turn of the twentieth century in the New York district of Greenwich Village, an avant-garde ghetto in a sea of cultural populism."[7] Since bohemianism was and is associated with all things urban it was only a matter of time that this romanticized, yet marginalized, grouping would begin emerging in American cities. As in Paris, they were drawn to parts of the city that were more rundown and dilapidated because they offered cheap rent and a lower cost of living. Since their lifestyle was more artisan than day-laborer, finding a low-rent urban district was paramount.

As with all things imported to America, bohemians began to adapt and re-form around a new cultural and economic narrative. "If the Greenwich Village version of bohemia borrowed liberally from Paris' example, it nevertheless took shape against the distinctive backdrop of the exploding American metropolis, fueled by immigrants and expanding industry."[8]

Bohemians from the beginning were countercultural. Not only that, but they also were and are creators of new culture, usually associated with creative endeavors such as art, music, and literature. Over the past 200 years bohemians have evolved. In the latter part of the twentieth century and into this new millennium, they even have become mainstream, much to their chagrin. In their evolution there have been various branches, versions, and adaptations making it problematic at times to explicitly identify them. From artists and writers to

---

6 McCracken, *Hipster Christianity*, 35.

7 *Neo-Bohemia*, 57.

8 Ibid.

hippies in the 1960s and 70s, to software programmers in the Silicon Valley, or bicycle frame builders in Portland today, they continue to evolve. From upstream to mainstream. "[Richard] Florida concludes that bohemia has morphed into something else, a new mainstream in which creativity, nonconformity and lust for visceral experience can coexist comfortable with grueling work schedules and the pursuit of massive profits."[9]

Today bohemians represent a growing swath in society from artists and bartenders in Wicker Park in Chicago to MTV hosts in New York to baristas and brewers in Portland. And similar to various "species" of animals, there are also today many different "breeds" of bohemians. A bohemian in the Pearl (upscale) is significantly different from a bohemian on North Williams.

One of the identifying markers of this burgeoning creative class is that they gain their livelihood through their intellect and creativity. Not surprisingly this finds expression in many different shapes and forms. And since Portland is a poster-child for this newly emerging and growing economic class, then certainly we'll find ample examples of these types throughout the city. "Other cities have their bohemian districts, but Portland stands alone as an urban economy that has broadly embraced the artisan approach to living and working."[10]

So who is this nebulous creative class? Richard Florida writes:

> The distinguishing characteristic of the Creative Class is that its members engage in work whose function is to 'create meaningful new forms' define the Creative Class as consisting of two components. The Super-Creative Core of this new class includes scientists and engineers, university professors, poets and novelists, artists, entertainers, actors, designers and architects, as well as the thought leadership of modern society: nonfiction writers, editors, cultural figures, think-tank researchers, analysts and other opinion-makers. Whether they are software programmers or engineers, architects or filmmakers, they fully engage in the creative process.[11]

Within this creative class (bohemians, artisans, hipsters) there is also a larger over-arching category that "includes 'creative professionals' who work in a wide range of knowledge-intensive industries such as high-tech sectors, financial

---

9 Ibid., 70.

10 Heying, *Brew to Bikes*, 17.

11 *The Rise of the Creative Class*, 69.

services, the legal and health care professions, and business management. These people engage in creative problem solving, drawing on complex bodies of knowledge to solve specific problems. Doing so typically requires a high degree of formal education and thus a high level of human capital."[12] The conversation about bohemians, hipsters, artisans, and the creative class is in actuality an economic conversation, because what separates them and makes them stand out is really all about their jobs and careers.

Henry Ford has had a significant impact upon American culture. While he didn't invent the automobile, he made sure that every American had the opportunity to buy one. Through creative genius, innovation, and determination he figured out how to use an assembly line to build cars by the thousands. This process has been dubbed "Fordism." "Fordism refers to the economic and institutional forms that became dominant in the late nineteenth century and reaches maturity in the post-World War II period. It is an economic system organized around mass production and mass consumption, and is so named because important aspects of the revolutionary restructuring of economic organization were introduced by Henry Ford."[13] Listed below are numerous attributes that have become synonymous with the American manufacturing economy.

- The standardization of the product (nothing hand-made: everything is made through machines, molds and not by skilled craftsmanship).
- The use of special-purpose tools and/or equipment designed to make assembly lines possible: tools are designed to permit workers with low skill levels to operate "assembly lines"—where each worker does one task over and over and over again—like on a doll assembly line, where one worker might spend all day every day screwing on doll heads.
- Workers are paid higher "living" wages, so they can afford to purchase the products they make.
- Other characteristics of the Fordist system are huge manufacturing complexes that anchor the urban economies of iconic locations such as Detroit and employ large numbers of unionized laborers who expect to

---

12 Ibid.

13 *Brew to Bikes*, 23.

be working for the company through most of their employed lifetimes.[14]

Uniformity is key. Everything is standardized. A McDonald's cheeseburger is designed to taste the same whether it's made in Seattle or in Miami. A Venti iced chai at Starbucks ought to taste the same whether it's made in Dallas or Detroit. This is Fordism: the celebration of uniformity, standardization, and consistency. On the surface that makes a lot of good sense. Regardless of what month we purchase a new car in, it should all be the same. It wouldn't quite work to have a "bad batch" in February, but March and August were "great months" for the Ford Fusion. There need to be consistent high standards throughout. To fail at that would jeopardize the whole system, or at least cost the company millions in recalls.

Workers in Fordist enterprises do not necessarily need to be skilled or educated. It could be all they do is pull a lever all day, eight hours a day, forty hours a week. They are just a part of the larger assembly line. They may be placing a key component or part into an automobile, a digital device, or a bicycle, but know little of the overall process or the mechanics of how the whole works. They simply pull their lever.

More than simply creating uniformity in a product, Fordism has created uniformity in mass cultural consumption as well. Most popular music or movies fit into this genre. Mass-produced for cultural consumption, the most popular music often is not even the best quality; it is simply what is popular because it follows the tried-and-true techniques and formulae that test-marketing shows appeal to the largest masses. The same can be said of most mainstream movies. In this regard we've become a consumers of global mass culture. It is a shared narrative regardless of where one lives.

Simultaneous with the Fordism narrative is Post-Fordism. This is what Charles Heying has labeled the Artisan Economy. As Fordism has crept into so many facets of our society and global culture, there has arisen a backlash of sorts. A growing group of people, disenfranchised by the excesses of Fordism, are opting to be more in tune and in touch with what they are buying or consuming. People want to be more intimately involved in the process and even production of what they use and consume. Rather than walking down the endless aisles of a

---

14 Ibid., 24.

national chain grocery store to purchase mass-produced food, for example, more and more people are either buying locally-sourced foods or are now growing their own. It is in this artisan economy of Post-Fordism that we find the neo-bohemians, the hipsters, and the creative class.

"Post-Fordism describes the phase shift in the market/industrial system in which the success and contradictions of the Fordist system are resolved in a new set of economic and institutional relationships. The watershed of this period of crisis and transformation is generally set around 1970."[15] Like Fordism, there are associated attributes that define this growing economic force.

- Small-batch production.
- Specialized products and jobs.
- New information technologies.
- Emphasis on types of consumers in contrast to previous emphasis on social class.
- The rise of the service and the white-collar worker.
- The feminization of the work force.[16]

What becomes immediately noticeable is the scale of output. From large quantity to small-batch. However, this small list represents only the beginning. The table below, taken from *Brew to Bikes,* details in more vivid detail the stark contrast between the two economies.

Artisan Economy	Fordist Economy
Product Qualities	
Handmade	Standardized
Similar but not uniform	Obsessive uniformity
Variation is appreciated	Low tolerance for variation
Authentic	Faux
Locally distinct	Universal, generic
Work Life	
Improvisational work	Routine work

15 Ibid., 25.

16 Ibid.

Work as vocation	Work for pay
Work follows rhythms of season, project	Work times fixed and monitored
Integration of work, living, socializing spaces	Segregation of work, living, socializing spaces
Organizational Structure	
Small and medium scale enterprise	Large scale enterprise
Higher work autonomy	Low worker autonomy
Clustered, collaborative firms	Hierarchically organized firms
Moral Economy	
Less is more	Structural imperative for growth
Reinvestment in social and ecological infrastructure	Exploitation of social and ecological infrastructure

"As urban economies shifted from Fordist industrial production to post-Fordist knowledge, and service industries and globalization increased competition between cities, a consensus developed that central cities had increasingly become sites of consumption rather than production."[17] This observation is pivotal to our topic about gentrification along North Williams Avenue. The geography of the artisan economy is concentrated in inner-city urban contexts. That is coupled with the reality that neo-bohemians and the creative class are located in their highest concentrations in these same districts and neighborhoods.

There's a new pecking order among cities that are reflective of this reality. Central cities and places such as along North Williams that are being revitalized and gentrified are seeing an increase in not only neo-bohemians, but in new artisan business start-ups as well. This bodes well for these reemerging neighborhoods in terms of economic viability. Heying writes, "To attract these high-income workers and the footloose new-economy industries to the city, many urban policymakers focus their entrepreneurial efforts on remaking the city into what Lloyd and Clark label 'an Entertainment Machine.'"[18] He adds, "Cities that have the cultural ambiance that resonates with the creative class will

---

17 Ibid., 27.

18 Ibid.

enter into a virtuous cycle of growth, attracting or growing clusters of new-economy industries that, in turn, become thick with opportunity and possibility for change."[19]

What this does is elevate the importance of place, and central cities in particular. These places are the habitat of hipsters. The Creative Class is drawn to cities (some more so than others) because these cities articulate the various factors that they value. This explains much of the "Portland phenomenon:" It intersects the artisan economy, the central city, and the influx of the creative class, hipsters, and bohemians. These macro-level changes are part of the storyline that is reshaping life along North Williams as it begins to answer the question as to why people are choosing to move there. As I will detail in the next section, this change in the economy and the presence of the creative class in Albina is expediting gentrification.

The Creative Class and the Artisan Economy as Catalytic for Gentrification

As I sat down to write this section, I glanced out the window of the four-story mixed-use residential building we call home at the four-story building across the street. The brand new, bright red "Now Open" banners adorning the building, which just opened yesterday, signaled to residents and newcomers alike that inner N/NE Portland continues to change and transform. Its website description and imagery selection reveal some of the developers' perceived hopes and aspirations for the building and who they are targeting. A logo designed around the building's name features a Portlandesque bicyclist. The scrolling images on the website's home page highlight the nearby library (with a bike in its bike rack), a local brewery (with a bike in its bike rack), and a French bakery and cafe (with a bike in its bike rack). Adding to the mix of the values that the building purportedly emits is the fact that prospective tenants will have no place to park their cars.

I decided to check out the new building and meet one of the leasing agents. I learned much about the building, how fast the units were renting out, the supposed controversy among the neighbors over no parking, the size of the units,

---

19 Ibid., 29.

and who is moving in. The units are small, ranging from roughly 500 to700 square feet. Surprisingly, the demographic profile of residents who've signed up to move in are not what one would think. While some are certainly young techies, there are also retired couples, elderly and middle-aged singles, young students, and young couples. All are white. Two blocks away the same company recently opened their other 47-unit apartment building. It was rented out quickly to a similar demographic.

These two new apartment buildings, although small, continue to change the neighborhoods of inner N/NE Portland. Along North Williams within the past few years several of these new apartment blocks with super-small units have gone up with even more under construction. Their presence, coupled with several other similar buildings in the neighborhood, are slowly changing the culture and flavor of Albina. Most of the new residents moving in, regardless of age, are white–collar, well-educated. They all have a common desire to live in Portland's central city … and they are all ethnically white. While this may not seem stereotypical of the creative class, they still are nonetheless. But why are people downsizing and willing to pay a premium price to live in rather small apartment units? What is the appeal in their choosing to forgo single-family detached homes with a two-car garage and a yard in favor of "cramped" units with little storage, no parking, and a bike rack on the bottom floor?

Are these incoming residents of North Williams part of Richard Florida's creative class? If so, then it would make sense to developers and civic leaders to court them knowing that they bring with them disposable incomes and a taste for an urban lifestyle. "In today's 'post-industrial,' technology-driven economy, people are more footloose than ever, frequently shifting jobs and geography to take advantage of new opportunities."[20] I wonder how much of the impetus behind the creation of these new apartment buildings grew out of a desire to attract and retain this "footloose" demographic.

Florida's creative class argument presumes, in essence, that a city's economic success hinges on the presence of these knowledge workers, the white-collar, cultural creatives[21] City after city across the United States has bought into this rhetoric and has begun reinvesting in and regenerating their central cities. Even

---

20 Bereitschaft, "Omaha's quality of living appeals to 'Creative Class.'"

21 Ibid.

old northern cities that were once the epicenter of industrialization are shedding old labels and industries in favor of wooing the creative class back into their declining downtowns. Florida points out that this very strategy is alive and working even in cities like Detroit. "Thousands of residents, including designers, techies and music makers, have moved to Detroit's old central business district. They are drawn, to borrow a phrase from Jane Jacobs' 1961 work, *The Death and Life of Great American Cities*, to the old buildings new ideas require."[22]

But not everyone is buying into Florida's thesis. After his book *The Rise of the Creative* was released in 2002 came a backlash among scholars who derided what they saw as his weak analysis and contrived conclusions. As Markusen points out, part of the dissonance is in how Florida lumps together various industries which may or may not be reflective of truly "creative" jobs:

> Florida's creative class groupings are based on major occupational groups—he does not look inside each of these to see what they contain. Business and financial occupations, for instance, include claims adjusters and purchasing agents. Managers include sales and food-service managers and funeral directors. Computer and mathematical occupations include actuaries and tax collectors. Engineers include surveyors and drafting technicians. Health care practitioners include dental hygienists and dietary and pharmacy technicians. These occupations may indeed be creative, but so too are airplane pilots, ship engineers, millwrights, and tailors—all of whom are uncreative in Florida's tally. The discussion of the creative class is fudged yet more by Florida's selective use of interviews and anecdote to suggest behaviors and preferences that are not representative of the 'class' as a whole.[23]

Regardless of this tension and pushback, cities from Portland to St. Louis to Milwaukee to Brooklyn have all bought into this creative economy and its creative class as a strategy for urban regeneration.

The discourse revolving around the creative class argument immediately begins to embrace other topics such as art, culture, tourism, and regeneration. The very nature of the term "creative" points to the need for and presence of the arts. If there were to be a flourishing of the arts in a city, what role would artists themselves play? Are they homegrown or imports from elsewhere, having been

---

22 Florida, "Detroit Shows Way to Beat Inner City Blues."

23 Markusen, "Urban Development and the Politics of a Creative Class," 1922.

drawn to a city that is "happening"? Is the burgeoning arts scene merely the product of a strategic economic effort and cultural push by civic leaders to reorient their city away from manufacturing to a more hi-tech, white-collar, creative- or knowledge-based economy? In addition to those initial questions there are bound to be a myriad more as the conversation can quickly turn to the creative class theory, how cities are all-in on this socio-economic grouping, and the resultant impact on the city of gentrification and urban revitalization.

Narrowing the conversation of the creative class specifically to artists, Elizabeth Currid asks, "How do we create places where talented people, who are footloose, capricious, and in high demand, want to live and work? What sort of place-based characteristics do they seek out?"[24] The arts, creativity, and innovation are integral to economic development which explains some of the reasoning behind the allure of the creative class and why cities are trying so hard to attract and keep them. One of the key components of the creative economy that Currid explores in her article "How Art and Culture Happen in New York" reveals that agglomeration is central to the success and vibrancy of a city's arts scene. "Planners and economic developers have long noted that clustering like-minded firms, labor pools, institutions, and resources is important to transferring information, supplies, and ideas efficiently, resulting in localized economic benefits. Agglomeration may be even more important to maintaining the social mechanisms by which the cultural economy sustains itself."[25] The appeal to planners and developers is that if a city can gather its share of cultural creatives then by proximity the benefits of agglomeration multiply. This bodes well for a city's prospects for nurturing the arts and ultimately its creative or artisan economy.

One of the challenges to cities that cater to the creative class, primarily artists and cultural creatives, is that, while they can serve as catalysts for urban regeneration, their efforts can make the very neighborhoods they moved into too pricey for them to stay there. Currid addresses this paradox where artists create desirable locations only to watch as non-artists move in and drive up housing costs which forces out the very people who had helped turn these neighborhoods around.

---

24 Currid, "How Art and Culture Happen in New York," 454.

25 Ibid., 460.

Artists in cities have been noted to favor more authentic, gritty neighborhoods. Their motivations range from aesthetic preference to simply the low cost of spaces in urban neighborhoods on the decline. These neighborhoods often have ample housing and studio stock for artists to move into and utilize. It could be argued that in some ways these places serve as "canvases" for artists and cultural creatives to create and frame space in the city. The potency is that for cities, image is everything. In the minds of elected civic leaders, planners and developers, the image their city projects either hurts or helps their economic outlook. "Yet the cultural power to create an image, to frame a vision, of the city has become more important as publics have become more mobile and diverse, and traditional institutions—both social classes and political parties—have become less relevant mechanisms of expressing identity."[26]

This sums up well the tensions surrounding the creative class theory. City after city, in the new "arms race" of city-branding, has bought into the creative class rhetoric. The challenge emerges when it comes at the expense of longstanding residents, most notably lower-income ethnic minorities. In some ways they are merely being pushed aside and marginalized even more so in favor of wooing white-collar knowledge workers who value certain cultural and lifestyle amenities. When investment in central city or neighborhood regeneration comes at the expense of the working class then this becomes problematic and arguably unethical. This is one more layer to the tensions to be found along North Williams.

Retail Gentrification in NE Portland

In the article "Retail Gentrification and Race," Sullivan and Shaw detail the transformation that has taken place in recent years on Alberta Street in NE Portland. Alberta intersects North Williams with commercial activity extending eastward. Sullivan and Shaw focus more on the retail implications of gentrification and even note the impact on the built environment. While they specifically address the changes that have taken place along Alberta, their analysis also reflects the changes taking place along North Williams. Sullivan and Shaw highlight the tension that residents feel due to the influx of new

---

26 Zukin, "Whose Culture? Whose City?," 283.

businesses in gentrifying neighborhoods. Oftentimes neighborhood change in gentrifying neighborhoods focuses on demographic shifts (i.e., who is moving in and out). Their article instead hones in on the transitions in retail and how neighborhood residents are reacting to the changes. "The majority of new retail, however, reflects the social class divide within gentrifying neighborhoods. Businesses such as art galleries, yoga studios, clothing boutiques, and restaurants appeal to the discretionary tastes and incomes of newcomers and nonlocal consumers; longtime residents are less likely to want or be able to afford these goods and services."[27] Their study revealed the mixed responses towards the physical changes taking place on Alberta as a result of new businesses moving in, regardless of whether they occupied existing space or were new commercial sites on vacant lots. On one level they appreciated the renewed economic vibrancy and how this new business activity even beautified the street. But they also complained that most of the new businesses did not cater to the established black community. Many, whether black or white, were averse to these newer "yuppie" businesses, but among the black community there was an outright rejection of these more "bohemian" enterprises.[28]

That last observation is key to understanding the changes happening on North Williams, namely who the businesses are catering to. Also of critical importance to the study of the intersection of racism, gentrification, and bicycles is to note and address who these neighborhood changes are meant to be for. Are these changes taking place to help the black community create a better neighborhood identity and sense of place? Or is the black community once again being excluded? Are these changes happening with or without their consent? In other words, *does gentrification continue the imbedded racism of black exclusion?*

The tension that Sullivan and Shaw's article reveals is in regards to who benefits from gentrification and the physical changes brought on by the process and who gets hurt by it. While longstanding residents, whether black or white, did indeed view positively some of the changes, what was problematic were precisely the types of new businesses that were coming in. Why should outside forces get to determine the future of neighborhoods when the future they envisage is not even what the neighborhood wants or desires? Why are the needs

---

27 Sullivan and Shaw, "Retail gentrification and race," 415.

28 Ibid., 422.

of the locals bypassed and ignored in hopes of wooing in this nebulous creative class who desire cafes, coffee shops, art spaces, and other urban amenities? Sullivan and Shaw conclude, "We find that, despite city officials, developers, new business owners, and members of the creative class embracing the principle of diversity and an ethos of progressivism, their actions privilege White 'creative' place entrepreneurs and undermine racial diversity by excluding longtime Black residents."[29] Tom Slater echoes this sentiment: "To label as anything other than gentrification the construction of upmarket housing aimed at young professionals in or on formerly working-class industrial spaces (for example, vacant dockyards or warehouses), and to use a term like 'revitalization' or 'regeneration' to characterize the implosion of low-income public housing projects in favor of mixed-income developments, is analytically erroneous and politically conservative."[30]

---

29 Ibid., 430.

30 Slater, "Gentrification of the City," 573.

Chapter 5

Gentrification, Bicycling, and Race on North Williams
Part 3: Bicycles and Urban Mission
Sean Benesh

The flashpoint for the gentrification conversation along North Williams revolves around the bicycle. As I mentioned previously, the cultural appetite for what the creative class likes and enjoys is in stark contrast to that of the African-American community. "North Williams Avenue wasn't hip back in the late 1970s. There was no Tasty n Sons. No Ristretto Roasters. No 5th Quadrant. Back then, it was the heart of the African American community. It was wonderfully colorful and gritty."[1] As Sullivan and Shaw noted in their article on retail gentrification, while the neighborhood appreciates seeing new businesses come in and the streetscape improved, these new businesses specifically cater mostly to ethnic white yuppies and bohemians. As the black community saw their own businesses close down through economic disinvestment, they weren't replaced with new businesses that they regarded as desirable. In the several hours I spent today at Ristretto Roasters I have seen roughly a hundred patrons come in and go out, plus others sitting outside in the patios of one of several nearby restaurants. Only three were African-American. As I mentioned earlier, the buildings that surround this coffee shop are home to many African-American families. And yet these new businesses do not appeal to their cultural tastes. Is the bicycle part of the same problem?

---

1 Smith, "This isn't the North Williams Avenue I remember."

This has all come to a head over the road project to reconfigure North Williams and Vancouver Avenue. Both are one-way roads a block apart that carry a high volume of bicycle traffic. Vancouver's southbound traffic flows carry cyclists towards the Lloyd Center and downtown Portland and so sees its heaviest usage in the mornings. Williams on the other hand carries northbound traffic away from the city center which means its highest use is in the afternoons and evenings when bicycle commuters are heading away from the city center. But the focal point of all of this controversy is specifically tied to North Williams Avenue because this is where most of the new businesses are coming in.

A *New York Times* article featured this stretch of the road including one of the business owners who opened up the Hopworks BikeBar that I mentioned earlier. "North Williams Avenue, one of the most-used commuter cycling corridors in a city already mad for all things two-wheeled. Some 3,000 riders a day pass by Mr. Ettinger's new brewpub, which he calls the Hopworks BikeBar. It has racks for 75 bicycles and free locks, to-go entrees that fit in bicycle water bottle cages, and dozens of handmade bicycle frames suspended over the bar areas. Portland is nationally recognized as a leader in the movement to create bicycle-friendly cities."[2] Other national newspapers and magazines have also picked up on all of the buzz happening along North Williams. In *Via Magazine*, Liz Crain writes, "With 3,000 commuters pedaling it every day, North Williams Avenue is Portland's premier bike corridor. Visitors, too, find plenty worth braking for on two blocks of this arterial, including two James Beard Award–nominated chef-owned restaurants and a slew of hip shops and cafés."[3] *Sunset Magazine* has several features on North Williams including "Go green on Portland's North Williams Avenue: Enjoy a low-key urban vibe thanks to yoga studios, indie shops, and cafes."[4]

With images of happy (white) hipsters pedaling bicycles, doing yoga, and eating gourmet food, the nation is given a taste of inner N/NE Portland that is not reflective of the reality of the neighborhood nor the tension surrounding gentrification. These magazines showcase things to see, do, and eat along North

---

2 Baker, "Developers Cater to Two-Wheeled Traffic in Portland, Ore."

3 Crain, "Portland's North Williams Avenue."

4 Manning, "Go Green on Portland's North Williams."

Williams with helpful hints like, "Scene: A low-key urban vibe, courtesy of yoga studios and green indie shops and cafes ... Dress code: waterproof jacket and jeans with right leg rolled up ... Native chic: A waterproof Lemolo bike bag ... The Waypost: Creative types come to this coffeehouse for locally produced wine and beer, as well as live music, lectures, and classic-movie screenings."[5] However, not all of the residents are necessarily in favor of these changes taking place. And there are certainly other national media outlets who have picked up on the "other side" of the North Williams story. "But not everyone is unreservedly enthusiastic about the district's new orientation. Located in a historic African-American community, the North Williams businesses are almost exclusively white-owned, and many residents see bicycles as a symbol of the gentrification taking place in the neighborhood."[6]

The tensions of racism and gentrification have culminated in the debates over North Williams' status as a major bicycle thoroughfare. Sarah Goodyear of *The Atlantic Cities* writes, "Sharon Maxwell-Hendricks, a black business owner who grew up in the neighborhood, has been one of the most vocal opponents to the city's plan for a wider, protected bike lane. She can't help but feel that the city seems only to care about traffic safety now that white people are living in the area. 'We as human beings deserved to have the same right to safer streets years ago,' she says. 'Why wasn't there any concern about people living here then?'"[7] This picks us on the tension surrounding the North Williams project in general, and in particular the controversy surrounding repainting the traffic lanes to incorporate new designs which cater to the growing number of bicyclists who use this corridor.

Goodyear goes on to lay out both sides of the controversy:

> Jonathan Maus, who runs the *Bike Portland* blog and has reported extensively on the North Williams controversy, thinks the city should have stood its ground and gone forward with the project, but wasn't willing to do so in part because of the political weakness of scandal-plagued Mayor Sam Adams, who has been a strong biking advocate and is closely identified with the biking community.

---

5 Ibid.

6 "Developers Cater to Two-Wheeled Traffic in Portland, Ore."

7 Goodyear, "Bike Lane Backlash, Even in Portland."

"There's been too much emphasis on consensus," said Maus. "I'm all for public process, but I also want the smartest transportation engineers in the country on bicycling to have their ideas prevail."

Maus, who is white, says the history of North Williams shouldn't be dictating current policy, and that safety issues for the many people who bike on the street are urgent. "At some point as a city, you have to start planning to serve the existing population," he said. "The remaining black community is holding traffic justice hostage. It's allowing injustice in the present because of injustice in the past."[8]

In light of this, why is North Williams the flashpoint for controversy? The tension and angst is more than simply repainting a roadway; it embodies the most visual representation of gentrification in inner N/NE Portland. For longtime African-American residents, as expressed by Sharon Maxwell-Hendricks above, she and others felt that they had simply been neglected for decades. This negligence took the form of economics, housing, and general concerns of safety. Their frustration is that it wasn't until middle-class whites began moving into the neighborhood that these issues began to be addressed and rectified. This notion of systemic racism helped created this area as a ghetto and these same forces are at play in gentrifying this once predominantly black neighborhood. The African-American community feels it has been slighted once again. The initial citizen advisory committee revealed the imbalance: "Despite North Williams running through a historically African American neighborhood, the citizen advisory committee formed for the project included 18 white members and only 4 non-white members."[9] This is why the push for safety along the North Williams corridor has caused such an uproar. "The current debate about North Williams Avenue—once the heart of Albina's business district—is only the latest chapter in a long story of development and redevelopment."[10]

For many in the African-American community the current debate over bike lanes along North Williams is simply one more example in a long line of

---

8 Ibid.

9 City Club of Portland, "Case Study."

10 Loving, "Portland Gentrification."

injustices that have been forced upon their neighborhood. Beginning in 1956, 450 African-American homes and business were torn down to make way for the Memorial Coliseum. "It was also the year federal officials approved highway construction funds that would pave Interstates 5 and 99 right through hundreds of homes and storefronts, destroying more than 1,100 housing units in South Albina."[11] Then came the clearance of even more houses to make way for Emanuel Hospital. For more than 60 years, racism has been imbedded in the storyline of what has taken place along North Williams.

For many, the North Williams project is more than repainting lines. Jonathan Maus reported, "A meeting last night that was meant to discuss a new outreach campaign on N. Williams Avenue turned into a raw and emotional exchange between community members and project staff about racism and gentrification."[12] In his article, Maus noted the painful history of Albina as the primary catalyst for the tension today.

> Lower Albina—the area of Portland just north and across the river from downtown through—was a thriving African-American community in the 1950s. Williams Avenue was at the heart of booming jazz clubs and home to a thriving black middle class. But history has not been kind to this area and through decades of institutional racism (through unfair development and lending practices), combined with the forces of gentrification, have led to a dramatic shift in the demographics of the neighborhood. The history of the neighborhood surrounding Williams now looms large over this project.[13]

It was at this meeting that a comment from one of those in attendance changed the entire trajectory of the evening as the conversation quickly moved away from the proposed agenda. Michelle DePass said, "We have an issue of racism and of the history of this neighborhood. I think if we're trying to skirt around that we're not going to get very far. We really need to address some of the underlying, systemic issues that have happened over last 60 years. I've seen it happen from a front row seat in this neighborhood. It's going to be very difficult to move forward and do a plan that suits all of these stakeholders until we

---

11 Ibid.

12 Maus, "Meeting on Williams project turns into discussion of race, gentrification."

13 Ibid.

address the history that has happened. Until we address that history and ... the cultural differences we have in terms of respect, we are not going to move very far."[14]

The crux of the conflict is not about bicycles nor bike lanes nor even new businesses and amenities. It is about racism. The push for creating a more bikeable and bike-friendly commuter corridor has raised the ire of longstanding residents who had felt neglected and voiceless for decades. "The North Williams case study is an example of the City inadequately identifying, engaging and communicating with stakeholders."[15] Now that more whites are moving in are changes are taking place. "Some question why the city now has $370,000 to pour into a project they say favors the bike community while residents for decades asked for resources to improve safety in those same neighborhoods. To the community, the conversation has polarized the issue: white bicyclists versus the black community."[16] The question is whether this is completely race-related or not. That is to say, Portland has been and continues to expand its bicycle infrastructure throughout the city, not just in N/NE Portland. There are also several other main bicycle corridors that receive a high volume of bicycle commuters, but since they do not go through any ethnic neighborhoods they have not created this much controversy. This does not minimize the tension and angst over the North Williams project; nor does it downplay the role that racism has played throughout the history of that community as well.

Minorities and Cycling

One of the questions that this case study reveals is the (supposed) connection between bicycles and racism. Are the use of bicycles really about ethnic identity and the preferred mode of urban transportation for a growing number of ethnic whites in central cities? Or is bicycling growing across the board among other ethnicities? John Greenfield, in an article entitled "Bike facilities don't have to be 'the white lanes of gentrification'" writes, "Bicycling

---

14 Ibid.

15 "Case Study."

16 Navas, "North Williams traffic safety plan gives neighbors a chance to delve into deeper issues of race, gentrification."

doesn't discriminate. It's good for people of all ethnicities and income levels because it's a cheap, convenient, healthy way to get around, and a positive activity for youth and families. So it's a shame that cycling, especially for transportation, is often seen as something that only privileged white people would want to do. And it's unfortunate when proposals to add bike facilities in low-income communities of color, which would be beneficial to the people who live there, are viewed as something forced on the community by outsiders."[17]

In his article, Greenfield explores a similar project in the neighborhood of Humboldt Park in Chicago. Like Portland, "People in Humboldt Park, a largely low-income Latino and African-American community on Chicago's West Side, once opposed bike facilities as well."[18] That was ten years ago. Since then attitudes towards bike lanes have changed. Over the last decade there have been concerted efforts to educate people, including low-income children, about the benefits of bicycling as well as related safety issues. The tide has turned, bike lanes have been installed, and the neighborhood has embraced them. In this case the city waited until the community eventually moved from resistance to acceptance to enthusiasm about a bicycle infrastructure before bike lanes were put in.

Again, this seems to be one of the points of tension in Albina because bike lanes were installed long before there was enthusiastic acceptance by the community. In essence, they felt that bike lanes were simply another in a long line of changes that were forced upon them without their consent. It appears that the City of Chicago did it right by taking their time. What it also reveals is the changing attitude among different ethnicities towards bikes and a bicycle infrastructure.

Recently a new report was released from the League of American Bicyclists and the Sierra Club called "The New Majority: Pedaling Towards Equity." Sarah Goodyear, in an article for *The Atlantic Cities*, highlights some of the findings from the report:

- Between 2001 and 2009, the fastest growth rate in bicycling was among the Hispanic, African American, and Asian American populations.

---

17 Greenfield, "Bike facilities don't have to be "the white lanes of gentrification."

18 Ibid.

Combined, those three groups went from making 16 percent of the nation's bike trips to 23 percent.

- Between 2001 and 2009, the growth in percent of all trips taken by bike was 100 percent among African Americans; 80 percent among Asians; 50 percent among Hispanics; and 22 percent among whites.
- Eighty-six percent of people of color surveyed said they had a positive view of bicyclists. (For the purposes of the survey, "people of color" includes African American, Hispanic, Asian, Native American and mixed race.)
- Seventy-one percent of people of color surveyed said that safer cycling would make their community better.[19]

What this article and this report reveal is the changing attitudes towards cycling among the American populace. This also dispels the notion that bicycling is strictly a "white" thing. Tanya Snyder writes, "Let's get one thing clear: People of color ride bikes. They commute to work on bikes. They ride for pleasure. It saves them money and time, and it keeps them healthy."[20]

In her article, Snyder highlights the tension of bicycling and racism. "'Nobody is against safer streets in their neighborhood,' said Hamzat Sani, equity and outreach fellow at the League of American Bicyclists. 'Cycling organizations just haven't done a good job communicating the message that streets that are safer for cyclists are safer for everyone.'"[21] In some ways this reveals part of the tension involved in the North Williams project. No one is against safer streets whether for adults or children. The crux of the angst is that the black community had been marginalized for so long that they felt they had lost their voice. This came to a head over the proposed bike lane changes because for them, it was more than white stripes on the road, it symbolized decades of marginalization and neglect.

The study by the League of American Bicyclists and the Sierra Club points out that bicycling ridership is on the rise among all different ethnicities. Not only that, but it is growing the fastest among the African-American community. The challenge is that, "Unfortunately, communities of color often lack for safe infrastructure. 'Data gathered by the Los Angeles County Bicycle Coalition

---

19 Goodyear, "The Surprising Diversity of the America Cycling Community."

20 Snyder, "Cyclists of Color."

21 Ibid.

revealed that neighborhoods with the highest percentage of people of color had a lower distribution of bicycling facilities,' the report says, 'and areas with the lowest median household income ($22,656 annually) were also the areas with the highest number of bicycle and pedestrian crashes.'"[22]

Case Study Conclusion

This case study reveals that there are multiple processes and actors involved in the gentrification process along North Williams Avenue. There are macro (global) and micro (local) forces at hand reshaping not only this part of Portland, but also inner-city neighborhood across the country in light of changing economies and cultural preferences as reflected in the rise of the creative class / artisans. The clash over bicycles appears to be at its core a sense of continued displacement symptomatic of the long history of racial exclusion. As a new report, "The New Majority: Pedaling Towards Equity," noted, the African-American community is not against bicycles. In fact they represent the fastest growing ethnicity in terms of new bicyclists, even at a faster rate than ethnic whites. The problem is not with bicycles or new bike lanes, but instead the systemic racism and injustice that have for so long oppressed the black community.

Injecting Urban Mission Into the Case Study

Over the past three chapters we delved into some of the nuances of the gentrification story along North Williams in Portland. As you can see by now, while there are similarities across cities and countries, each setting has been shaped in unique ways. Also, within each city where gentrification is taking place or has already happened, the process has not been uniform. One of the scenarios that makes the Portland story unique are those factors that are specific to the city, such as a relatively small minority population, in this case African-American, and the growing presence of bicycling. However, this book is not meant to be purely about theories and concepts. Instead, wherever possible, it is my intention as both an editor and contributor to inject thoughts and ideas

---

22 Ibid.

91

about urban mission into these settings and conversations. In the case of North Williams in Portland, what bearing does the Gospel have on what is taking place?

Throughout the book are chapters written by church planting practitioners who are starting churches either in gentrifying neighborhoods or in neighborhoods outside the central city on the receiving end of those displaced by gentrification. From the tenor of their perspective, experiences, and writings, you will be able to discern they are friends or foes (or both) of the whole gentrification process. My hope is to expose you to a wider range of opinion on the topics at hand from those who are planting churches among the creative class and hipsters in contrast to those who are planting churches among minority populations or the more marginalized. The truth is, both communities need to hear the Gospel. No one church can reach the full spectrum of the populace in gentrifying neighborhoods … which is why they need more new churches of various shapes and forms.

In light of this case study, what are the missiological implications? How does urban mission enter into the conversation and help frame what both the casual and informed observers see? In sharing some of my own observations I will highlight my own interactions and experiences here in Portland which may or may not be normative in many other neighborhoods and cities not only nationally but globally.

All of my adult post-college life I have been a pastor and a church planter. Sometimes pastors are fearful that the general public views them through the lens of Ricoeur's *hermeneutic of suspicion.* That somehow we are shallow imperialists who are colonialists in what we do, as if we were some post-modern version of the Crusades. There is an underlying conversation about *us* versus *them.* We fear being misunderstood. When I first entered state university academia following seminary to take classes to expand my understanding of the city I kept my "pastor card" tucked into my back pocket. It is not that I am ashamed of the cross or of Christ, but I instead wanted to discern a helpful way to communicate what I do and Who I belong to. Initially I would hem and haw when people asked what I do for a living, but after diving deeper into urban studies I soon discovered that one cannot swing a proverbial stick in the discourse on urban renewal, community development, or gentrification without hitting a church whether it be evangelical, mainline Protestant, or Catholic.

In reading countless articles, journals, and books on the various topics of urban revitalization I soon discovered that in many cases it was the church and professional clergy who helped create some sense of stability in destabilized neighborhoods. I read of pastors and priests standing in the midst of violent gangs while preaching the peace of Christ. I read of churches engaged in real estate development and economic development, and helping their congregations buy homes and stay rooted in their gentrifying neighborhoods. Bolstered by this I took my "pastor card" out of my back pocket and began again to wear it proudly. It has given me the opportunity to freely share *why* I am so passionate about cities, community development, and equitable gentrification. I am driven by a theological "Gospel-centered" ethic that God desires to redeem both urban people and urban places.

In the case of what is transpiring along North Williams in Portland there are ample ways for both new and established churches to be engaged in reaching out to and loving both the longtime residents and those newcomers who we would label as gentrifiers. In the next chapter I will continue to focus on this latter grouping. As I explained in the Preface, I write from and approach the topic of gentrification from a specific socio-economic, ethnic, and cultural background. While I can observe and note what is transpiring in neighborhoods around me, experientially I cannot pretend to be something or someone I am not. That is why I invited multiple contributors to help flesh out a larger perspective. But before they begin to do that, allow me to discuss the appeal of gentrification from the gentrifiers' vantage point.

Chapter 6

The Appeal of Gentrification
Sean Benesh

There are a lot of myths, assumptions, and conspiracy theories circulating around the topic of gentrification. Admittedly, much of it is warranted and deserved. However, in the discourse on gentrification one of the flash points of controversy we need to dispel and demystify are the intentions, motives, desires, and cultural preferences of those deemed as gentrifiers. Why are middle-class white people moving back into central city urban neighborhoods? Are their intentions imperialistic? Is it their desire to "take over" these declining neighborhoods and kick out the long-tenured ethnic residents? Is there a collective secret society of gentrifiers who plot and scheme how they will move into urban neighborhoods, fix up old homes a certain way, grow hipster mustaches, drink artisan coffee and hand-crafted beer, listen to only indie rock, start creative businesses, just so they can evict who's different from them? While these notions may seem absurd, the fact is many do claim to see gentrification as nothing more than a conspiracy to improve their lot in life by pushing out those who stand in their way. So what is the truth of what's taking place? Why are people moving back into the city?

Jane Jacobs is famously attributed with a statement that I have quoted for years: "New ideas require old buildings." I believe that statement helps frame much of the appeal of gentrification. Cities in essence can be viewed as grand cultural experiments of what society thinks and believes about certain values. The twentieth century was a unique aberration in the historical development of cities as changes in mobility from evolving transportation technologies allowed cities to sprawl and grow horizontally at an unparalleled pace. This created a need for mass-produced housing akin to Henry Ford's assembly lines. The result was suburbia in its current form. As we left the central city for greener suburban pastures in some ways there was also a cutting of ties. Old ethnic urban neighborhoods that were once heavily German or Italian or Puerto Rican saw their young adults leave in favor of the new sparkling suburbs with expansive lawns and open space. Who could blame them?

Fast forward to today and in some ways it is as though pockets of society are awakening from this car-induced slumber to realize they have lost touch with their cities, their history, and their roots. Slowly people started moving back in. This is not new to life in this new millennium; it has been taking place for decades. But what is different is how the pace has picked up. Maybe we simply got tired and bored of every fourth house in our neighborhood looking virtually the same, with the same color palette as our house, and our neighbors virtually the same demographic and socio-economic cross-section as ourselves. For many, Jacobs' quote was and is a clarion call wooing them (i.e., us) back into the city to experience its true grit, vitality, rawness, variety, and vibrancy. And so they (i.e., we) moved back into the city.

What was it in Jacobs' statement that resonates? It is though it gave expression to what millions of Americans, Canadians, and others are feeling and desiring. What changed? What is changing? Why is it changing? Academics are keen on their methods of research, controls, variances, and so on, but how do we qualify and quantify this back-to-the-city movement? How do we measure a "gut feeling" and a desire? My intention in this chapter is to simply try to answer those questions from the perspective of one making casual observations of these changes. This is more "gut" than "brain" as I simply offer a social commentary on some of the changes, desires, preferences, and leanings of those who we would classify as gentrifiers.

The Quest for Authenticity

It seems that the more virtual, detached, and complex life becomes, the stronger we yearn to return to what's authentic, what's real, what can make us "feel alive" again. Maybe it was after watching one too many movies like *The Matrix* that something stirred within us, a recoiling in our core to get back to where we felt alive, that our life really does matter and make a difference, and that what we are experiencing is truly life and not some faux version or a lie. Maybe this is only a First World problem in that we have such a comfortable lifestyle that we don't fuss or worry too much about simply survival. Our chief complaints seem nowadays to be about spotty wifi, a data plan for our smart phones that's too expensive, our commutes are too long, too many of the commercials during the Super Bowl are just plain bad, *The Office* television series has come to an end, or that our favorite coffee shop has raised its prices 25 cents.

I can recall numerous songs and movies where an underlying theme is a desire to feel pain in order to ensure that we are really alive and conscious. Maybe this is a lingering outcome of the postmodern hermeneutic, but it can also explain the rapid rise and continuation of extreme sports. You see, if your life is simply about survival you don't have time nor are you tempted to do anything more extreme than eat. But in a culture where all of our basic needs are met (and then some) then maybe we have "moved on" from simply surviving. Even our homeless population here in Portland has it better now than a generation ago, and certainly better than for millions of people in other countries. I see them sipping on $4 lattes while checking emails and updating their Facebook status on their smart phones. In a time in history, particularly in Western and Northern countries, where comfort and security have moved from being a necessity to a commodity, with the result that in order to feel alive we push ourselves to new extremes.

As an urban cyclist it is a thrill to ride my singlespeed (not a fixie, mind you) through crowded downtown streets, cutting through narrow spaces in-between cars. It sure makes for exciting commutes and it keeps me alert and focused. Just last night I was watching a film about alley cat races in such places as New York City and Tokyo where fixie bicycle riders race from checkpoint to checkpoint for a truly urban race. The only rules are that the bikes have to be fixies and have no hand brakes. The footage of the race, filmed via helmet camera, is of riders zigging and zagging through congested Manhattan traffic all the while blowing through stop lights and stop signs, holding onto moving cars for extra speed, and taking risk after risk. If life is about survival and the assumed self-preservation then risks like that are not worth taking.

Sometimes this quest for authenticity drives us to reconnect with our past, whether real or imagined. Maybe that partly explains why hipsters always don the fashion of yesteryear ... the grizzly beards, mustaches, glasses, hairstyles, and clothing. The more mobile and detached we've become the more rootless we feel and the more we desire some sort of anchor to the past. I can honestly admit that the older I get the more this inner desire for connectivity to the past grows. Not "past" in terms of my childhood per se, but something even older. A few days ago as I was in VeloCult bike shop across the street from us and there was a patron sipping on a beer next to his refurbished 1920s English-built bicycle. It was a thing of beauty and we talked about the details of the bike and how he rebuilt it. Many of us desire connections to a past which we somehow deem to be more authentic than the life we experience today.

While I thoroughly enjoyed living in Vancouver, BC, by the end I was growing weary of seeing the proliferation of shiny new high-rise residential towers. The city's skyline is new, sleek, and modern. I began to long for something old ... cobblestone streets, old brick buildings, and a sense of grittiness, rawness, and authenticity. It is not that the new and the modern are not authentic, but in my mind I longed for something old. That explains why I loved spending time among the more historic buildings of Gastown in downtown Vancouver, or downtown New Westminster, and or Lower Lonsdale in North Vancouver. The first time I visited Montreal I was enthralled and still am to this day because of the historicity of the place.

Japonica Brown-Saracino picks up on this mindset in an article entitled, "Social Preservationists and the Quest for Authentic Community," "There is an ethic and set of practices, unnamed and little noticed, that shape both urban and rural communities. I call this ethic and set of practices *social preservation*; the culturally motivated choice of certain people, who tend to be highly educated and residentially mobile, to live in the central city or small town in order to live in authentic social space, embodied by the sustained presence of 'original' residents."[1] And so it is here, in this notion of social preservation, there emerges the heart of gentrification's appeal. The desire for authentic experiences ties in with what we would deem authentic places which for most of us are the older

---

1 Brown-Saracino, "Social Preservationists and the Quest for Authentic Community," 261.

historic parts of the city. It just happens to be where, in many cities today (even though it is rapidly changing) that ethnic minorities also live.

When most of the mobile white middle class fled for the suburbs throughout the twentieth century, they left behind lower-income ethnic minorities who were not so mobile. Their lack of mobility stemmed from economic exclusion as well as racism that sought to keep them "contained" in these deteriorating older pockets of the city. However, decades later when there is renewed interest among the mobile white middle class to move back into these same neighborhoods that this becomes the focal point of tension and conflict. Admittedly, I don't harbor any conspiracy theories of those who left these urban neighborhoods a generation or two ago and I still don't harbor any conspiracy theories in regards to those who desire to move back. That doesn't mean, as we have explored in earlier chapters, that there were not (and are) larger systemic sins of racism which played out in redlining, market exclusion, or even the government playing a role in promoting suburbanization to keep the economic engine humming along after World War II. As Neil Smith explains, suburbanization and gentrification are inextricably linked, "Suburbanization and gentrification are certainly interconnected. The dramatic suburbanization of the urban landscape in the last century or more provided an alternative geographical locus for capital accumulation and thereby encouraged a comparative disinvestment at the center—most intensely so in the US."[2] However, what is essential in this conversation are the reasons why those that we have labeled gentrifiers are moving back into these old central city neighborhoods. I contend that one of their motives is an honest desire for authenticity and a connection to the past.

Tim Butler, in a 1997 article wrote, "Inner-city gentrification permits a style of life that can still be considered positively attractive."[3] He goes on to highlight this longing for something old and this notion of authentic places. "Oldness, or images of oldness, are important to a new class that is trying to emphasize its 'place' in the social structure; just as the industrial middle class married and bought its way into the aristocracy in the early nineteenth century so the service

2 Smith, "A Short History of Gentrification," 35.

3 Butler, "Consumption and Culture, 235.

class is doing so in the late twentieth century."[4] Authenticity and appeal of the old which many gentrifiers desire begins to frame the conversation around of what has been deemed a "loft lifestyle."

Who Doesn't Want to Live in a Loft?

Lofts fascinate me. I have named a book after them (*View From the Urban Loft*) as well as a publishing company (*Urban Loft Publishers*) and yet I have never lived in one. The closest we have come as a family is a fourth-floor apartment in a mixed-use building. Sometimes we jokingly refer to it as our "loft" but it is obviously far from one. So why this fascination with lofts and loft living?

The first time I came across lofts was in Tucson. As a former Church Planting Strategist I spent considerable time in the downtown and inner-city neighborhoods trying to get the pulse of the area and the changes that were slowly beginning to take place. Unlike other cities, apart from a few pockets here and there, Tucson does not offer much in the form of urban density which dampens potential would-be vibrant walkable urbanism. However, that is slowly changing as well. Over time building by building began to make the slow conversion from warehouse to apartment lofts or condos. From my vantage point I was interested in figuring out how we could start churches in these neighborhoods. I vividly recall scouring the websites of some of these conversion lofts and being fascinated with what I saw.

Lofts are not new and nor is this notion of loft living, but in the grand scheme of things they are relatively new. Sharon Zukin explains:

> Until the 1970s, living in a loft was considered neither chic nor comfortable–if the possibility was considered at all. Making a home in a factory district clearly contradicted the dominant middle-class ideas of "home" and "factory," as well as the separate work environments of family and work on which these ideas were based. Since the 1950s, suburbia had so dominated popular images of the American home that it was almost

---

4 Ibid., 236.

impossible to imagine how anyone could conceive the desire to move downtown into a former sweatshop or printing plant.[5]

Somewhere along the way the urban fabric of cities began changing as did the way that people viewed cities. The details go beyond the scope of this book,[6] but it should be noted the Industrial Revolution created certain factors that made cities unpleasant and unsavory, namely (a) rapid urbanization which meant overcrowding and (b) the close proximity between factory and home. Given the lack of sustainability practices in cities, factories with belching smokestacks combined with cramped housing, unsanitary conditions and unsustainable practices made for cities that were gritty and filthy. It's no wonder people were not keen on living in old factories. In fact, loft living was not on people's minds until the industrial city began to fade into history leaving empty buildings in its wake.

However, the key changes that were taking place which were (and are) reshaping the cultural preferences of Americans (and Canadians) were the lofts themselves in tandem with shifting middle-class consumption patterns.[7] This was all part of the larger reshaping of cities. Part of the newfound longing ties into the previous section on the quest for authenticity which also ties into Brown-Saracino's assertion of people's desire to live alongside the original residents of these older neighborhoods, to which I would add a preference for older historic buildings. Never mind that part of this longing was a somewhat naive romanticization of the past. "Only people who do not know the steam and sweat factory can find industrial space romantic or interesting."[8] Nonetheless, the continued growing appeal for loft living is an identification with the past and a desire for a new and even chic way to live.

Lofts are appealing to many and not simply among young 20-something hipsters. As lofts become even more fashionable and desirable they also become expensive and exclusive. Usually when one thinks initially of loft living the

---

5 Zukin, "The Creation of a 'Loft Lifestyle,'" 175.

6 A good primer on the changing downtowns read *Downtown: Its Rise and Fall, 1880-1920* by Robert M. Fogelson.

7 "The Creation of a 'Loft Lifestyle,'" 175.

8 Ibid., 176.

images that are conjured up are of starving artists squatting in an open former industrial building with a bed, a lamp, and design table amidst 10,000 square feet of emptiness that gets bone-chilling cold in the winter due to the lack of heat or any other basic amenities. The skinny-jeans-wearing artist in a beret and scarf throws outlaw-type weekend raves in his place which is known locally and inside the scene as "the spot." Fast forward to today and many loft residents are retired baby boomers who sold their massive suburban homes to move into and experience urban life as empty nesters (which I applaud). Just this morning while sitting in one of my favorite local coffee shops I watched a man in his late 60s walk in wearing cycling shoes, his bike helmet on, and a fashionable Chrome messenger bag slung over his shoulder. Not everyone who lives in the Pearl District or the other inner-city neighborhoods are poor hipsters and bohemians.

Lastly, loft living is the appeal of design and architecture from another era. There is an appreciation of different design facets which create a truly authentic experience in contrast to hyper-modernism.

> Loft living is part of a larger modern quest for authenticity. Old buildings and old neighborhoods are "authentic" in a way that new construction and new communities are not. They have an identity that comes from years of continuous use, and an individuality that creates a sense of "place" instead of "space." They are "New York" rather than "California," or "San Francisco" rather than "Los Angeles." Such places grow organically, not spasmodically. Because they are here today *and* tomorrow, they provide landmarks for the mind as well as the senses. In a world that changes moment by moment, anchoring the self to old places is a way of coping with the "continuous past." So loft living rejects functionalism, Le Corbusier, and the severe idealism of form that modern architecture represents.[9]

Gentrification, despite popular mythology, is not about rich white people moving into poor ethnic neighborhoods in order to evict people and create trendy neighborhoods. Instead, the appeal of these neighborhoods and such things as loft living is the attempt to reconnect with the past, carve out a sense of identity, cultivate a deeper sense of place, and evade the negative effects of all-things hyper-modern. The only problem is when there are many others who also desire this space which brings this group into close proximity with the lower-

---

9 Ibid., 181.

income groups and minorities in these historic places and neighborhoods. This is where the fulcrum of controversy takes place.

Connection with Historic Roots

This section seamlessly blends in with the previous as in many ways it is a continuation of the same thought, because this appeal for a connection to the past as it explains one of the motivations people have moving back into central city urban neighborhoods. As Tim Butler rightly states, "The desire to live in an old house emerges as a powerful reason for living in the inner city."[10] It appears that prolific suburbanization has left a certain void in the hearts, lives, and imaginations of people living in the city. We desired the new, the sleek, the efficient, the modern, the manicured, and the zoning that separated commercial from residential, only to realize a generation or two later how much we had missed what previous generations once had.

Small-town Iowa where I grew up is certainly by no stretch of the imagination "urban." Needless to say, I certainly did not have a big city upbringing. I actually disliked cities and was deathly afraid of their sheer girth and all of the negative associations with urban life. However, where and how I grew up really was not that different for many who grew up in central city urban neighborhoods. Let me explain. First of all, I grew up in a house that was more than a hundred years old. We even had a carriage barn as our garage came complete with a loft where hay was stored which made for great opportunities to jump out of second-story windows. A few blocks away was the old corner store where we'd go and buy all sorts of candy and sweets. Above it is where the owners lived.

When I left home for university I went to Grace University in the heart of Omaha, Nebraska, on the southern flank of the downtown area. Part of the neighborhood was an old bohemian ethnic enclave and since my family came from an actual country called Bohemia and the part of Iowa I grew up in had been settled by Bohemian immigrants it was fun to be there, especially since I could find some delicacies like *kolaches*. But that was about as far as my interest went because I had a difficult time adjusting to city life, especially transitioning

---

10 "Consumption and Culture," 248.

from a small town to an inner-city neighborhood. It was old, historic, and all of the things that we find appealing today, but in 1993 all I wanted was something new. People were not flocking to this part of the city to live out their hipster existence. It was blue-collar and a bit on the gritty side, but not bad or rough. A lot of the people living there had been there a while.

After growing up in an old historic home and living in a historic district I would on occasion drive out to the suburbs and be somewhat in awe of the new tract homes. I had no preconceived notions of the urban-suburban cultural conflict or dichotomy. All I knew was that the homes were nice and new, the landscaping was immaculate, and it was clean and seemed safe. I was neither hypercritical about the supposed sterility of the suburbs nor their homogeneity. It simply was appealing to me.

For the next ten years following college my wife and I had the opportunity to live a fully suburban experience, and not only that, but in sprawling Sunbelt cities. We lived in and loved our tract home that was the same as every fourth home on the block. Again, we didn't have any preconceived notions of the supposed lack of cultural couth in the suburbs. It was new, nice, clean, uniform, modern, and quite enjoyable. We liked our two-car garage that from the front street seemed to dominate the house. Our neighbors were all socio-economically in the same boat since housing prices were roughly the same, but we enjoyed that as many of the neighborhood children were the same ages as our own. There was a sense of community among the neighbors and we would have barbeques together, celebrate holidays together, and even be there for each other during times of crisis. It was a great experience and I still recall those times with fondness. But then something changed.

Through my ministry as a Church Planting Strategist I would spend a considerable part of my time in the central city of Tucson. My perceptions of the city began changing. Most of those former college experiences began to fade and the allure of the central city grew. Over time I grew to appreciate and even long for the old, historic districts, and buildings that were not mass-produced. Fast forward the storyline and our lives are now housed in the central city of Portland. We live in a district full of hundred-year-old houses and buildings like the Hollywood Theater. Strangely, this is the most like small-town Iowa than anywhere else we have lived. Both feature old homes, mixed-use zoning, and a street canopy of large old trees. When we walk the dog we chat with the neighbors and our boys spend their days in the neighborhood skateboarding with friends.

If my life is a microcosm of a larger cultural phenomenon, then this growing desire to connect with and become rooted in the past is certainly strong. As I analyze my own feelings it is not something that can necessarily be quantifiable, but instead it is a longing. I wonder how much of it is the resultant impact of a mobile society where we have become separated from our roots and life for most us after high school took us all over the country and the globe? The craving for new adventures and experiences can indeed be a rush, but in the end it can lead to loneliness and a longing for stability and roots.

Am I saying that people are motivated to moving into urban neighborhoods because they are in some way feeling disconnected from their past and thus seeking to subconsciously rectify it? No, not necessarily. But what I am saying is that in a world that is fast-paced and hyper-modern (sleek, new, uniform) there is a collective longing for what is old, rooted, historic, and unique. The appeal of gentrification, i.e., the middle class moving into lower-income neighborhoods, is partly this desire to have some connection with the past. "What matters most for those gentrifying the inner city is that their houses are moulded from 'real history.'"[11] Where conflict ensues is when the middle class who fled a generation or two ago decide to come back, they find the neighborhood has changed.

Participants in a Cultural Experiment

Another motivation people have for wanting to relocate in central city neighborhoods is the strong desire to be part of a new trend, business, or movement from its "grassroots beginnings." How many people have kicked themselves because they passed up a chance to get in on the ground floor with innovators like Bill Gates or Steve Jobs or Mark Zuckerberg? Or maybe they missed out on an opportunity to invest in a fledgling little start-up company that became a multi-billion-dollar company? The same impetus to some degree drives gentrification. When I see homes valued at $500,000, $750,000, or $1.25 million I often wonder why I didn't move to Portland back in the mid-1990s when I could've bought it for $55,000?

---

11 Ibid., 236.

It is not uncommon for people to want to be part of something new and exciting and cutting-edge. Gentrification is just as much a social movement as it is an economic investment or a means to connect with the past. We even have labels for people who first move into "pre-gentrified" neighborhoods ... *pioneer gentrifiers*. We apply the label of "pioneer" to these "brave souls" because they choose to risk life and limb to move into the "hood" before the rest of their fellow white middle-class folks. The term itself betrays an arrogance by as much as suggesting that simply by moving in, these "pioneers" had a civilizing effect on these neighborhoods or districts, which until they arrived were on the verge of urban barbarism. It is basically the same mindset by which we view those pioneers of yesteryear who settled the West and made something good out of seemingly nothing. Yet this glosses over the fact that Native Americans had already been living on the land for thousands of years. But because they didn't look or act or believe like us, we have made the newcomers into heroic "pioneers." This is troubling because when used in this context the term itself in many ways assumes an ethnic white cultural superiority ethic.

Neil Smith tackles this frontier mentality head on in his article "Building the Frontier Myth." He writes, "The social meaning of gentrification is increasingly constructed through the vocabulary of the frontier myth, and at first glance this appropriation of language and landscape might seem simply playful, innocent. Newspapers habitually extol the courage of urban 'homesteaders,' the adventurous spirit and rugged individualism of the new settlers, brave 'urban pioneers,' presumably going where, in the words of *Star Trek*, no (white) man has gone before."[12] When seen through this lens, gentrification thus becomes nothing more than ethnic whites courageously moving into the inner city as "pioneer homesteaders" among those they deem to be less civilized or educated than they are. Not surprisingly this perspective just reinforces the tensions and divisions between established residents and the newcomers.

This desire to participate in such a social experiment also evokes images of colonial expansion. Atkinson and Bridge allude to this in their article on globalization and gentrification: "Contemporary gentrification has elements of colonialism as a cultural force in its privileging of whiteness, as well as the more class-based identities and preferences of urban living. In fact not only are the

---

12 Smith, "Building the Frontier Myth, 113.

new middle-class gentrifiers predominantly white but the aesthetic and cultural aspects of the process assert a white Anglo appropriation of urban space and urban history."[13] This notion of gentrification as a social cultural experiment is dangerous in that it borders on a colonialist mindset and creates a dichotomy between "them" and "us." It conjures up negative images of colonialism past and present. "At the neighbourhood level itself poor and vulnerable residents often experience gentrification as a process of colonisation by the more privileged class."[14]

With that said, I want to make it clear that not all gentrifiers are colonialists or pioneers, because many are simply drawn to the greater vibrancy of multicultural urban neighborhoods. I often tell the story of when we moved to Vancouver, Canada. We purposely moved into the most ethnically diverse neighborhood that we could find. At one point I heard our local Member of Parliament describe our neighborhood as the most ethnically diverse neighborhood in the world. Its residents spoke more than a hundred different languages. It was commonly claimed that everyone there was foreign-born. We had grown accustomed to and loved living in almost exclusively non-white communities. At times when I was sitting in one of the local coffee shops I would look up and realize that out of the thirty to forty patrons in the place I was the only white person.

These were precisely the reasons why we moved there. We loved the daily joy of navigating the socially complex neighborhoods as we interacted with people from India, China, Pakistan, Iran, Sudan, Bangladesh, Japan, and so on. As parents we were humbled and grateful that our children had this opportunity to catch a glimpse of the global village all within one neighborhood. I suppose one could argue that in some ways we were drawn to this notion of being part of a social experiment. It appealed to us to be living in a complex urban environment. But there was nothing pioneering or colonialist about it ... we simply loved it. As a matter of fact, we didn't want the neighborhood to change.

Many gentrifiers find themselves in the same boat. There are certain aspects about moving into ethnic urban neighborhoods that simply appeal to them. They have no questionable motives. Their intent is not to be pioneers or plant the flag

---

13 Atkinson and Bridge, "Globalisation and the New Urban Colonialism," 52.

14 Ibid.

of ethnic superiority, even to cause displacement. Not everyone desires to live in low-density homogeneous suburban settings. People who move to Manhattan do so because they love the density and diversity that New York City offers. People move to Vancouver, San Francisco, Toronto and many other major cities for no other reason. Like us, they simply want to participate in a cultural experiment of living in a multicultural neighborhood.

Practical Reasons

In contrast to the foregoing, the final reason that motivates gentrifiers to move into central city urban neighborhoods is not controversial. In fact it is somewhat benign. As cities expand outward travel times have increased to the point where it is not unusual for commuters to drive two hours just to get to work. To avoid that, people who work downtown have instead opted to move into the central city because of the ease and access that living there affords them. I see this reality every day of the week as I ride my bike into and through downtown Portland. Depending on my route I will usually cross two different interstate freeways. It is not uncommon to see traffic backed up for mile after mile, either at a standstill or barely crawling. Instead, I happily pedal my bike either over or under the freeway on residential streets. My bicycle commute takes all of fifteen to twenty minutes. I arrive home relaxed and stress-free having enjoyed a nice pedal through the city. I can't say the same for those gridlocked on the freeway.

"One of the reasons that many people are attracted to inner-city living is that it involves minimal travelling time to work (this is particularly so when both partners are working)."[15] For many, the appeal for gentrification is it allows for short commutes and gives them close access to urban amenities. I have noticed the difference for my family and me living in central city Portland compared to Tucson. Here my life is housed within probably a four-mile radius. I rarely leave inner NE, inner SE, and the downtown. In Tucson I lived exactly four miles away from the nearest coffee shop and my place of work was twenty miles away on the other side of the city. It was not uncommon for my commute to take an

---

15 "Consumption and Culture," 242.

hour one way. We had to drive twelve miles to get to downtown Tucson. As a result we needed two vehicles whereas here we can get away with only one.

Other practical reasons for quitting the suburbs include living life on a smaller scale and reduced transportation costs. If the average annual cost to simply own and operate a car is $8,000 ($10,000 in Canada) and the average annual cost to own and maintain a bicycle is $300 then people living close-in can live car-free or at least be less dependent on a vehicle and simply use a bicycle for their primary mode of transportation (or walk or use public transit). This can even offset higher housing costs in the central city. If rent is $400 a month higher in the city compared to the suburbs, but one can get rid of the car and save $300-$600 per month by not having to pay for insurance, gas, upkeep, or even car payments. Then there's the added benefits of a reduction in the stress caused by commuting and the time spent in gridlock.

Conclusion

To lump the appeal of gentrification into one category or chapter is a challenge because the only unifying theme is the appeal itself. I would argue that for the most part, those who actually move into these central city neighborhoods do so for helpful, hopeful, and practical reasons. I don't hold to the notion that white people move into ethnic neighborhoods to displace people or to homestead or indulge in colonialist ambitions, but because they desire things like the opportunity to buy an affordable house, live in a multicultural neighborhood, experience shorter commute times, live in an historic neighborhood and house, and have access to urban amenities. That does not diminish the presence of developers, realtors, speculators, and others looking to turn a profit at the expense of the established neighborhood residents.

Having addressed the appeal of gentrification, we can now expand the conversation onto a more global level. Gentrification is not simply a movement taking place in North America; it is happening all over the world.

The Appeal of Gentrification

Chapter 7

Gentrification Gone Global
Michael Crane

My Christmas shopping took a somber tone this year when I was forced to encounter the ugly side of gentrification in the process of buying a gift for my wife. I was looking for this gift while I was in the Malaysian island city of Penang. While I was there teaching a class, my hosts told me about Johnny who has a shop that sold just what I was looking for at a discounted rate. The shop was an old family business that sold Malaysian crafts in the George Town municipality. This shop is a shop house, a traditionally Chinese urban structure designed for a shop on the ground level with living quarters for the family above it. These are typically built in rows, each sharing a wall with its neighbor. Johnny, by now in his 50s, was raised in the house above the shop and has never lived anywhere else.

George Town was named as a UNESCO World Heritage Site in 2008 because of its charming combination of colonial heritage and vintage multicultural shops. The streets of George Town are lined with old British buildings and Chinese shop houses built during the Art Deco era. It is the kind of place where one can visit family-owned shops selling Indians linens, Chinese tea sets, and Malaysian pewter. Even the back alleys offer culinary treats sold from mobile carts. Once this quaint municipality was dubbed with the World Heritage tag, in entered the business and land speculators. Property prices rose by up to 40 percent in 2010.[1] A businessman from a neighboring country bought the whole row of shop houses where Johnny has his store and plans to renovate the whole block. This means Johnny's store needs to close for at least a year. Johnny does not have the means to move his business elsewhere and so this means Johnny's store and his home are in their final days.

The conversation around the topic of gentrification is happening in Malaysia as it is in America, except the term "gentrification" is rarely used. Instead, more positive terms are used like "urban renewal." A discussion of gentrification around the globe is nearly impossible to encapsulate in this chapter except to aver that gentrification is happening around the world and therefore cannot be written off as a purely western phenomenon. But it also needs to be said that the issues surrounding gentrification will vary considerably from place to place.[2] Land laws, urban policies, and degree of economic development will significantly affect how gentrification plays out in each city in the world.

In this chapter, as we examine issues of gentrification from a global perspective, we hope to achieve three things: push and stretch the definition of gentrification, articulate some of the issues and obstacles related to gentrification in the cities of Malaysia, and address opportunities and challenges facing the church in the context of Kuala Lumpur. An accurate account of gentrification trends and issues around the world is not possible in this chapter. My goal is simply to broaden the conversation on gentrification by highlighting the realities in Malaysia's conurbations (urban areas).

Some say that gentrification is a phenomenon that has occurred primarily in cities of developed nations.[3] It's true that little gentrification has taken place in many cities in developing nations where there has been a presence of wealthy

---

1 Yeoh, "Not Easy Housing Malaysians," 37.

2 These works demonstrate the diversity of issues related to gentrification around the world: Neil Smith, "New Globalism, New Urbanism: Gentrification as Global Urban Strategy," *Antipode* 34:3 (2002) 427–450; S. Sabri and A. Yakuup, "Multi-Criteria Expert Based Analysis for Ranking the Urban Gentrification Drivers in Developing Countries," in *Built Environment in Developing Countries*; Nilgun Ergun, "Gentrification in Istanbul," *Cities* 21:5 (2004) 391–405; Laurence Crot, "'Scenographic' and 'Cosmetic' Planning: Globalization and Territorial Restructuring in Buenos Aires," *Journal of Urban Affairs* 28:3 (2006) 227–251.

3 Conn and Ortiz, *Urban Ministry*, 292; Smith, "Gentrification, the Frontier, and the Restructuring of Urban Space," 260.

residential communities that never left the city centers.[4] These communities, often gated, are in close proximity to poor communities which provide service-related employees for the wealthy. The wealthy communities continue to change and modernize, but the demographics remain the same.[5] Around the world, even in developing nations, however, there are many cities that are dealing with gentrification issues.[6] As it occurs in cities in the United States, there are some general similarities in patterns and municipal governance. The differences around the world are more pronounced. For example, gentrification in the United States occurs partly as a result of a free market economy, whereas in other countries the totalitarian government might be the root cause of gentrification.[7]

Stretching the Definition for the Global Context

In Chapter 2, Sean Benesh defined gentrification as the transformation of a poorer community in the city center into a middle-class community. This has been the trend in American cities because there was a stage when the urban core of many cities hollowed out due to suburbanization and deindustrialization. In cities around the world, this dynamic of urban communities undergoing dramatic change due to the middle class replacing the lower class is a reality, but the geographical patterns and land-ownership dynamics are different.

Kuala Lumpur (called KL by the locals) is a decentralized metro area with multiple central business districts (CBDs).[8] This collection of municipalities

---

4 Ward, "Mexico City in an Era of Globalization and Demographic Downturn," 179.

5 The Southeast Asian megacities of Manila and Jakarta both demonstrate this phenomenon.

6 By way of example, the following cities are experiencing gentrification: Cape Town in South Africa, Mumbai in India, and Shanghai in China. This representation just skims the surface, but demonstrates the diversity of global cities undergoing gentrification. A quick study of each of these cities reveals the unique contextual issues in each city. Cf. Gustav Visser and Nico Kotze, "The State and New-build Gentrification in Central Cape Town, South Africa," *Urban Studies* 45:12 (2008) 2565–2593; Andrew Harris, "From London to Mumbai and Back Again: Gentrification and Public Policy in Comparative Perspective," *Urban Studies* 45:12 (2008) 2407–2428; Shenjing He, "State-sponsored Gentrification Under Market Transition The Case of Shanghai," *Urban Affairs Review* 43:2 (2007) 171–198.

7 He, "State-sponsored Gentrification Under Market Transition The Case of Shanghai."

8 Sardar, *The Consumption of Kuala Lumpur*, 75.

connected by freeways has earned it a comparison with Los Angeles (LA).[9] This more postmodern urban geography of LA and KL means that gentrification can occur in communities that are not close to a traditional city center but become gentrified for other reasons.

As cities stretch into urban agglomerations growth can occur along corridors that connect these pivotal points. The KL metro area has connected KL to the port city of Klang in the west and to the airport, twenty miles to the south. These corridors have witnessed considerable growth, which has displaced working-class communities once on the periphery of the city, and now finding themselves in prime real estate.[10]

The same thing is happening in the southern tip of the Malaysian peninsula. Johor Bahru is a large city directly across from the island nation-state of Singapore. Due to limited land, the whole city of Singapore has experienced some of the characteristics of gentrification.[11] Enterprising Malaysians have recognized an opportunity to build a new development right across from Singapore that will offer international-standard healthcare, education, entertainment, and housing for a lower price. A lower price than the Singaporean market is an exorbitant price for the local of Johor Bahru, thus they are getting priced out of their own communities. In both KL and Johor Bahru, gentrification is not impacting the old city centers as much as the urban growth corridors.

Issues and Trends with Gentrification in Malaysia

The Upside of Gentrification

The renewal of communities is generally a positive sign for the well-being of the city. As each community in a city ages, there is a need for old buildings to be replaced by newer buildings and old infrastructure to be replaced by newer

---

9 Rimmer and Dick, *The City in Southeast Asia*, xviii.

10 T Bunnell, PA Barter, and S Morshidi, "Kuala Lumpur metropolitan area: A globalizing city–region," *Cities* 19:5 (2002) 357–370; King, Kuala Lumpur and Putrajaya, 2.

11 Singapore as a nation is only 687 square kilometers. By way of comparison, it is roughly half the size of London.

infrastructure. Dilapidated and neglected buildings and blocks become nesting grounds for unsavory activities. In KL, the old rubber plantation estate of Bangsar has gone through a lot of change over the last twenty years. It has changed for good reason. Bangsar's proximity to the business districts of KL makes it prime real estate for working professionals. The old rubber plantation is long gone and anyone depending on that industry for their livelihood has likely relocated. The need for nicer housing near the business districts is a positive sign for the economy of the city. Rebuilding higher density housing close to the urban core places less strain on the infrastructure of the city. Today Bangsar is the paragon of trendy in KL with thriving boutique shops, eateries and housing lots of artists and activists.

Difficulties Presented by Gentrification

Near Bangsar is an area called Brickfields. It is the old train yard from the British colonial era. Over time, Brickfields became home to a bustling Indian population which provided labor for the train industry. Today, a walk down the streets of Brickfields can be a sensory overload with pulsating beats of techno Indian music, wafts of strong curries, and overwhelmingly colorful sari shops and Hindu temples. But this only tells half the story. Directly across from Brickfields is the enormous hyper-modern KL Sentral complex, the transportation hub of KL where buses, trains, and monorails come and go at all hours. This ever-expanding complex has luxury hotels, corporate office buildings, and enough coffee shops to give the whole city a caffeine buzz. Large-scale construction projects surround KL Sentral on every side, building luxury condominiums, shopping complexes, and more office buildings. At first glimpse, this seems like a positive development. But underneath the sparkly new development is the reality that KL Sentral's development is bursting over into Brickfields. The old Indian enclave in Brickfields can no longer afford to stay there, and they are moving to cheaper areas in the suburban belt. The fallout is twofold: 1) the urban poor are getting pushed out; and 2) the vibrant cultural production of the ethnic enclave is disappearing.

Most of the conversation surrounding gentrification in Malaysia is concerned with the potential benefits gentrification brings.[12] If negative consequences are considered, it is more often about the community's loss of character or the potential of making the whole city generic. Rarely have I heard much concern over the displacement of the poor that happens as a result of gentrification. There is even sometimes an optimism that the poorer residents will rise with their changing community. Research shows, however, that gentrification rarely improves poverty.[13] The poor simply move to other places. In the case of Brickfields, the poor have had little choice but to move to communities farther away. This means they are moving away from the job opportunities, public transportation, and a supportive cultural community. As a minority ethnic group, Indian families can benefit from living in a community that supports their language, culture, and religious needs. What remains of Brickfields is a "Little India" made for tourists but lacking authenticity and a vibrant Indian community.

Responses to Gentrification by the Church

The smell of fresh-baked chocolate chip cookies is breaking down my willpower to watch what I eat as I sit in the café of Harvest Centre talking with Pastor Elisha Satvinder. Harvest Centre is in the middle of a part of KL known as Sentul. Elisha tells me that thirty years ago Sentul was infamous with a reputation for violent gangs, drugs, and alcoholism. Once a community built around a railway factory built by the British, it became a squatter community where mafia bosses were in charge.

Sentul is another KL neighborhood that is undergoing drastic changes now. Elisha Satvinder and his wife Petrina are in Sentul precisely to help the poor and oppressed of KL. They discovered teenagers who were illiterate and had no drive to learn.[14] The people of Sentul have never had control over their land. Since it is

---

12 Chong, "The Gentrification of KL - Around Town." Even as former Brickfields resident, Balan Moses, laments the changes of Brickfields, he says the KL Sentral development "augers well" for Brickfields. Moses, *Brickfields*.

13 Squires, "Partnership and the Pursuit of the Private City," 244.

14 Wong, "A Heart for the Poor," 25.

now in the hands of developers, the old squatter communities have been torn down and large, low-cost apartments have been built. At first this might seem like a positive step for the people. But the process of moving this traditional community into impersonal concrete towers had a damaging impact. Even though a squatter community may have appeared tattered and unreliable, they had control over their space. On ground level, they provided for a sense of community, safety, and opportunities for informal businesses (micro-enterprise). The high-rise apartments gave them private spaces separate from each other and public space that was no longer their own. Nearby vacant land disappeared, taking away cow pastures, vegetable gardens, and fields on which the kids could play soccer. What remains is a population with fewer economic opportunities and children with fewer recreational opportunities.

Now, Sentul is moving into a new phase. As I drove into Sentul to meet Elisha, I drove by brand-new luxury condominiums and towering cranes building yet more. A sign on one new development said: "This is the new Sentul." Just north of the financial center of KL, Sentul is now prime real estate for developers. The inclusion of a new creative arts center, swanky condominiums and new boutique shops spells trouble for the already troubled residents of Sentul. Just like those in Brickfields, many of the poor have moved to areas further on the periphery of the city. But not all of the poor have left. Many refugees from surrounding nations have taken up residence there.

Harvest Centre has remained through all of the changes. During such difficult times for people in the community, Elisha and Petrina have been able to provide help, encouragement, and even advocacy when needed. Harvest Centre has a school for underprivileged children with a goal of breaking the vicious cycle of poverty in that community. Theirs is not a short-term drop-in and drop-out vision; rather, they are in it for the long haul. They are educating a new generation of leaders with strong moral character who can shape their communities for the better.

I asked Elisha about the changing demographics of Sentul and how it would affect their work. My question did not catch him off-guard; he has already been wrestling with these realities. Their school will need to provide transportation for those children getting pushed further out. They are also looking at new communities of the poor in which to invest. In this, they remain committed to investing in the least of these. But he also recognized that the wealthier, trendier new arrivals were troubled in other ways, particularly emotionally. Harvest Centre has started a counseling center in order to minister to everyone in their changing community.

Elisha recognizes the signs of gentrification, but he is not under the illusion that such reformation of the neighborhood will provide any lasting change in hearts of the locals. He says, "There is no reform, because there is no transformation of the heart." Through the church they have planted in this transitioning community, they are able to provide opportunities to experience hope. Because of their sustained presence and commitment to the people of the community, they have become integral to the future well-being of Sentul.

Church Responses to Gentrification

How should ministries and churches respond to changes such as these? As the church seeks to make disciples of people and care for the least of these, we need three responses. First, the church needs to stay and adapt. Elisha and Petrina demonstrate this well by their willingness to serve everyone in their community. Because of their long-term sacrificial presence, their relationship with the community is irreplaceable. People in communities that are enduring such transitions have few who they can trust. By staying, Elisha and Petrina become a source of trust and stability for those who need it. But staying is not the same thing as maintaining the status quo. Change is a reality of life amplified by the urban context.[15] Elisha and Petrina understand this and continue to adapt and adjust the ways in which they help the people of Sentul. Ministries like theirs also rely on the church of the city to provide continuous support so they can be most effective.

Second, the church needs new initiatives in changing neighborhoods. It is during these points of transition that new and innovative churches and ministries are needed. Cities are centers of innovation, and, as such, the church must experiment and innovate as it reaches an ever-changing urban context.[16] There are a number of studies that have shown that it is far easier to start a new

---

15 Fischer, *The Urban Experience*, 216; Hiebert and Meneses, *Incarnational Ministry*, 273.

16 Hall, *Cities in Civilisation*; Kotkin, *The City*.

church in a changing community than in an old, stable community.[17] These new initiatives will be most effective at engaging those moving into the neighborhood. And new churches more naturally reach those not attending any church rather than those attending older churches.[18] In Sentul, a creative arts center has been attracting artists and appreciators of art to the area. There is a need for a new church by and for artists that brings in their creativity in worship and proclamation of the gospel.

Third, the church needs to be ready to work with those who are being displaced into new locations. This will involve established churches and new churches working together for the sake of those new to the neighborhood. I saw this demonstrated beautifully recently when a student of mine wanted to start a church among a population of migrant workers from Myanmar. A local Chinese church offered to let them use their worship facilities so they can have a place to meet that is large enough for their group. My student initially approached another church. This other church wanted to charge a high hourly rate and dictate exactly when they could use the facility. Fortunately, a willing and established church was able to partner with this young church planter in order to reach out to the thousands of migrant workers from Myanmar. Other ministries will be needed in order to help those displaced by gentrification begin a healthy life in the new community. And, just like the reasoning for the new initiatives in the gentrifying neighborhood, the displaced urban poor will experience a loss of social structure and community. Ministries and churches need to be ready to welcome and help those who have been pushed out. It is not an easy step for the established churches because their natural inclination will be to withdraw out of concern for higher crime. But this will only make things worse. Churches and individuals need to be ready for those who are being displaced and need to be open to listening to them with a willingness to help.

---

17 Big changes in the urban context disrupt the former social structures and people experience a loss of community. Churches starting in neighborhoods of transition can help foster new community. Stark, *Cities of God*, 81; Hinton, *Growing Churches Singapore Style Ministry in an Urban Context*, 91; Smith, "Towards the Transformation of our Cities/Regions."

18 Timothy Keller says that new churches bring new people into the church at six to eight times the rate of older churches. Keller, *Center Church*, 359; Wagner, *Strategies for Church Growth*, 171; Stetzer, *Planting Missional Churches*, 8.

Conclusion

Gentrification is a reality. The vibrancy of urban communities will ebb and flow. Around the world, neighborhoods undergo types of renewal that end up pushing out the poor and the marginalized. The church cannot necessarily stop gentrification, but it can and must help everyone affected by such changes to thrive holistically (spiritually, socially, and economically).

Chapter 8

Is Gentrification Positive or Negative?
Sean Benesh

In the previous chapter Michael Crane addressed both the positive and negative elements in gentrification. It is not all one side or the other, but instead a mixed bag. For me, there is not a week that goes by without the topic of gentrification coming up in a conversation. More than any place I have ever lived, given the nature of inner city Portland, gentrification seems to be on the tip of everyone's tongue. Not only that, but I have found many people are actually quite aware of the dynamics surrounding the topic. Before when I used to term people would look at me rather oddly. Or they would comment that I'm obviously using "deep academic" terminology. In hindsight, I now realize that many of those people live in the suburbs. For those living in the city, in central cities in particular, gentrification is as normative a term as hipster, PBR, Mumford and Sons, microbreweries, or skinny jeans. It is on their radars.

Of all of the chapters in this book, this one in particular is the most daunting. The term "gentrification" brings up a conversation that can be very volatile in nature. It ranks up there with partisan politics and gun control. However, the conversation is certainly one-sided, kind of like talking about gun control in rural Iowa where every farmer has multiple guns for hunting, trapping, or protecting his chickens from raccoons. In terms of gentrification, the conversation is *always* slanted towards the atrocities that it leaves in its wake. For many, there is nothing good or wholesome about gentrification. But is it all bad?

Is there anything good about it? Can the process be redeemed? And is there ... or could there be ... such a thing as *equitable gentrification*?

Like Michael indicated in the previous chapter, it would be difficult to deny the *lifting process* that gentrification brings to a neighborhood whether in *classical gentrification* or *new-build gentrification*. Anyone who's familiar with the changes that have taken place in Portland's Pearl District, Wicker Park in Chicago, or LoDo in Denver can testify to that. "Gentrification has occurred in many U.S. cities that have charming inner-city homes."[1] While many could argue about the *how*, these places have been transformed into trendy urban entertainment districts that have brought economic vitality into these once-degraded areas. So why the big fuss over gentrification?

I have referred previously to the book *Gentrification* by Loretta Lees, Tom Slater, and Elvin Wyly, and will to do continue so, particularly in this chapter. In their Chapter 6, "Gentrification: Positive or Negative?" they do a remarkable job of walking the reader through the pros and cons of the process. My intention here is to utilize their framework to construct this chapter. I will then overlay it with missiological ramifications and applications as well as my own insights.

"Gentrification, of course, has both positive and negative aspects to it."[2] While intellectually many may agree, it is on the emotional or social level that others resist the process of gentrification and the collateral damage it can cause. I am not suggesting that unemotional people "get it" while the rest "don't get it." What I am trying to say is that gentrification is multi-faceted; there are numerous layers with which to view the dynamics at hand. If you were to pick up an armload of books, articles, and resources on gentrification, more than likely each will deal with some feature or aspect of it that is taking place during the metamorphosis. This is where it gets convoluted.

Some authors, urban ministry practitioners in particular, write about the evils of gentrification on the social level. They have experienced firsthand the process of poverty diffusion, relocation, and even prior to that the redlining where neighborhoods were purposely disinvested so they would degrade even more. Then once the bottom falls out banks and real estate speculators and investors can swoop down into these prime urban locations and make millions.

---

1 Phillips, *City Lights*, 546.

2 Lees at al, *Gentrification*, 195.

Urban ministry workers living and ministering in the trenches, as it were, who are watching this horrific reality, cry "foul" as they advocate for the least and the last. From this perspective gentrification is certainly negative.

Wayne Gordon, an urban ministry leader and practitioner echoes this sentiment: "Gentrification. A dreaded word to many of us in urban ministry and a major issue."[3] Not only that, but Gordon sees gentrification as contrary to the process of Christian community development. "Rebuild, raise up, restore: these are the buzz words most of us use in our ministry in under-resourced communities. As we live and work in poor neighborhoods, it has always been our goal to rebuild our communities and to restore the streets where people live, walk, and play. In many ways gentrification is the secular response to dilapidated neighborhoods."[4] Is that true? Is gentrification an evil secular process? From an urban ministry standpoint gentrification certainly seems to have negative implications.

In her book *Naked City*, Sharon Zukin also laments over the effects of gentrification. In her introduction, she aptly names one chapter "The City That Lost Its Soul." Throughout the book she notes neighborhood after neighborhood that has "lost its soul" through the gentrification process. Whereas the urban ministry worker like Wayne Gordon watches with pain the process of redlining, relocation, and the painful effects of congregants, the sociologist and professor Sharon Zukin observes how ethnic urban neighborhoods lose their distinctiveness. "In the areas where hipsters and gentrifiers live there's a new cosmopolitanism in the air: tolerant, hip, casual. And that isn't bad. But little by little the old ethnic neighborhoods they have moved into are dying, along with the factories where longtime residents plied their trades and the Irish bars, Latino bodegas, and black soul food restaurants where they made their homes away from home. The people who seemed so rooted in these neighborhoods are disappearing."[5]

These two examples are obviously very negative towards gentrification. However, the process is not so clear-cut that we can label it "evil" versus "good" or "hurtful" versus "helpful" because it all depends on the particular dynamics at

---

3 Gordon, "Gentrification," 39.

4 Ibid., 40.

5 Zukin, *Naked City*, 8.

hand as well as the particular stage of gentrification. "There is a temporal dimension to all of this, for arguably pioneer gentrification ideologically and practically has more positive aspects associated with it than later waves of gentrification. For example, pioneer gentrifiers desired social mixing, whereas second- and especially third-wave gentrifiers are much more individualistic."[6]

The table below is a snapshot of some of the pros and cons of gentrification. Below I will unpack some of the points on both sides.

The Positives and Negatives of Gentrification	
Positive	Negative
	Displacement through rent/price increases
	Secondary psychological costs of displacement
Stabilization of declining areas	Community resentment and conflict
Increased property values	Loss of affordable housing
	Unsustainable speculative property price increases
Reduced vacancy rates	Homelessness
Increased local fiscal revenues	Greater take of local spending through lobbying/articulacy
Encouragement and increased viability of further development	Commercial/industrial displacement
	Increased cost and changes to local services
Reduction of suburban sprawl	Displacement and housing demand pressures on surrounding poor areas
Increased social mix	Loss of social diversity (from socially disparate to rich ghettos)

6 *Gentrification*, 195.

The Positives and Negatives of Gentrification	
Rehabilitation of property both with and without state sponsorship	Under occupancy and population loss to gentrified areas

Source: Atkinson and Bridge, *Gentrification in a Global Context*, 5. Summarized and reposted in Lees, et al., *Gentrification*, 196.

Positive

Given the foregoing you might already assume that nothing really positive can be brought about through gentrification. That is not the case. A trip up to Portland's Alberta Arts District reveals a vibrant and robust street scene with shops, galleries, restaurants, and new businesses whereas twenty years ago it was a boarded-up wasteland. No one is longing for the "good old days" when this area was blighted. This raises the question: Should we who are followers of Jesus living and ministering in the city make it our biblical aim and mandate to stop the process of gentrification? Or is there a better way? Wayne Gordon alludes to this when he asks, "How do we use the gentrification process for our mission and the good of our community?"[7] While Gordon articulates the negative effects of the process he still sees it as an ever-present reality. "It is imperative for us not to see gentrification as the enemy but to embrace it."[8]

Gentrification is an ever-present reality that is here to stay. Over time it will continue to morph and evolve into new and varied mutations. It is a mixed bag, a mixed blessing. "Some observers applaud this development. They say that gentrification brings back the white middle and upper middle classes to the city, thereby upgrading the housing stock and increasing the tax base."[9] With that said, I will start my analysis of the process focusing on the positive elements of it. Again, many will resist this part by purporting that nothing truly beneficial can come about through gentrification. I will argue that certainly is not true.

7 "Gentrification," 43.

8 Ibid., 47.

9 *City Lights*, 546.

Example 1: Stabilization

Gentrification can bring about a certain level of stability to a neighborhood. According to the report of the United Kingdom's Urban Task Force, the British government is seeking to bring some stability to low-income neighborhoods by encouraging members of the middle-class to move there. "The idea is to diversify the social mix and dilute concentrations of poverty in the inner city through gentrification."[10]   Some may perceive this as harsh, insensitive, and rogue. However, if it is a catalyst to stabilize the neighborhood to make it safer, which in turn brings in more investment, is it always wrong? While many decry gentrification as a great social evil, we need to be honest and say that there is nothing glamorous or wholesome about urban neighborhoods that are war zones and pockets of social unrest. So what is the solution?

My brother-in-law is a criminology graduate who lives on the edge of a "pre-gentrified" inner city urban neighborhood. As a result of his studies and knowing a lot of police officers, including those on the gang task force, we have had many enjoyable and lively conversations about urban neighborhoods. One day he plainly stated, "You know, Sean, there's no other way to put it. Low-income neighborhoods are hotbeds of crime. There's a direct statistical correlation." What many politicians, city planners, police officers, educators, social workers, ministry leaders, and residents hope gentrification will do is that it would not only break the cycle of poverty but also "break up" the density of this economic and social demarcation. The question then becomes, "How?" Some policy-makers propose what is sometimes called "poverty diffusion," i.e., placing middle-class families in the midst of these neighborhoods. Does it work? Is it fair? Is it equitable?

"The current trend in the U.S. housing redevelopment is to replace existing high-rise, high-density, 'projects' with new lower-density mixed income communities, for example, Cabrini-Green in Chicago."[11] The concept behind poverty diffusion is to seek to remedy what ails these neighborhoods. When poverty is spatially concentrated, some policy-makers see it almost in terms of a

---

10 *Gentrification*, 198.

11 Ibid., 203.

contagion spreading behavioral pathologies.[12] Thus the need for diffusion and stabilization. Unfortunately, what we find as a negative effect of gentrification is that this can oftentimes lead to displacement. No one denies the need for stability and social mixing, but it is easy by this so-called remedy to cross the threshold into rampant abuse.

Done well, social mixing and poverty diffusion can indeed be helpful as well as stabilizing. Having lived in a "living urban laboratory" where this was an everyday reality I watched first-hand how this process works. While far from perfect, it was an everyday adventure living in a high-density urban neighborhood full of immigrants (middle-class and lower-class) including low-income refugees holding on for dear life. At the grocery store, public library, public school, or McDonald's, I observed all of the disparate ethnicities and socio-economic classes merge together, interact, and enrich the community. I vividly recall watching a millionaire eastern European developer sit across from an under-resourced homeless woman chatting and laughing. Affluent mainland Chinese lived across the street from low-income Iraqi refugees. It was intriguing watching my three sons learn to navigate these waters in public school where their friendships crossed all these classes and lines.

The tension arises because the reverse occurs only rarely. Governments can fund programs and initiatives to woo middle-class people to move into low-income neighborhoods, but as Lees et al explain, "there are very few examples of government support to allow the poor to move into affluent suburban communities."[13] Positives can easily become negatives, thus creating tension and conflict in the process.

As we find throughout Scripture, in God's economy, the widow, orphan, foreigner, and marginalized were always to be given preferential treatment. I believe that we should go forward with that same template in mind. The difficulty behind gentrification is that it carries both positive as well as negative ramifications. Anytime it slips into the negative or does not favor the marginalized then we can and should cry foul. The stabilization that gentrification creates is a double-edged sword: Done well, it can be healthy and inclusive, but taken too far it leads to displacement which is always harmful.

---

12 Ibid.

13 Ibid., 207.

As followers of Jesus we're to play a healthy stabilizing presence in the neighborhood. Can urban missionaries or practitioners move into degraded inner-city neighborhoods, districts, or slums without helping to be a catalyst for gentrification, or at least its negative aspects? John Hayes, the director of InnerCHANGE, a mission order among the global urban poor, writes, "When we move into a poor neighborhood, we send the message that if love is costly, then those who are the object of such love are worth much. This is especially important to the poor who bear the weight of the world's low opinion of them."[14] Many urban missionaries and practitioners with whom I am acquainted both nationally and globally are mostly well-educated middle-class ethnic whites. Are they the bearers of gentrification without realizing it? Theirs is an incarnational approach to live out and proclaim the Gospel in word and deed. Among other things, they hope that they truly would be a stabilizing agent in the neighborhood, but not at the cost of displacement.

We must step cautiously forward even in addressing the positive elements of gentrification. The next positive element is less controversial.

Example 2: Reduction of Suburban Sprawl

A positive marker of gentrification is that it affirms development, redevelopment, renewal, regeneration, and investment in central cities. Rather than outward suburban sprawl, the focus instead is on infill or back fill. All one has to do is drive across Los Angeles or Phoenix to see and experience firsthand the effects of sprawl. Michael Dear in *From Chicago to L.A.* makes the claim that "Los Angeles is the prototype for a different kind of city, one increasingly prominent in the late 20th century, but not the type of older city facing decline that draws the attention of federal problem solvers. Los Angeles is the paragon of sprawling cities throughout the Sunbelt and located even on the growing edge of otherwise large, stagnant northern cities."[15] Many grimace at the thought. It's worth noting that the consternation is not about polycentrism, but instead rampant sprawl.

---

14 Hayes, *Sub-merge*, 117.

15 Dear, *From Chicago to L.A.*, 28.

Cities like Portland, with our urban growth boundary, are demonstrating the effectiveness of infill/back fill and densification. As a former cycling guide leading numerous tours a week, I was privileged to spend time with national and international visitors and show them why Portland is America's Bicycle Capital. During our bicycle rides many visitors commented on how inner-city Portland (and our CBD) is a remarkable place despite its density. I inwardly chuckle because we don't have the density of the Loop in Chicago, or Vancouver, BC, or Manhattan, and yet we have enough density whereby it is easy to live a car-free or low-car-usage lifestyle. Much of that is attributable to our urban growth boundary which encourages infill.

Throughout inner-city Portland I have watched empty lot after empty lot go on the market, sell, and then become developed. Oftentimes, especially along transportation corridors, new developments are of a higher density (more vertical) than what used to be there. In some neighborhoods there are "canyons" being constructed with four-story buildings lining both sides of the street. These mixed-use buildings create a vibrant streetscape. Locally we do not have to look much further than the Pearl as an example of infill. Smith mentions these kinds of districts as ripe for development. As he notes, "Many post-industrial landscapes exist as vague spaces: underdeveloped spaces, spaces left over from development, or spaces abandoned post-development."[16]

The positive elements of gentrification which create infill positively affect cities in terms of densification. As we looked at in Chapter 2, different kinds of gentrification (*classical, new-build*) bring about various kinds of development and redevelopment. Here in inner NE Portland are abundant examples of *classical gentrification*. Many homes have been improved as have corridors of new development such as along Mississippi Avenue and North Williams Avenue. On the other hand, one of my favorite stops on our bicycle tours is South Waterfront which sits on the southern edge of Portland's CBD. It offers the benefits of density which Glaeser highlights:

There is great value in protecting the most beautiful parts of our urban past, but cities shouldn't be embalmed in amber. Too much preservation stops cities from providing newer, taller, better buildings for their inhabitants. Height restrictions, in Paris and New York and Mumbai, may seem like

---

16 Smith, *Events and Urban Regeneration*, 37.

obscure arcana of interest only to planning professionals. Nothing could be more wrong. These rules are shaping the future of our cities and our world. If the cities' history becomes a straitjacket, then they lose one of their greatest assets; the ability to built up.[17]

Glaeser is a passionate supporter of the need for more construction in central cities and in gentrifying neighborhoods because it actually lowers housing prices, or at least keeps them affordable. It is when infill is not encouraged, along with lower height limits, that central cities housing prices soar. "People in an affluent society want and expect comfortable, spacious homes. Today America builds those homes in the suburbs of the Sunbelt, which pulls people out of cities and toward Texas. But spacious, affordable homes can also be built in our older cities. There *can be* an urban future where people live in central cities, but to do that, the most desirable of those cities must reduce the regulatory barriers that limit the construction of taller buildings."[18]

Example 3: Increased Social Mixing / Tolerance

Another significant element that gentrification brings, as alluded to earlier, is increased social mixing. And to that I'll add, tolerance. That assertion needs to be thoroughly clarified and explained. In the section above on stabilization I referred to social mixing. Certainly stabilization and social mixing go hand-in-hand. In the same way, tolerance can be viewed as a positive element of gentrification. Instead of tolerance, perhaps a more appropriate term would be *refuge*. One of the facets of gentrification that is rarely discussed, especially in Christian circles, is how gentrifying neighborhoods serves as a refuge for various groups fleeing oppression on various levels, especially women and those of alternative sexual identities. "The inner city allows more flexible family identities for middle-class women, as well as men."[19] Drawing from various research initiatives (Rose 1984, Markusen 1981, Mills 1989, Beauregard 1986, Holcomb 1984, and Williams 1986) Lees et al draw out this theme. "If we consider all this research as a collective, there is no question that a central theme is how

---

17 Glaeser, *Triumph of the City*, 136.

18 Ibid., 152.

19 *Gentrification*, 212.

gentrification is playing a positive, emancipatory role in the lives of middle-class women who have physically and mentally rejected the oppressive, patriarchal conditions of suburbia."[20]

But there's another group. "Researchers also noted the emancipatory qualities of the inner city for the gay community."[21] As I mentioned earlier, oftentimes the gay community is fleeing from white suburban evangelicals. This is problematic on many fronts, especially when Jesus was a "friend of sinners." Obviously this brings up an uncomfortable and controversial conversation about the role of followers of Jesus in the city. There's a wide spectrum of response to the gay community among Christians that ranges from outright rejection (and oppression) to inclusion and even an affirmation of their lifestyle and sexual orientation. It is not my goal or intention to spend a lot of time discussing how one should respond because as a researcher and author I want to bring to light current urban realities that we need to address. Apart from Christ, we're all dead in our transgressions whether straight or gay.

What this brings up, though, is that the gay community represents the first wave of pioneer gentrifiers. "Gay gentrified neighborhoods are also seen to be spaces from which the gay community can combat oppression, develop economic and political clout, and gain access to the state apparatus."[22] Richard Florida has researched and written extensively on this phenomenon. The more tolerant the cities are as a whole, the greater their economic outlook is. "The key to understanding the new economic geography of creativity and its effects on economic outcomes lies in what I call the 3T's of economic development: *Technology, Talent, and Tolerance*. Each is a necessary but by itself insufficient condition. To attract creative people, generate innovation and stimulate economic growth, a place must have all three."[23]

Florida goes on to research the correlation between the gay community and the location of high-tech industries. "The same places that were popular among

---

20 Ibid.

21 Ibid., 213.

22 Ibid.

23 Florida, *The Rise of the Creative Class*, 249.

gays were also the ones where high-tech industry located."[24] The point Florida is making, and how I am tying it into gentrification is this: The gay community is drawn to places and districts within the city that are more open and tolerant of their lifestyle. This is why many have an aversion towards the suburbs, where conservative "family values" are most likely to be upheld. As a result, many find themselves moving into degraded and neglected inner city neighborhoods because they tend to be more tolerant and open-minded. "There is also a strong relationship between the concentration of gays in a metropolitan area and other measures of diversity, notably the percent of foreign-born residents. These results reiterate the impact of diversity on a broad section of society. Low barriers to entry thus seem to be good for the whole economy."[25]

I affirm the positive element of gentrified neighborhoods being a refuge for well-educated, professional, middle-class women as well as the gay community. Certainly people did not seek refuge *away* from Jesus as he drew together most of society, especially social outcasts, while marginalizing the religious elite. We've done exactly the opposite. People sought refuge *in* Jesus. There was something about his nature and character that drew even the most ardent sinners to him. What was it about Jesus that made it possible for prostitutes, weighed down by guilt, oppression, and social exclusion, to find refuge *in* him? As the church, and as individual followers of Jesus, we are his body ... his hands and feet here on earth. We're to be incarnational in the same way that Jesus was and adopt this posture in gentrified urban neighborhoods. My prayer is that people would find a true refuge *in* Jesus *through* us.

Negative

Now we turn our attention to highlighting some of the negative elements of gentrification. As I did with its positive elements, the examples below are certainly not an exhaustive list, but merely representational. Also, I am mentioning only three for each category rather than getting bogged down in minutia. There are great books, articles, and resources that address these topics in

---

24 Ibid., 255.

25 Ibid., 258.

more detail. My intention here is to highlight only a few while tying in some missiological insights and implications.

Example 1: Displacement

Those familiar with the gentrification process cry foul most often in regards to the displacement that occurs. Whether intentional or not, when neighborhoods are revitalized or gentrified, housing prices climb which in turn pushes up rental costs. As a result, those most affected are the lower-income working class who are forced to find more affordable housing. This causes a continuous reshuffling cycle in cities. While some claim that gentrification brings stability to neighborhoods, oftentimes it is the opposite. "As real estate developers gentrify these neighborhoods, displaced tenants move to places they can afford–slums, in many cases."[26] However, in the life cycle of the neighborhood more than likely those currently living there most often came in on the heels of another immigrant or ethnic group that was moving out or dispersing.

Internationally, particularly in developing nations, gentrification is synonymous with slum removal. Not only that, but the political climate of various nations means little to no resistance to this process as citizens have no voice. I saw this firsthand while walking the streets of Beijing before the 2008 Summer Olympics. The entire city seemed like one massive construction project. Interestingly enough, slums were either completely removed or high walls were constructed to hide them from public view. Phillips writes about this dynamic: "In Beijing, for example, slum-clearance projects accelerated after 2001 when the city's bid to host the 2008 Olympic Games was accepted. Many residents were displaced, and some poor, vibrant neighborhoods were demolished in the effort to rebuild for the Olympics."[27]

Displacement is a reality in gentrification regardless of whether ethnic blacks or ethnic whites are the ones moving out. Some are forced out while others simply throw their hands up in the air and leave with the rest of the diaspora. An article in the *Portland Monthly* by Aaron Scott reveals the pain,

---

26 *City Lights*, 48.

27 Ibid., 548.

tension, and fallout as a result of this process. "Over the past two decades, the gentrification of inner North and Northeast has displaced much of this community. Urban renewal policies and a broader trend in favor of inner-urban living brought a sea change for new residents—most white and Hispanic—into Portland's historically black neighborhoods. An influx of trendy businesses, like those Alberta Street coffee shops, and upscale development followed. But as the neighborhood rose, much of its longtime population moved away, pushed into Portland's hinterlands."[28]

Scott describes not simply what is taking place in Portland, but how this is a current reality facing differing ethnic groups in cities across the nation.

> In America's cities, racial and ethnic enclaves come and go. New York's Little Italy has been virtually swallowed by Chinatown, which itself is shifting white; Chicago's "bungalow belt," once the segregated heartland of that city's white working class, is rapidly turning Hispanic. In one sense, then, the movement of blacks from North and Northeast Portland to the city's fringes is merely the latest chapter in a 130-year history of forced dislocations of the African American community. Yet with no other black neighborhood to move to, the ramifications are greater, especially when it coincides with a troubling development: Portland's African Americans now rank at or near the bottom of almost every socioeconomic measure, below Native Americans, Hispanics, Asians, and Caucasians.[29]

Displacement is at the forefront of the tension surrounding gentrification. Surveying the changes he's seen take place in his inner northeast Portland neighborhood, one African-American resident of inner northeast Portland says, "I just don't really agree with all these white folks around here now. It seems like we're getting pushed out. To me, I call it ethnic cleaning. I do. That's the way I feel."[30]

"Displacement is, however, extremely difficult to quantify."[31] That brings up again the other side of the question of displacement in gentrification. Does gentrification "force" people out? Or do people simply leave because they no

---

28 Scott, "By the Grace of God."

29 Ibid.

30 Rommelmann, "There Goes the Neighborhood."

31 *Gentrification*, 218.

longer like the changing nature of their neighborhood? One study in New York City revealed that "between 1996 and 1999, lower income and lesser-educated households were 19 percent less likely to move in the seven gentrifying neighborhoods studied than those elsewhere, and concluded that displacement was therefore limited. They suggested that such households stay put because they appreciate the public service improvements taking place in these neighborhoods and thus find ways to remain in their homes even in the face of higher rent burdens."[32]

I mention the other side of the displacement debate because many of the points themselves are debatable on some levels. In broad generalities, we can, if pressed, find arguments to support our theses whether we note the trend of displacement in our neighborhoods and cities or just the opposite. We also move easily beyond data and statistics into emotions and preferences which is why this dynamic is so volatile and polarizing. Nonetheless displacement does happen, but not as uniformly as one might assume.

Example 2: Community Resentment and Conflict

Whether it's ethnic blacks in inner-city U.S. cities displaced by the influx of middle-class whites, or white residents moving out to the city's edge because of the rapid infusion of ethnic Chinese, or low-income day laborers in large Chinese cities being displaced through forced removal, the resultant impact is the same ... bitterness, resentment, and conflict. In some regards this is where data, studies, and statistics get thrown out the window as gentrification becomes personal, especially when it happens *here* instead of *there*.

In scouring numerous articles about the gentrification process, in Portland in particular, the same storyline appears time and time again. Whether having been forced out or leaving voluntarily, those who've left "their" neighborhoods because of an influx of different ethnicities or those in higher socio-economic categories, are frustrated, angry, and bitter. In an interview in the *Willamette Weekly*, one respondent shared his thoughts on the changing neighborhood. "It was quiet, calm and peaceful,' he says. 'It was all black people up in here ... then all of a sudden, all the black families just start moving out, moving out, next

---

32 Ibid., 219.

thing you know, I said, "Dang, all these white folks coming back over here?'" He laughs. 'Look, how it used to be was, "How you doing? What's up, man?" Now, you walk down the street, [say to] the white, "How you doing?" They will walk right past. I hate that.'"[33]

As I mentioned earlier, many who moved into urban neighborhoods do not do so with the purposeful intent of gentrifying the neighborhood or eventually displacing the current residents Instead, they are drawn to the current dynamics of the neighborhood, the opportunities for affordable rent or homeownership, as well as an appreciation of the cultural landscape at hand. In his book *Neo-Bohemia*, Richard Lloyd has a chapter entitled "Grit as Glamour." In other words, it is precisely a neighborhood's grittiness that is a draw for many, particularly young artists. "Artists are committed urbanites, and they fold representation of urban decay into their picture of authentic urbanism, even if their presence contributes to the reversal of many of its effects."[34] Lloyd expands on that thought as he researches and writes about Wicker Park in Chicago. "In part, artists' interest in locating in marginal neighborhoods whose majority population is poor and nonwhite involves the desire to occupy inexpensive space adequate to their needs. They are a transient population, breaking ground in marginal urban areas that many be targeted for redevelopment."[35]

The clash happens when more and more of one ethnic group moves in. Racial tensions ensue, especially when the incoming group is in a higher socio-economic strata. An *us*-versus-*them* mentality can develop. In cases like Wicker Park, when the starving artists move in at random they seem to blend into the neighborhood as is their desire. However, their presence also signifies (or potentially signifies) a harbinger of things to come. These first-wave unintentional gentrifiers often inadvertently act as catalysts to change the very dynamics of the neighborhood or district that drew them in to begin with.

It is at this intersection that I believe that churches, including new church plants, have the potential to step in and bridge the gap. I realize that my views may be muted by the fact that I write from the standpoint of a middle-class ethnic white. Some may claim that I write from a position of power since ethnic

---

33 "There Goes the Neighborhood."

34 Lloyd, *Neo-Bohemia*, 78.

35 Ibid., 80.

whites are responsible for bringing hardship to many different ethnicities throughout American history, be they Native-Americans, Chinese, Japanese, African-Americans, and so on. I own that and I continuously repent in the same way that Nehemiah repented of the sins of his ancestors and forefathers (Nehemiah 1:4-7).

Both sides need to own the tension and conflict that gentrification brings. Whether established churches or new church plants, followers of Jesus need to step in to be brokers of reconciliation. Reconciliation not only between humanity and God, but with one another in the power of the Gospel. Being one with Christ doesn't mean that all of a sudden the conflict and tension caused by gentrification will be removed. However, we have the power of the indwelling Holy Spirit to remedy what ails urban neighborhoods.

One of the troubling elements revealed in the article "By the Grace of God," quoted earlier was that rather than changing with the neighborhood, the African-American church the author mentioned brings in for Sunday worship its diaspora from twenty to thirty miles away. A van driver literally drives one hundred miles to pick up black congregants from all over the city. Many writers, myself included, have called out and challenged white congregations who have left, or are leaving, urban neighborhoods because of their changing ethnic make-up. As many inner cities became degraded beginning in the 1950s through to the 1990s many ethnic whites fled the city. Like the church mentioned in the article, many would come back into the city to worship with other ethnic whites. This is problematic on both fronts. As followers of Jesus we're neither slave nor free, black nor white, but on an equal footing before the cross of Christ. Missiologically speaking, aren't we to adapt to the changing nature of the city?

Does some of the conflict and tension therefore stem from our unwillingness to change and adapt? German immigrants lived in inner North and NE Portland before the African-Americans came. This is part of the changing tide of the city as wave after wave of groups come and go throughout the years. The older the city, the more the transition. If we're to think and act like missionaries rather than staying ethnically separated, wouldn't it better to integrate? What if the church in gentrifying neighborhoods really did reflect the surrounding area? Blacks and white, middle-class, low-income, families, singles, and so on all worshipping as one the Triune God? In an article on CCDA's blog, Jin S. Kim discusses this tension:

137

The ministry of reconciliation will be the most urgent ministry in the 21st century. Our divisions, arrogance and hateful passions will be broadcast instantly in today's globalized world. Our fractured witness will be more a stumbling block to evangelism than ever before. Our brokenness will dilute our efforts at peace and justice. Let us now confess our wretchedness together instead of pointing fingers at one another. Perhaps God will have pity on us and show compassion on us. To paraphrase Paul: Wretched church that we are! Who will rescue us from this body of death? Thanks be to God through Jesus Christ our Lord![36]

Instead of gathering their diaspora from all over the city, what if the church intentionally sought to be reflective of its changing neighborhood? Maybe the church started off reflecting its ethnically white neighborhood but over the past decade it's now become 71 percent Hispanic. There is something off missiologically if that church is still all white. In the same way, an ethnic black church that now finds itself in a majority white neighborhood needs to take steps towards integration. In both cases, this involves repentance, forgiveness, and reconciliation. The tension that gentrification causes is valid and real. However, as followers of Jesus the Messiah we're not to simply sit and stew about it but instead be ambassadors of reconciliation between man and God and with one another.

Example 3: Loss of Affordable Housing

The last negative point about gentrification that I'll highlight is the loss of affordable housing. Donald Conradson gets to the heart of the issue in addressing not only gentrification, but the topic of housing with a biblically rooted ethic. "Righteousness then emphasises the fair treatment of poor and otherwise-marginalised individuals, condemning exploitation in forms such as non-living wages, crippling interest rates, forced labour and human trafficking."[37] Righteousness, God's righteous, and His economy have always given preferential treatment to the poor and the marginalized. That means that the church and individual followers of Jesus in gentrifying neighborhoods ought to show

---

36 Kim, "The Uprooted Church."

37 Conradson, "Expressions of Charity and Action towards Justice."

preferential treatment for the last and the least. This means tackling the housing issue head on.

In *View From the Urban Loft*, I spent a chapter looking at the Mosaic Law and how the whole of Scripture reveals God's heart for those on the margins. "I'm convinced that if one were to read the entirety of Scripture in one sitting, one theme that would not or could not be missed is God's simple and unadulterated love, concern, and preferential treatment for the poor, the widow, the orphan, the foreigner, and the marginalized. Often it is a direct challenge to a culture that marginalizes the have-nots while we obsess on self and accumulating stuff."[38] Affordable housing then is something that is near and dear to the heart of God.

Part of the challenge is the reality that what makes a city rank high in terms of livability, creativity, and economic vitality, also means that it leaves a wake of destruction among those who don't directly contribute to a city's coolness. "As cities aggressively compete to make themselves attractive places to live in and for investors, they are more willing to impose harsh penalties on those people seen as undesirable by wealthy visitors, tourists, shoppers, commuters, and investors."[39] However, this stands in stark contrast to what God desires for cities. Can a city that ranks high in terms of livability and creativity be considered great? "Is this not the litmus test of what makes a city great? That the needy residing within are cared for? Can a city be truly great and neglect this admonition?"[40]

For years I've been tracking and following the creative class, creative cities, and the creative or artisan economy. I dedicated a good portion of my book *Metrospiritual* to the creative class and church planting in gentrifying neighborhoods among this economic grouping. It has been an intriguing and fascinating journey as I've looked at numerous cities, both nationally and internationally, and the resultant impact of this creative economy that comes on the heels of post-industrial cities. However, as much as it has helped cities, in many ways it catalyzes gentrification and creates a greater gap between the haves and have-nots. Lees at al pick up on this and combine Richard Florida's

---

38 Benesh, *View From the Urban Loft*, 68.

39 *Gentrification*, 226.

40 *View From the Urban Loft*, 74.

creativity index with a revanchist urban hierarchy and conclude, "Note in particular how San Francisco and Seattle, two of the cities with the 'meanest' policies towards the homeless and marginal populations, come second and third, respectively, on Richard Florida's creativity index. This raises the crucial issue of disturbing ordinances deployed to make way for the influx of his 'creative class.'"[41]

Given the changing global cityscape this is not simply about ethnic whites moving into ethnic black neighborhoods. "Influxes of new inhabitants, particularly from places without any urban tradition, are seen as making the development of any civil infrastructure perplexing."[42] This is where we must not get bogged down in the minutia of our own cities in order to recognize global trends and movements. As Glaeser noted, people move to the city for a better life. "Cities aren't full of poor people because cities make people poor, but because cities *attract* poor people with the prospect of improving their lot in life."[43]

It is at this intersection that a follower of Jesus can step in to bridge the gap. Glaeser aptly states that one of the ways to keep housing prices down in cities, and city centers in particular, is to build ... and even build up. "If the cities' history becomes a straightjacket, then they lose one of their greatest assets: the ability to build up."[44] He argues in favor of building in central cities to keep down housing costs. "The cost of restricting development is that protected areas become more expensive and more exclusive."[45]

I spent the second chapter in *The Multi-Nucleated Church* looking at and exploring high-density urban contexts. "Whether with immigrants or North American born citizens, there is a growing preference for an urban lifestyle which centers around public transit, walkability, and being bike-friendly."[46] Even in gentrifying neighborhoods I advocate that we find ways to build up and

---

41 *Gentrification*, 226.

42 Davey, *Urban Christianity and Global Order*, 47.

43 *Triumph of the City*, 70.

44 Ibid., 136.

45 Ibid., 150.

46 Benesh, *The Multi-Nucleated Church*, 55.

densify. Density reduces sprawl, keeps a wider selection of housing stock available, and lowers demand so prices potentially remain more affordable.

But where does the church fit in? How exactly does the church in gentrifying neighborhoods work towards this end ... or should it? Is this simply in the realm of city planners, developers, and realtors? "We are called to model a better way more than we are called to criticise the existing one. We are called to be the solution we want to see in the midst of moral and social fragmentation of western societies. We are called to measure our effectiveness not by the size of our churches but by their impact on our communities and the radical discipleship of their members."[47]

Maybe churches could raze their current facilities or campus and in their place build a four- to six-story building that includes housing units (both affordable and market rate) as well as commercial business on the ground level to help pay for the new building. The church could occupy one of the floors. In the end everyone benefits. There would be more housing options, more affordable units, new economic initiatives (including new jobs) and cash flowing into the neighborhood as businesses relocate to this new building. The church would also be seen as being a blessing to the neighborhood by demonstrating that all is sacred and that there are has physical elements and applications to the spiritual.

Conclusion

These then are a few of the positives and negatives that come about through the gentrification process. My encouragement to the followers of Jesus is to see this process through a missiological lens. At each point, at each key intersection in the process, the church (collectively and individually) has the potential to step in and embody the Gospel in word and deed. We should not shy away from gentrification but instead run towards it carrying with us the Gospel as ministers and ambassadors of reconciliation. We will affirm what's positive and advocate for those adversely affected by gentrification.

---

47 Edwards, *An Agenda for Change*, 98.

Is Gentrification Positive or Negative?

Chapter 9

Demographic Changes, Gentrification, and Religious Preference
Orvic Pada

The discussion of demographic change is key to understanding religious preference in light of gentrification. Although the core of gentrification studies is focused on economic structures, there are other variables that need to be explored, especially when we take into consideration the socio-cultural elements of urban transformation.

The demographic changes in the U.S. reflect the transformation in the country's religious landscape. Research on religion and demographic trends suggests that there are major differences between the religious affiliation of immigrants and those born in the U.S.[1]

Studies also find that "immigrants and young adults are significantly less Protestant than are native-born and older Americans."[2] There is also the observation that younger adults are less likely to be affiliated with any particular religion. Others also suggest that religiosity is greater among females than males.[3]

It is important to consider factors of age and gender when studying religious preference as it gives us some clues as to why people prefer some groups over

---

1 *The Pew Forum on Religion and Public Life.*

2 Ibid.

3 Roth and Kroth. *"Risky Business."*

others. Although the reasons might appear obvious to some, there could be deeper reasons why people affiliate or disaffiliate with religious institutions, specifically Christian churches.

The discussion on religion and social stratification is rooted in the classical sociological theories of Max Weber and Emile Durkheim.[4] Although some people's religious preference are based on achieved status, for others it is based on ascribed status of race and sex because of hegemonic ideologies, religious patriarchy and gender bias. Additionally, Von der Ruhr and Daniels state that "religious denominations embrace certain values and beliefs in their social teaching that will impact the economic life of their members."[5] This implies that there is a relationship between religiosity, income, and work.

Finally, the literature on gender and religiosity suggests that females report higher religiosity than males. It also suggests that religions perpetuate gender ideologies, norms and stereotypes.[6] In effect, this can lead to displacement, marginalization, and exclusion from groups or tasks based on ones gender.

The implications of research on demographic change and religiosity in light of gentrification propose that although gentrification encourages diversity, it leads to homogeneity. Thus, from a sociological standpoint, there are ramifications for socio-economic disparities either based on pre-existing religious institutional social structures or the revamping of the social structure of religious institutions in gentrified areas.

A number of religious institutions in urban areas cater to the religious affiliations of adherents who practice religiosity. For example, Christian churches offer services ranging from youth programs, education, clothing distribution, food distribution, feeding programs, vocational training, and rehabilitative programs for substance abuse.[7] This is a reflection of ethical and religious traditional "value-rational"[8] social action. Churches carve out a religious

---

4 Taylor and Merino, "Race, Religion, and Beliefs about Racial Inequality."

5 Von der Ruhr and Daniels, "The Relationship between Religious Affiliation, Region, Race, and Attitudes toward Globalization."

6 Seguino, "Help or Hindrance? Religion's Impact on Gender Inequality in Attitudes and Outcomes."

7 Unruh, "Religious Elements of Church-Based Social Service Programs."

8 Weber, *Economy and Society.*

institutional identity motivated by a sacred spiritual dimension of their calling and religious expression.[9]

Churches are faced with an identity crisis as gentrification transforms the urban landscape. Identities and institutional structures undergo significant change due to the shift from a machine-driven economy to a culturally centered paradigm.[10] They face economic challenges as the cost of real estate rises.[11] Old religious dogmas are challenged by the influx of new dwellers who predominantly emphasize secularization or rationalization and diminish the emphasis on traditional belief systems. Religious institutions face the danger of extinction and are challenged to move out or adapt to the changes by forming a hybrid identity. What are the implications of demographic changes to a church's identity in a gentrified neighborhood?

The statistical analysis shows a significant relationship between religious preference, race, age, and gender. Religious preference varies based on race given that although some religious institutions claim openness and inclusion of other racial groups and promote a form of multiculturalism, religions maintain and attract specific gender, age, ethnic or racial groups.

In regards to age, younger people prefer less conservative religions or will be more likely to be unaffiliated with any particular religion. As for gender, the expectation is that traditionally male-dominated religions such as the Judeo-Christian and Islamic religions have a higher percentage of males who prefer these religions, despite previous studies positing that a higher percentage of females report religious preference.

Data Description

The dataset for the analysis is from the General Social Survey 2008 conducted by the National Opinion Research Center (NORC) to analyze social trends. This dataset is significant to the study because it has a large sample and is widely considered as the single best source for examining social trends in the

---

9 "Religious Elements of Church-Based Social Service Programs."

10 Landry, *The Creative City.*

11 Mian, "Prophets-for-Profits," 2143-2161.

U.S. The survey contained a wide range of questions to measure demographic characteristics and attitudes of people living in the United States. The survey includes questions on- from race relations, religion, economics, and gender issues, to name a few categories. The sample for the GSS was independently drawn from English-speaking persons 18 years of age or over who are not institutionalized.[12] Data was collected by face-to-face interviews, computer-assisted personal interviewing (CAPI) and telephone interviews.[13]

Sample Description

The sample has an average age of 47 and is about 54 percent female. It is racially and ethnically diverse and the sample mostly represents White, Black or African-American, Hispanic, and Asian/Pacific Islander. In regards to religious preference, about 51 percent indicated Protestant, about 4 percent Other Christian, about 23 percent Catholic, about 2 percent Jewish, 16 percent responded "None." and less than 1 percent for Eastern/Islam. In regards to age, 20.5 percent of the sample is between the ages of 45-54, while 9.1 percent of the population is between the ages of 18-24.

The sample population shows a growing number of the aging population (75th percentile are about 60 years old), a median age of 47, and 25th percentile of the sample is 34 years old. There is a wide distribution in age of people in the sample, ranging from 30 to 65 years old.

The largest groups in the sample are White (76.8 percent), Black (13.9 percent), Hispanic (4.1 percent) and Asian/Pacific Islander (3.5 percent) (see Table 1). The highest percentage of religious preference in the United States based on the sample are Protestant (51.6 percent), Catholic (23.3 percent), Other Christian (3.9 percent), and None (16.5 percent).

There is a statistically significant relationship between gender and religion. Females report a higher percentage than males in religious preference in almost all the categories for religion, except for religions under the categories of None

---

12 Smith, et al, *General Social Surveys Codebook, 1972-2010.*

13 www3.norc.org.

and Eastern/Islam where males report a higher percentage of religious preference.[14]

There is also a statistically significant relationship between age and religion. As people grow older, response to religious preference decreases. Yet it is interesting to note that Protestants and Catholics age 75 and older have a very high percentage when responding to religious preference compared to other religions in the survey.[15]

Summary

There is a notable trend of racial groups self-reporting for specific religious categories.[16] Blacks have a significantly higher percentage in the Protestant religion, Hispanics have the highest percentage in the Catholic religion, Whites moderately comprise Judeo-Christian, Protestant, and Catholic religions, Asian/Pacific Islander and Other comprise Islam/Eastern religions.

As for gender, females have a higher percentage than males in the Christian, Catholic, Jewish and Other Christian religions but lower in Eastern/Islam, Other, and None. This is noteworthy as the initial suggestion was that females will have a lesser religious preference for male-dominated religions such as Judeo-Christian, Catholic and Eastern/Islam, but other than the religions of Eastern/Islam, they have a higher percentage in the Judeo-Christian and Catholic religions.

In regards to age, there is an overall decrease in response to religious preference as people grow older, but there is a notable increase in response to religious preference in the Protestant, Catholic and Jewish religions as people grow older. Overall, the highest percentage of self-reporting for religious preference is between the age of 25-44.

Based on the analysis, there is statistical evidence that religious preference varies by race, gender and age in the United States.

---

14 Appendix, Figure 1.

15 Appendix, Table 2 and Figure 2.

16 Appendix, Figure 3.

Christian Enclaves

As people struggle to share or make their claim on space in gentrifying urban centers, religious groups and institutions take on the form of cultural enclaves. According to Durkheim's theory, diversity can be problematic.[17] The challenge of working together and communicating rises as diversity increases. Thus, in religious institutions, cultural integration and social solidarity are weakened and cultural values change because of diversity. In Durkheim's view this can lead to *normlessness*.[18]

For example, Christian groups or churches, instead of being a beacon, turn inwards for self-preservation, most noticeably in areas where diversity increases. This is done to preserve mechanical solidarity where people adhere to the same norms and values. In societal systems, groups are preserved by adhering to the same practices, values, cultural norms, and religious practices. Those who deviate are considered disruptive to the equilibrium of the group, and are often expelled or excommunicated. Other adherents opt out and prefer to be unaffiliated, such as younger people, immigrants, or second-generation immigrants.

The creation of such preservationist enclaves is also possibly due to xenophobia, land displacement, financial derailment, and "Christian flight." Cultural or institutional preservation often overshadows the core message of Christianity, but for some, increasing diversity, and possibly gentrification, is a great opportunity to live out the core beliefs and practices of Christianity. So for some groups, cultural or institutional preservation is not the goal but a hybridization of practices, structures and models based on core values to preserve the essence of the belief system and invite new adherents. But the question remains, "Who prefers what group?" This is not a spiritual question but rather a sociological observation. Why does this matter? It matters because despite noble intentions, systems are perpetuated that displace, marginalize, and promote social inequalities. "The socio-economic transformation of the resident

---

17 Durkheim, *The Division of Labor in Society.*

18 Ibid.

population has its own 'autonomous' effect on space in the city."[19] As an urban place is gentrified, new identities are shaped.[20]

Religious Ethnocentrism

For example, the statistical analysis in this chapter demonstrates that a form of ethnocentrism emerges. Social inequalities such as gender, economic, and racial inequalities persist despite the hope of multiculturalism or a diverse ideal urban world.[21] Respondents from the sample self-report a preference for certain religious institutions that attract specific groups. The discussion centers on gender, age, and race, but further statistical analysis is needed to test the effect of income and other possible variables on religious preference. Although nothing is wrong with people preferring specific groups, there is a looming danger of marginalization, displacement, and I daresay colorblind racism.[22] What is interesting to observe is that despite the exterior façade of the promotion of diversity, inequalities are perpetuated in gentrified urban places by the homogenization of the economy.[23]

Major issues of race, class, and gender are ongoing, despite the changes in laws, cultural norms, and religious institutional policies and practices in mainstream U.S. society. The significant relationships tested in the statistical analysis from the GSS sample show some evidence for this but do not specifically determine if it is caused by demographic factors of race, gender, and age or by the economic forces of gentrification. Further research can be done to test the relation between religious preference and the aforementioned variables. Other research methods can also focus on an ethnographic study of gentrified cities in the United States, focusing on religious preference and socio-economic status.

---

19 King, *Re-presenting the City.*

20 Hackworth and Rekers, "Ethnic Packaging and Gentrification."

21 Karner and Aldridge, "Theorizing Religion in a Globalizing World," 5-32.

22 Silva, *Racism Without Racists.*

23 Barnes, et al, "Community and Nostalgia in Urban Revitalization," 335-354.

Uncovering Theological Responses

What are the implications of these attitudes or outcomes in light of a Christian worldview? Based on the Christian Scriptures, the good news of the gospel is for all people and it welcomes all people. Are there social forces at play that are theologically ignored that displace and marginalize people? The discussion on race, gender, and age are big issues that need continued theological reflection in urban contexts. It is noteworthy that there are groups and individuals who contextualize and adapt to the changing neighborhood with sincere intentions of living out love, justice, and compassion. These groups strive to create an atmosphere that encourages people to "come as you are" regardless of race, gender, and age. What are they doing that is successful and what is counterproductive or damaging? Yet there are other groups that consciously exclude people or groups based on their interpretation of biblical texts or theological standpoints. What social forces cause churches to indirectly exclude certain people or groups?

The followers of The Way (Christians) during the historical period of Jesus' life were constantly challenged to reflect and uncover a response to social structures and forces. Classic examples can be seen in how Jesus deviated from cultural and religious norms to get at the heart of the essence and meaning of a transformed life. His actions during the Sabbath (healing and working), associating with "sinners" and tax collectors, his interaction with women, some of whom were social outcasts (prostitutes), and his inclusiveness towards children in social gatherings are clear indications of his diversion from norms to emphasize forgiveness, compassion, justice, and love.

One of the most striking pictures I see when I read through the historical account is Jesus' choice of people to be his disciples and the parables he taught. Most contemporary teachings usually focus on the seemingly random assortment of characters in this ragtag band of disciples. But what interested me most is that upon closer inspection of these characters, there were people in this group who would never associate with each other due to social norms or preconceived notions of the group they came from.

For example, one of the disciples, Simon the Zealot, was associated with the aggressive Jewish sect concerned with the national and religious life of their people and which wanted to overthrow Roman rule. And then there was

Matthew the tax collector, a Jew who collected taxes for the Romans. How could both of these people coexist on a daily basis!? Clearly, there are numerous examples of similar characters in Christian churches today who come from diametrically opposite spectrums. Yet when Jesus called them to follow him, they laid aside their differences to work and learn together. Much can be said about the transformational elements of the teachings and experiences they absorbed as they followed Jesus. The importance of this example is it speaks to the possibility of unity in diversity.

Another key text is the Parable of the Good Samaritan.[24] This is a timeless example of how to answer the question, "Who is my neighbor?" This parable teaches us how to treat anyone we encounter in society regardless of the social construction of race, class, gender, political affiliation, or age. It teaches us to treat others with mercy and grace. In light of demographic changes and increasing diversity in gentrified neighborhoods, we can take steps towards living and advocating for these goals that transcend personal, cultural, social, and religious norms. It might actually be helpful to identify differences and the cultural, social, and religious norms to which we are accustomed or bound to so we can realize how to transform our way of living or response to other people or groups.

The kingdom of God is a place where there is justice and peace. It is a place where people are free, forgiven, and where love covers all. We can utilize the sociological imagination and empirical research to provide evidence and facts as foundational data for structural revisions or changes in established churches or new hybrid expressions of church. Empirical studies can shed light on social structural systems and practices that indirectly or directly promote inequalities, injustice, and elitist structures and cliques that displace people and groups. These structures are both knowingly and unknowingly perpetuated in the name of proclaiming Christ and a life-transforming gospel.

Structural practices and cultural values often overshadow the focal points of Christ's life and teachings. He taught and lived out unconditional love, compassion, mercy and justice. Are these concepts obscured because of the motivation of economic, cultural and religious preservation, leading to displacement, marginalization, and social inequalities? Theological reflection will

---

24 Luke 10:25-37.

benefit from integrating empirical studies in order to address urban issues deeply rooted in gender, age, and racial discourses.

PART II
CHURCH PLANTING AND GENTRIFICATION

Now that some of the preliminary foundation is laid, it is time to build on it by expanding our understanding of gentrification in terms of how it is viewed, experienced, and lived out at street level. Having been involved in pastoral ministries in general since college and church planting specifically over the past ten years it is difficult for me to address any topic without a view towards its impact on church planting or the other way around. In a time where church planting continues to gain momentum and the conversation has taken many course corrections along the way, it is time to put another proverbial iron in the fire by bringing up gentrification in light of church planting.

Church planters tend to start churches among people most like themselves. For the most part, sociologically speaking, that's normative. For example, we would assume that a first-generation Korean would plant churches among other first-generation Koreans, or that a converted Punjabi Sikh would in turn seek to bring the Gospel to other Punjabis. We would assume cowboys plant cowboy churches and bikers (the Harley-Davidson kind) plant biker churches. However, when it comes to gentrifying neighborhoods, or those parts of the city on the receiving end of the gentrification process, who starts new churches? Not only that, but for *whom?*

If a white church planter starts a church in a gentrifying neighborhood many assume it will be hipster/bohemian in nature. If a black church planter starts a church in a gentrifying neighborhood many assume it will be among the established black community. But is there another way? Should white church planters start churches that reach blacks and should black church planters start churches to reach whites? Or should both church planters seek to reach *all* residents, or is that simply a foolish notion? Also, is one plant considered ethnocentric while the other is not? Again, these are the types of questions that need to be addressed and for which we need to have the humility, the grace, and the boldness in order to have an open dialogue where we lay all of our cards out on the table.

The dynamics of gentrification are messy in and of themselves. Adding church planting into the mix makes it even messier. The following chapters are written by church planters who are in the midst of hammering this out on the anvil of life and ministry. There are to be commended for their efforts and applauded for their boldness. Nothing they are attempting is neat and tidy. At times you will find yourself nodding in agreement with what they say, and at other times you will find yourself in sharp disagreement. Embrace the tension. This book is not about packaged answers. I purposelessly invited a wide variety of contributors who represent not only the Reformed and Anabaptist traditions, but also represent planting among different cultures and ethnicities. One thing they all have in common is they've all been impacted in some way by gentrification. But before we get into their stories let us delve into a little research.

Chapter 10

The Geography of Church Planting in the City
Part 1: Agglomeration Economies
Sean Benesh

It was my first class at Portland State University. *Urban Economics and Spatial Structure*. I walked into a crowded room as nervous as if it was my first junior high dance. My palms were sweating and my heart was racing. To say that I was intimidated would be an understatement. I have been in school pretty much continuously since I graduated from high school twenty years ago. Three degrees later, including a doctorate, and my nerves were still frayed. I had gone to a Bible college and to seminaries where I studied the Bible, theology, church history, church planting, church growth, and a theology of the city ... but urban economics?

I quietly slipped in and to my horror the only spot available was right in the front of the class (gulp). As the class started the professor went around the room and we had to introduce ourselves, our educational background, and what we hoped to get out of the class. I listened as student after student explained their background ... political science, urban planning, sociology, economics, and so forth. When it was my turn I even think my voice cracked like a junior higher ... "Theology and ministry," I said.

After the introductions the professor jumped right into his lecture. I was soon lost as he drew all of these diagrams and charts that looked nothing like the end-times charts I had once studied or the graphs showing different versions of sanctification. At the conclusion of the class I walked out with my heading spinning wondering what medieval form of torture I had unwittingly signed up for.

Surprisingly I quickly caught up and learned the lingo. It turned out to be one of the most stimulating classes I have ever taken. I learned the relationship between a city's economics and how it affects its built environment. I was also happily surprised that my DMin from Bakke Graduate University prepared me well for this adventure. What this class did, including thousands of pages of reading, was to open my eyes up to new (to me) ways of marrying an urban theology or urban missiology with urban planning and the social sciences.

Portland is an intriguing city on many fronts. From its abundance of cultural creatives and hipsters to the activist scene to food carts, it is a city unlike others. Church planting is no different. For many years Portland was like a slumbering giant within the city limits (in contrast to the suburbs) with seemingly little effort being made to plant churches in the urban core and first-ring urban neighborhoods. Most church planting, which mirrored most other cities, was indeed in the suburbs. Then something changed; numerous seismic cultural, sociological, transportation and infrastructure, and spiritual forces all coalesced at once to create a ripe environment for church planting in the city. Through gentrification and urban revitalization the city became safer, more aesthetically appealing, and provided the cultural and architectural soil for a flourishing of cultural creatives, hipsters, and neo-bohemians. The central city is truly a fun place to be. "Today successful cities, old or young, attract smart entrepreneurial people, in part, by being urban theme parks."[1]

A quick perusal through the urban development of the past two hundred years reveals the ubiquitous reality that transportation in many ways dictates urban form. As Glaeser notes, "Transportation technologies have always determined urban form."[2] Like most other North American cities, Portland has been shaped by the car and still is for the most part. However, retrofitting the city with light rail[3] and a modern streetcar[4] have helped to reshape the city

---

1 Glaeser, *Triumph of the City*, 11.

2 Ibid., 12.

3 Wikimedia Foundation LLC, "Max Light Rail."

4 Wikimedia Foundation LLC, "Portland Streetcar."

center and first-ring urban neighborhoods. In addition Portland's already robust bicycling commuter scene[5] gave rise to the city's transportation infrastructure which has become internationally known. "The bike network, combined with the city's transit system and planners' focus on developing amenities in neighborhoods allows people to access work, shopping, and social and recreation destinations without a car. Portland's emerging reputation for a car-free lifestyle is a significant draw for a new creative class, especially bike-related artisans."[6] Portland State University recently hosted a delegation of Chinese urban planners who spent weeks in the city studying the unique features of Portland's urbanism. Again, ripe conditions for church planting in the city. The only thing needed now was a spark.

I recall hearing how Martin Luther lit the match that sparked the Protestant Reformation. Through such movements as the Renaissance[7] and the creation of the printing press the cultural environment was ripe for change. The only thing needed was a spark. Luther provided that with his *Ninety-five Theses*. In terms of church planting in the central city of Portland that spark came through the convergence of the aforementioned cultural conditions mixed in with the planting of Imago Dei Community[8] and the release and cult-like popularity of Donald Miller's *Blue Like Jazz*[9]. Church planting in urban Portland took an enormous leap forward. In the same way technology firms began clustering in the Silicon Valley or Bangalore, India, so the same dynamics began reshaping the church planting fabric of Portland. Innovation of all kinds is directly tied to the urban advantage of density and proximity. "Innovations cluster in places like Silicon Valley because ideas cross corridors and streets more easily than continents and seas."[10]

---

5 For more about Portland's bicycling community visit http://bikeportland.org.

6 Heying, *Brew to Bikes*, 110.

7 William Estep traces this in *Renaissance and Reformation.* Grand Rapids: Eerdmans, 1986.

8 www.imagodeicommunity.com

9 Donald Miller, *Blue Like Jazz: Nonreligious Thoughts on Christian Spirituality.* Nashville: Thomas Nelson, 2003.

10 *Triumph of the City*, 36.

Just as artistic talent tends to cluster in certain areas so do various companies and firms. "In most countries, economic activity is spatially concentrated."[11] The same concept is also true of sports. Those who follow collegiate football know that the recruiting hotspots are where there is a disproportionate amount of talent clustered in various geographic locales; southern California, Texas, and Florida top out the list. A quick perusal through the top-tiered college football programs in the country whether Ohio State, Oregon, USC, Alabama, Oklahoma, or LSU, shows their rosters have an ample number of recruits from these locations.

For numerous reasons I continue to revisit the concept of a geography of church planting. The push-and-pull factors taking place across cities is almost like a series of invisible forces or dynamics at hand influencing people and policies. There are simply a complexity of dynamics that are shaping the built environment of cities, where firms and businesses locate, and by default, where churches are being planted. It is my contention that most church planters are not aware of these influences. This has a direct bearing on the rise of church planting in gentrified neighborhoods. But why?

When I first set out to focus my dissertation endeavors and later on my book *Metrospiritual* on this idea of the geographic location of church planting in cities I had assumed the topic was one of a long list of obscure subjects and ideas that most people involved in planting are not even remotely interested in. In many ways that still may be true. However, once I stepped outside of the world of occupational ministry and church planting and into academia and urban economics, all of a sudden I realized that I had inadvertently stumbled onto something. Getting a DMin from a seminary has taught me to view the city through the lens of theology, ministry, and the Kingdom of God. Now that I am lurching out of the starting gates working on a PhD (regardless if I finish or not) from a state university my framework or perspective on the city has become significantly more thorough, in-depth, and rounded. The great irony is that both sides are two halves of the same urban coin. Both perspectives are equally valid and inform one another. Both offer perspectives on the city which ultimately create a whole rather than separate parts. This division is more a categorical creation based upon prevalent worldviews than how God views the city.

---

11 Greenstone, et al, "Identifying Agglomeration Spillovers," 537.

Portland-area Warner Pacific College Professor of Urban Studies Caleb Rosado writes, "I would suggest that a chief reason for the persistent existence of this conflictual division to this day has to do with the continued prevalence of Greek dualistic thinking, brought to its peak expression by Newtonian physics and Cartesian dualism."[12] If we were to apply holism to viewing the city then we would realize that we are to care for both urban places and urban people.

Agglomeration Economies

For the purposes of this chapter I will take my initial research on the geography of church planting that I wrote about in my dissertation[13] and published in *Metrospiritual: The Geography of Church Planting* and apply concepts from urban economics and spatial structure; namely agglomeration economies and location theory, and how they relate to church planting in gentrified neighborhoods. While my hypothesis, research, and findings are still foundational, I can begin expanding on it and investigating with a better set of tools. In *Metrospiritual* the scope of my research was the metropolitan areas[14] of various cities out West.[15] For example, instead of focusing solely on Seattle, the data compilation included other cities that make up the Seattle metropolitan area such as Tacoma, Bellevue, Everett, and so forth. For the geographic parameters of this chapter and book I will continue to narrow the scope to the city proper. For Portland that means the sum total of around 580,000 inhabitants.[16]

The first influential factor as to why and where church planters decide to plant where they do ties into the concept of *agglomeration economies*. For starters,

---

12 Rosado, "Context Determines Content," 2075-2076.

13 Sean Benesh, "Church Planting in the Central City: An Examination of the Causes and Consequences in Seven Western Cities from 2000-2009 with a Deeper Look at the Creative Class in Gentrified Districts and Neighborhoods." (DMin diss., Bakke Graduate University, 2010).

14 The term metropolitan area refers to a region consisting of a densely populated urban core and its less-populated surrounding territories, sharing industry, infrastructure, and housing. Wikimedia Foundation LLC, "Metropolitan Area."

15 Seven cities were used in the research of *Metrospiritual*; Denver, Albuquerque, Tucson, Phoenix, Portland, Seattle, and Vancouver (BC).

16 Wikimedia Foundation Inc, "Portland, Oregon."

agglomeration economies is defined as, "savings which arise from the concentration of industries in urban areas and their location close to linked activities. E.g. a car factory attracts component suppliers to locate close by, saving on transport costs. Other savings are made in labour and training costs, and the use of the services found in urban areas, e.g. housing, banking, roads, electricity, etc."[17] In essence firms locate close to one another to reap the benefit of spillovers. "Economists have speculated that this concentration of economic activity may be explained by cost or productivity advantages enjoyed by firms when they locate near other firms."[18]

In other words, there are many advantages to locating firms or manufacturers close to one another. "Cities are the absence of physical space between people and companies. They are proximity, density, closeness. They enable us to work and play together, and their success depends on the demand for physical connection."[19] It is to this agglomeration or clustering phenomenon that Richard Florida traces the collecting of talent. "Today's key economic factors–talent, innovation, and creativity–are not distributed evenly across the global economy. They concentrate in specific locations. It's obvious how major new innovations in communications and transportation allow economic activity to spread out all over the world. What's less obvious is the incredible power of what I call the *clustering force*. In today's creative economy, the real source of economic growth comes from clustering and concentration of talent and productive people. New ideas are generated and our productivity increases when we locate close to one another in cities and regions."[20] The same applies to church planting on many fronts.

Greenstone, Hornbeck, and Moretti identify five possible reasons for agglomeration in cities. I will list them and then unpack their relevance for church planting in gentrified urban neighborhoods.

---

17 Barcelona Field Studies Centre , "GCSE Industry Glossary."

18 "Identifying Agglomeration Spillovers," 537.

19 *Triumph of the City,* 6.

20 Florida, *Who's Your City?,* 9.

First, it is possible that firms (and workers) are attracted to areas with high concentration of other firms (and other workers) by the *size of the labor market*.

A second reason why the concentration of economic activity may be beneficial has to do with transportation costs. Firms located in denser areas are likely to enjoy cheaper and faster delivery of local services and intermediate goods.

A third reason why the concentration of economic activity may be beneficial has to do with *knowledge spillovers*.

It is possible that firms concentrate spatially not because of any technological spillover, but because *local amenities* valued by workers are concentrated.

Finally, spatial concentration of some industries may be explained by the presence of *natural advantages* or *productive amenities*.[21]

Let me rephrase each point inserting and using church planting language. "First, it is possible that church plants (and church planters) are attracted to areas with high concentration of other church plants (and other church planters) by the *size of the labor market*." At first glance this may seem somewhat untrue. Church planters most often look for neighborhoods, districts, or pockets with little to no church or Gospel presence at all. There is certainly a pioneering spirit among planters regardless of modes or methods. Certainly church planters won't locate in neighborhoods experiencing a high proportion of church planting. However, what may not be applicable on a small neighborhood scale does not negate this reality on a larger city-wide or regional scale. In other words, there is most definitely a magnetic pull in cities that are experiencing a high proportion of church planters compared to other cities. The reasoning behind this has not been documented or researched, but I will set forward several hypotheses as to this phenomenon.

First of all, cities that are more attractive draw more church planters. "This begs the question: Why do creative people cluster in certain places? In a world where people are highly mobile, why do they choose to live in and concentrate in

---

21 "Identifying Agglomeration Spillovers," 542-544.

some cities over others and for what reason?"[22] When a decision is made as to where to locate a church plant is it surprising that such cities as Austin, Seattle, or Los Angeles top the list? These cities also rank high in terms of livability with abundant cultural amenities. They also are hotbeds for creativity and innovation. While beauty is indeed in the eye of the beholder there is little doubt that strictly in terms of appeal and desirability San Francisco ranks higher than Cheyenne or Bismarck.

There appears to be a direct correlation between a city's built environment and cultural climate and the amount of church planting within. Gentrifying neighborhoods hold a special allure. This then leads into the second hypothesis, that church planters are influenced by the same cultural and social forces that others in the Creative Class (hipsters or neo-bohemians) experience. What my research revealed was that outside of the top response ("God's will") the primary motivating factor for site selection among church planters was cultural identity, compatibility, and familiarity. They simply planted churches in those places they most enjoyed and identified with. When a combination of spiritual and cultural dynamics round out "God's call" it becomes challenging to differentiate and analyze, as I alluded to in *Metrospiritual*:

> As a researcher, to study the motivating factors for church planting site selection becomes problematic. What are the criteria to be used? How do I navigate through those who take a methodical approach versus those who felt God prompt them in a certain direction? Often times I liken God's calling or will to the black box found on passenger jetliners. The whole plane may crash leaving nothing but flaming debris but somehow the black box is always intact. Often times, when everything around us crashes and burns, it is that calling we cling to.[23]

Church planters are drawn to an "agglomeration dynamics" of existing networks, affinity, and support structures present in cities as the above quotation from Greenstone et al reveals. In the same way high-tech companies are drawn to Bangalore or the Silicon Valley, church planters are drawn to cities and neighborhoods within cities where "it is happening." Such cities provide ample educational opportunities from seminaries to conferences, existing and emerging

---

22 Florida, *The Rise of the Creative Class*, 223.

23 Benesh, *Metrospiritual*, 92-93.

networks of church planters (Acts 29 for example), and the ability to rub shoulders with one's peers. "Highly skilled people are highly mobile. They do not necessarily respond to monetary incentives alone; they want to be around other smart people. The university plays a magnetic role in the attraction of talent, supporting a classic increasing-returns phenomenon."[24]   Glaeser affirms this when he writes, "Ideas move from person to person within dense urban spaces, and this exchange occasionally creates miracles of human creativity."[25]   The agglomeration dynamics found in many cities prove to be a strong drawing point for potential church planters whether they rise up from within or relocate from outside.

The next point I've adapted from Greenstone, Hornbeck and Moretti's list is, "A second reason why the concentration of church planting may be beneficial has to do with transportation costs. Church plants located in denser areas are likely to enjoy cheaper and faster delivery of local services and intermediate goods." How does this directly correlate to the realm of church planting? This becomes problematic in that currently there is little to no research or data available to draw from. We've yet to see substantial research towards urban advantage due to density and proximity in the realm of ministry in general and church planting in particular. But we can find examples elsewhere which parallel to church planting. "There are two aspects to density in the growth of cities. *Proximity* reduces the time and energy and therefore the cost required to move people and materials around the achieve any objective. When mutually supportive activities are located in proximity to each other, their *concentration* has a further synergistic effect."[26] However, church planting is not about shipping or receiving goods whereby this becomes a factor. On the other hand, put in purely economics terms, the religious "goods" or "offerings" that churches provide leads to them being in accessible areas. That is why in suburban settings it is not uncommon to find churches at intersections or just off the on- and off-ramps of a freeway. In urban settings the benefit is to be found in its density.

Density and proximity create an urban advantage in church planting. As I noted in *View From the Urban Loft*, "Those who live in higher-density

---

24 Florida, *Cities and the Creative Class,* 151.

25 *Triumph of the City,* 19.

26 Brugmann, *Welcome to the Urban Revolution,* 28-29.

neighborhoods have more accessibility to your church and its body life. Socio-economics no longer is a dividing line, because people are not excluded because they can't drive to any of the gatherings."[27] The benefit of density is that "church planting and walkable churches in denser urban environments is that the foundation of community is found in the communal."[28] While churches in gentrified neighborhoods are not shipping goods per se, transportation is still a shaping force. Oftentimes due to denser environs, the "goods" (the spiritual life of a church) are more easily accessible.

"A third reason why the concentration of church planting may be beneficial has to do with *knowledge spillovers*." This directly ties into the first reason that Greenstone, Hornbeck and Moretti mention. Church planters are drawn to cities that offer robust resources, educational opportunities, and networking options because of this spillover factor. Talent collects unequally in cities. "The concentration of inventive and innovative activities in urban areas is often interpreted as providing evidence for the importance of information spillovers in generating new ideas."[29] Of the seven cities in my dissertation research, those that had the strongest networks, plus ample educational institutions cranking out church planters, had the largest concentration of church planters. We find this with the Mennonite Brethren's Church Planting[30] network in Vancouver, BC which is serviced by such institutions as Regent College, Trinity Western University, and Carey Theological College, or by the Acts 29 Network[31] in Seattle with schools like Northwest University, Seattle Pacific, and so forth in the metro area. These are good examples of this *knowledge spillover* phenomenon. In cities such as these are ample opportunities for church planters to rub shoulders and network, learn from one another, and have various opportunities for higher education and ongoing training.

Here in Portland we find the same dynamics with a proliferation of great schools that are church planter and urban ministry factories such as Multnomah,

---

27 Benesh, *View From the Urban Loft*, 165.

28 Ibid., 167.

29 Kim and Margo, "Historical Perspectives on US Economic Geography," 40.

30 Visit Church Planting BC at www.churchplantingbc.com.

31 Visit Acts 29 Network at www.acts29network.org.

George Fox, Warner Pacific, and Western. I regularly come in contact with congregants, pastors, leaders, and church planters who were educated at these schools or are currently attending there. This also explains Portland's meteoric rise as a hotbed for church planting and cultural innovation. "To thrive, cities must attract smart people and enable them to work collaboratively. There is no such thing as a successful city without human capital."[32] The same applies to church planting.

The fourth point that stems from Greenstone, Hornbeck and Moretti's reasons behind agglomeration in cities is, "It is possible that church plants concentrate spatially not because of any technological spillover, but because *local amenities* valued by church planters are concentrated." Glaeser points out, "Urban enjoyments help determine a city's success. Talent is mobile, and it seeks out a good place to consume as well as produce."[33] This reveals something that is all too familiar in today's global economy, which ironically has the same influence upon the geography of church planting. Again, as economists, Edward Glaeser and Richard Florida are observing much of the same trends in that talented people are unequally pooling in specific cities. There are clear winners and losers in this talent arms race. "As humankind becomes wealthier, more people will choose their locations on the basis of pleasure as well as productivity. To understand why cities are succeeding and whether they will continue to thrive in the future, we must understand how urban amenities work and how consumer cities succeed."[34] This is why Wicker Park in Chicago is more desirable as a church planting destination than South Omaha or South Tucson. "People today expect more from the places they live. In the past, many were content to work in one place and vacation somewhere else, while frequently getting away for weekends to ski, enjoy a day in the country or sample nightlife and culture in another city. The idea seemed to be that some places are for making money and others are for fun. This is no longer sufficient."[35]

---

32 *Triumph of the City*, 223.

33 Ibid., 118.

34 Ibid., 119.

35 *The Rise of the Creative Class*, 224.

Where conflict arises is over how does the allure of urban amenities that church planters are drawn to correlate with the values of the Kingdom of God? Church planters are unequivocally drawn to cool cities and cool neighborhoods. It is this that Brett McCracken highlights when he asks, "Are the purposes and/ or effects of cool compatible with those of Christianity? If we assume that *cool* necessarily connotes the notion of being elite, privileged, and somehow better than the masses, how can we reconcile the idea with that of Christianity, which seems to beckon us away from self-aggrandizement or pride of any kind?"[36] What should the motivating factor for site selection in church planting be? This becomes poignant in reference to planting in gentrified neighborhoods. "All the cool places in every city are occupied by a proliferation of church planters. Either in the far-flung suburbs or gentrified neighborhoods, that is where we're seeing a bumper crop of church plants."[37] Does the draw for planters have to do with urban amenities and a lifestyle choice or is it about broken people in need of a Savior? There is no doubt that the answer lies somewhere in between, but church planters need to proceed forward cautiously with humility and gut-wrenching honesty.

The final parallel to the reasons for agglomeration in cities as set forth by Greenstone, Hornbeck, and Moretti is, "Finally, spatial concentration of some church plants may be explained by the presence of *natural advantages* or *productive amenities.*[38] This sounds strikingly familiar to the first and fourth points because it highlights the urban advantage of density and proximity as well as spillovers, networking, and the allure of cultural amenities. The reality is that "People with more human capital live in denser counties"[39] whether in business, education, or ministry.

This last point provides a good opportunity to summarize our foray into applying agglomeration economies to church planting. No doubt there are numerous parallels that can be made and applications drawn. My point here is to reveal some of the subterranean influences that church planters face which have

---

36 McCracken, *Hipster Christianity,* 13.

37 *View From the Urban Loft,* 177.

38 "Identifying Agglomeration Spillovers," 542-544.

39 Glaeser and Kohlhase, "Cities, Regions and the Decline of Transport Costs," 224.

a direct correlation to gentrified neighborhoods and districts. As we've seen thus far in this book, there are clear winners and losers in the gentrification process. How well are church planters, pastors, and followers of Christ in general standing in the gap? How well are they acting as the glue holding the neighborhood together which gentrification seeks to tear apart?

Chapter 11

The Geography of Church Planting in the City
Part 2: Location Theory
Sean Benesh

I have always been a geography nerd. I like maps. As an elementary student I had prided myself on knowing all fifty states as well as their capitals. Even today the spatial layout of cities and their relationship to their regions and states/ provinces intrigue me. For example, last fall I visited Montreal, Quebec, with others for a week to explore the city. Part of my preparation was pouring over maps; maps of the city, maps of the region including other prominent cities up and down the St. Lawrence River, and so forth. Maps give us context and grounds us in a place. Each place has a relationship with other places.

Since returning to the States from Canada sometimes at the dinner table we'll bring out a map of Canada and quiz each other about the names and capitals of the various provinces and territories. While not as daunting as knowing all fifty states it is still fun. We usually get stuck remembering the capital of New Brunswick or Nunavut. We then turn to a map of the world and one by one the boys take turns picking some obscure country and we then have to remember (or guess) which nations border it. They like to pick nations like Togo, Moldova, or one of the -stan countries (Tajikistan, Uzbekistan, etc).

I have always had a fascination with place in regards to the geography of church planting. Where are new churches being planted and why? I am baffled and curious as to where people decide to plant new churches. What was their reasoning? Why here? Why there? What went into the decision process? How aware were they of the push-and-pull dynamics at hand shaping and influencing their decision?

Another way to help understand the spatial distribution or clustering of church planters is to delve into *location theory* as to why firms and plants locate where they do in cities. Whether in reference to large professional sports venues, manufacturing plants, or something seemingly small and insignificant like a gas station, why did they locate where they did? What were the factors involved and how does this apply to where churches are being planted whether in gentrified districts or the slums? "Location theory is concerned with the geographic location of economic activity; it has become an integral part of economic geography, regional science, and spatial economics. Location theory addresses the questions of what economic activities are located where and why."[1]

Location theory plays a significant role in church planting and ministry in both gentrified neighborhoods or a city's degraded neighborhoods. In purely economic terms the decisions revolving around site selection for new businesses are intended to put themselves in locations which they can leverage for maximum profit. This could be a suburban business park, an industrial site just outside the central business district, or a gentrified neighborhood for a new trendy coffee shop. How much of this factors in to where churches are being started or where new ministries are being launched? We've already explored the concept of agglomeration that is drawing talent to certain cities, which includes church planters. Delving into location theory offers insight into specifically where in cities new churches are located and how that helps or hurts gentrified neighborhoods. Also, it could very well explain why desirable parts of the city receive more church plants compared to locations like outer SE Portland.

One of the challenges in applying an urban economics template over site selection in church planting is that it is to some degree limiting. On the one hand, new insights can be gleaned by the value of studying location theory and its impact on gentrified neighborhoods or the resultant lower income areas. On the other, the template does not factor in key insights from theology including missiology and ecclesiology. With that in mind, we'll cautiously seek to reconcile both perspectives and how each relates to the topic of gentrification and cultivating a thoroughly Christian and biblical framework of response.

---

1 Wikimedia Foundation Inc., "Location Theory."

As a whole, the concept of the spatial distribution of churches across cities is an intriguing topic. In the course of a city's history, whether a newer city like Seattle or an older one like Buffalo, NY, or Quebec City, Canada there has always been an ebb and flow phenomenon in regards to the starting of new churches. For example, where I live in inner NE Portland is home to a myriad of old church buildings. Seemingly on every other block one can find an assortment of these buildings punctuate the skyline. The apogee of this construction boom was eighty to a hundred years ago in and among the various ethnic immigrant groups. Throughout the past one hundred years any new church that was established and built ultimately sought to target one of the existing ethnicities or socio-economic demographics whether immigrant Germans or the African-American community. The same can be said of new church plants today, which is why location theory has much to add to this discussion.

Looking back on this neighborhood's history, site selection for new churches wasn't even questioned. It made sense to start an ethnic German church for new immigrants in the same way later to transition that same building for use as an African-American church in keeping with the shifting demographics. Now that same building is again under renovation for its rebirth as a new mostly white hipster church. Is the discussion on site selection for new churches therefore the same as the reasoning as to why a new Chinese grocery store opens up in a neighborhood with a large Chinese population? What then are the implications for gentrification as well as for those locations as a result of this process? For the rest of this chapter I will apply some segments of the location theory template to church planting in the city and note how they affect churches being planted in both gentrified neighborhoods as well as those in outlying areas that are on the receiving end of the diaspora. Some of the features to be explored are locational advantages, how the decision-making process factors into social equality and income equity (or the lack thereof), and site selection in relation to transportation availability.

As I've mentioned before, the decision-making process of where to locate a new business in the context of a metro area is of key importance. "First, what is an *efficient* location or pattern of locations? According to location theory, the location patterns of all activities will be efficient or optimal when profits are maximum in a perfectly competitive system. Any shift in location or intensity of production at a location away from the optimum would reduce system profits and efficiency."[2] Again, this could be a multi-million- (or billion-) dollar technology plant like Intel or Google, a branch office for a Fortune 500 company, and so on down the list. It is a laborious process indeed that, in some cases, takes years to finalize. Should church plants follow suit? How thorough, investigative, and toilsome should the process be? Is the process already this in-depth or are decisions made mostly on intuition? The reason why companies go through an extensive and sometimes multi-year research process, is that site selection is key in leveraging long-term profit and economic sustainability. However, a church's "bottom line" is assumedly going to be different. If the goal is Great Commission- (and Great Commandment-) driven then the measurables for long-term success, based upon a location, are going to look markedly different than a business start-up. However, location is still key. There are no guarantees either in church planting start-ups or business start-ups. Chapman and Walker affirm this when they write, "Industrial location decisions clearly involve considerable *risk* and *uncertainty*."[3]

What are the locational advantages in the city? When it comes to church planting do some places simply make more sense to plant in than others? Does the proliferation of suburban church plants over the past several decades reveal as a whole North America's shift in this direction? "Since World War II, much of the industry in metropolitan areas in the United States has moved to the suburbs. The principle reason for this movement is that plants need more land because one-story buildings are better suited to today's production processes and because vast areas are needed for workers' parking. Since much more land is needed, plants go to the suburbs, where is it cheaper."[4] How much of that applies to the locational choices for new churches?

As disinvestment took place in urban neighborhoods in regards to banks, real estate, and businesses, I can't help but think that in some ways this trend also took place in the church as well. That does not mean that the church ceased to exist in these urban neighborhoods or that new churches weren't started to connect with the changing demographics, but there seem to be parallel patterns of disinvestment, White flight (even among evangelicals), and the rise of

---

2 Morrill and Symons, "Efficiency and Equity Aspects of Optimum Location," 215.

3 Chapman and Walker, *Industrial Location*, 52.

4 Alonso, "Location Theory," 58.

suburban church planting. In urban neighborhoods across North America, as reinvestment has occurred and the streets have become safer again, there has been a boom both in business and new church start-ups in these locations which is now bringing church planters back into the city. It was only five years ago that I didn't hear much about church planting in the city, now it seems as if the urban is the new suburban.

Economically, it makes great sense to position new businesses for maximum profit, and gentrifying neighborhoods are hotbeds for this. From my vantage point this morning at an inner-city coffee shop, the place is buzzing with activity. Trendy (white) urbanites, young and middle-aged, flock to this coffee shop as agglomeration economies on a smaller neighborhood scale draw the local masses to this area which houses not only this coffee shop, but also the new modern condos and numerous other businesses that cater to this growing demographic. The same principles apply in church planting. Planters, like business people, seek to locate their new churches in locations that are on the upswing of population growth and momentum. This is why brand new suburban master-planned communities have a magnetic draw for planters who can capitalize on social and cultural dynamics that can lead to people's openness to spiritual matters and the Gospel.

Where this becomes problematic is when neighborhoods no longer hold wider cultural appeal. What happens when these areas become neglected, disinvested, and forgotten? Is the bottom line for site selection and locational choices in church planting simply about a neighborhood's desirability and livability? While suburbia and hip gentrified neighborhoods and districts are on the winning side of this equation, are we neglecting our higher calling? That doesn't mean we cease to plant churches in the suburbs or gentrified urban neighborhoods, but what it does mean is that we have to continue to push through the cultural entrapments of comfort, success, and desirability to also plant in locations that are in spiritual, emotional, economic, and social need.

This is where the church does diverge from location theory as it pertains to the business world. Instead of running away from blighted areas we need to run to them. But it seems as though most[5] church planters shy away from these locations. As Brandon Rhodes notes in a *Christianity Today* article entitled

---

5 I am writing in broad generalities and focusing on larger regional and national trends.

"Where Church Planters Fear to Tread," "Hawthorne and other 'corridors of cool' are also where you find most of the city's church-planters. In age and technological preferences, they're not too different from their non-Christian counterparts in Portland: mostly smartphone-savvy, denominationally financed white men in their 30s."[6]

This then brings up a second pertinent issue regarding site selection in church planting: equity. As Morrill and Symons note, speaking of businesses and site selection, "The notion of distributional *equity*, or justice with respect to location, is much less clear."[7] What is equitable or just in site selection in church planting? Is there such a thing? How would we know if there is or is not? Is it even measurable? Morrill and Symon continue, "The idea of measuring equity only arises, of course, if society feels that some of its members may not be receiving fair or adequate goods and services."[8] Those questions are asked in the business world. Do we dare ask them in the world of church planting? If site selection of church planters means agglomeration dynamics in certain parts of the city and overall neglect in the downtrodden and blighted parts what does that mean? Do we have a framework where we can measure or a platform to even have these conversations?

Much of the equity conversation revolves around transportation issues. One of the benefits of living in high-density urban areas is that most often they are serviced by a greater concentration of transportation options. "The location and orientation of transport networks is a significant factor in the real world. Such infrastructure is expensive to build and confers special benefits on particular locations."[9] For example, where I live I have access to several bus routes, the MAX light rail, plus the area is thoroughly bike-friendly. But most of the city is not like this. Murray and Davis point out such discrepancies: "Most transportation agencies stipulate that an important planning goal is to provide equitable and just public transport services. However, who is to be served and the

---

6 Rhodes, "Where Church Planters Fear to Tread."

7 "Efficiency and Equity Aspects of Optimum Location," 217.

8 Ibid.

9 "Location Theory, Location Factors and Location Decisions," 42.

type of service that should be provided has been ambiguous."[10] Oftentimes lower income people who have historically lived in dense central city neighborhoods benefitted from transportation accessibility. However, through gentrification and the resultant displacement of many of these families, they now find themselves in neighborhoods with little access to a variety of transportation options.

That brings up issues in regards to equity and justice. "In general, the notion of equity, justice, or fairness deals with principles that determine the distribution of income, goods, or services."[11] This is related to transportation accessibility as Newman, Beatley, and Boyer point out. "The evidence of the poor becoming more and more isolated on the car-dependent urban fringe is very clear in Australia and increasingly so in North America as the focus of social policy has been on creating affordable housing on cheap land. The emphasis has not been on creating affordable housing in urban areas that is walkable, transit accessible, and energy efficient."[12]

Where this conversation and this reality come crashing into the world of site selection in church planting is how aware church planters are of these conditions if at all. Do they know the dynamics that are shaping both urban gentrified neighborhoods and those areas that are on the receiving end of gentrification? How does this conversation affect where and how we plant churches across cities? To try to answer this question I return to the work of Morrill and Symons. While they are writing about appropriately placing public facilities (i.e., hospitals and such) there are some lessons we can glean about an equitable distribution of church plants. Concerned about achieving greater equity in accessibility they set forth three points worthy of consideration as they apply to church planting:

1. Raising the average level of access of people to a set of facilities implies simply a larger number of perhaps smaller facilities located closer together.

2. To reduce the proportion of people more than some critical distance from a facility, facilities must be shifted toward less dense (or poorer) areas from more dense (or richer) areas.

---

10 Murray and Davis, "Equity in Regional Service Provision," 577.

11 Ibid., 578.

12 Newman, et al, *Resilient Cities*, 50.

3. Reduction of the variability of access or distance traveled implies perhaps simply the imposition of a regular central-place-like lattice of facilities, irrespective of variations in density or income.[13]

Would some of these points apply when it comes to the geography of church planting across cities? Or is that simply nonsensical ? Do such dynamics as agglomeration economies and its effect on church planting deter any concept of equally distributing new churches across cities so as to create equal accessibility for all urban inhabitants? Why are all of the great coffee shops found in urban neighborhoods that are gentrifying? In the same way, why are most of the new church plants in the city limits in similar neighborhoods? While we may not get to the point of a spatial equilibrium of church plants across the city we can at least posit that "equitable church planting" needs to be grounded in care and concern for the whole city. If not we'll continue to plant mostly in the suburbs and trendy gentrified neighborhoods all the while neglecting blighted areas. This is not right. But how do correct the course of the trajectory we're on? DeVerteuil contends that, "Welfare economics makes value judgments about the distribution of resources in society, and determines if such distributions are equitable."[14] If any group should seem to have a corner on the market of equity in economics, redistribution, and accessibility it would be the church. Does this reflect where we're planting churches?

In the past two chapters I attempted to apply the template of agglomeration economies and location theory to church planting. It is a messy process but worth the risk. The church is about extending common and saving grace to the city, therefore we must be concerned with both urban places and urban people. The former affects the latter more than we realize. The place we live in the city is more than an address and a zip code. It affects our worldview and ultimately our lives. Life is markedly different if one grows up on the 17th floor of a run down tenement building in a blighted neighborhood in South Chicago compared to a lush agrarian suburban setting in The Woodlands, outside of Houston, Texas, or the upscale False Creek or Yaletown neighborhoods of downtown Vancouver,

---

13 "Efficiency and Equity Aspects of Optimum Location," 222-223.

14 DeVerteuil, "Reconsidering the Legacy of Urban Public Facility Location Theory in Human Geography," 50.

BC. We find a proliferation of church planting in such places compared to neighborhoods like South Chicago or outer SE Portland. Exploring agglomeration economies and location theory is one way to address where churches are being planted, the push-and-pull dynamics shaping site selection, and then how they correlate with the Kingdom of God. Although its context is the site selection of industrial locations, the following quotation highlights even more so the need for the church to be sensitive and thoughtful as to where it plants new churches: "Whatever reasons promote the search for a new location, the question of how this search is made is clearly important, bearing in mind the optimizing approach assumed by location theory."[15] Gentrified neighborhoods need more new churches not fewer. However, so do the blighted neighborhoods that are experiencing the fallout from gentrification.

---

15 "Location Theory, Location Factors and Location Decisions," 55.

Chapter 12

Church Planting in Gentrifying Neighborhoods
Part 1: Church at Argenta (Little Rock, AR)
Michael Carpenter

Argenta. The heirs of territorial and early statehood politician Thomas W. Newton Sr. planted the town of Argenta in 1866. The name, derived from the Latin *argentum* (silver), recognized Newton's leadership during the late 1840s and early 1850s in the Southwest Arkansas Mining Company that operated the Kellogg lead and silver mine about ten miles north of Argenta.

A majority of the population on the town's north side in 1870 was African-American, including many former slaves. European immigrants began arriving in the 1870s to take the railroad jobs and other employment connected with the railroads, fueling Argenta's development . Argenta soon gained the unwanted nickname of "Dogtown" from its working-class origins. According to oral tradition, people in Little Rock on the south side of the river dumped their unwanted dogs in Argenta.

Fast-forward 140 years. The "white flight" to the suburbs of the 1970s and 80s left Argenta's storefronts empty, its housing dilapidated, and the area all but forgotten. Churches left for the contrived landscapes of suburban sprawl and abandoned their buildings. The crime rate increased exponentially as gangs began to occupy the territory once home to a vibrant neighborhood. The old First Baptist Church building became a bar and strip club that served as a front for most of the criminal activity in Argenta. The town quickly became the unwanted dog of metro Little Rock.

Fearful and angry residents became weary of the many problems that were plaguing their once thriving Argenta neighborhood—high crime, disinvestment, and abandoned homes. In response they formed the Argenta Community Development Corporation (CDC) in 1993. According to the CDC's website:

> By developing strategic partnerships with the private and public sectors, the CDC created a vision of how their neighborhood could be-a safe, thriving, strong community for residential, cultural and commercial growth.
>
> Nearly two decades later this vision has evolved into a Historical District with numerous small businesses, private investments, low crime, recreational and entertainment venues, an emerging arts district and proud homeowners who have experienced a 200% increase in property values. At present, Argenta CDC has newly constructed and rehabilitated over 200 units of affordable housing (purchase and rental) and owns one-third of the properties in the district. This ownership has minimized gentrification in a now vibrant, mixed-income community.[1]

Yet the church remained absent. Fear of urban neighborhoods, fear of the "other," and the love of convenience rather than the Bible, prayer, and meaningful discussions among fellow Christians have driven the church's perception of neighborhoods like Argenta. Not surprisingly, this perception is largely negative. We have moved our homes and congregations to the fringes of our historic neighborhoods and to suburban enclaves. Moreover, we have learned to speak of these neighborhoods as places in need of rescue missions rather than places in which to live, work, and play.

Urban Church Planting in the Deep South

Because of the predominantly negative perception of urban neighborhoods, we, as the Church, must deal with the issue of faithfully communicating the Gospel. We are not the first ones to deal with this problem. Like the Church throughout history, what we must continually ask ourselves is if we, the church, are biblically faithful, acting as the presence of Christ in the community at large, and able to relate Christ to people in a culture. In other words, the Church exists in a cultural context and has a responsibility toward that context. It is to live out

---

1 Argenta Community Development Corporation, "About Us."

the reality of the redeemed life within its context and to bring the power of redemption to bear on its culture by making disciples. This will mean taking a long view of success and being realistic about the fact that the world in which people are living in is working against the Church.

Church planting in the Bible belt of the Deep South can often feel like being sent into the "Burned Over District" of western New York after the Second Great Awakening. I would argue that familiarity with the Gospel in the Southern United States has bred contempt for the Gospel which stems from the fact that people are looking for a faith that can change them and allows them to be a part of changing the world, yet they are unable to find this in Sunday "worship" services. The climate is as if people have been inoculated and are now immune to the Gospel that once stood at the center of Southern culture. In other words, Argenta is not Babylon where the culture knows little about Christianity. Rather, Argenta is like Samaria where they know plenty about Christianity, but have a definite grudge against it and/or have been taught a false Gospel. The problem is not that the Church is strange. The problem is that the Church is familiar.[2]

If Southern culture is merely taken at face value by the church community, then we will spend our time manipulating aspects of culture until they are redeemable rather than pointing out what is truly redemptive. We need to constantly evaluate and reevaluate how we are engaging the people within culture. Primarily, our action is to engage people and use the culture rather than to engage the culture and use the people. Christ lived in the culture. He did not isolate himself from sinners, regardless of how the religious leaders felt about it. He ate with a tax collector, touched a leper, forgave an adulterous woman, and spoke to a woman at a well. At the same time, Jesus did not allow the surrounding culture to change him. He used everyday objects to teach spiritual lessons, but on more than one occasion, he told sinners to sin no more. He was gracious and just—a combination that we should strive to achieve rather than settling for one swing of the pendulum or the other.

However, the question is, now that we are planting a church, how the story of Argenta will be retold in the generations to come remains. We believe that to answer this question we must first answer the question, "What does

---

2 Stafford, "This Samaritan Life," 47.

transformation look like?" Our answer to that question will reveal our assumptions regarding salvation, redemption, and the nature of God. Creating the perfect, problem-free neighborhood will never redeem humanity. However, we cannot ignore the context to which we have been sent. In other words, we must learn how to work out our discipleship in the specific context of our neighborhood. While cities began as physical manifestations of our rebellion against God, God took our rebellion and redeemed it for his purpose.[3] And as the covenant people of God, we have been given a mandate in respect to our city. As witnessed throughout the story of the Bible, God has continually led his people back to communion with himself in the context of a city. And since God is already at work in our city, our neighborhood, and in the lives of the people who call and will call Argenta home, our job is to simply reveal his universal reign. This may be revealing the beauty of Argenta in its residential streets, its commercial endeavors, local economies, and being patrons of various artistic ventures. And it certainly includes entering into the places of profound heartbreak and need offering the reconciliation and forgiveness required.

Where You Live Matters

Church planting in gentrified neighborhoods like Argenta requires "landing" over "launching" a Sunday morning church service. This may seem obvious, but by "landing" I mean people must move into the neighborhood. Earnest Goodman on his blog, *Missions Misunderstood*, states that for some reason, "Christians often use criteria such as cost, square footage, neighborhood, good schools, low crime, return on investment, etc. when deciding where to live. This, however, is heavily informed by the American Dream and stands in direct conflict with Kingdom values. When we adopt these kinds of values, following Jesus is entirely accidental."[4] In other words, when believers are faced with a decision about where to live, we need to adopt values that are informed by the Kingdom rather than our right to life, liberty, and the pursuit of happiness.

---

3 Jacobsen, *Sidewalks in the Kingdom*, 68.

4 Goodman, "Where You Live Matters."

Goodman then gives us some questions to ask as we decide where to plant our lives. First, we need to ask, "Where can I be a blessing?"[5] Since God's covenant with Abraham, God's people have been blessed in order that they may be a blessing to others. The exiles in Babylon faced a similar dilemma. How would they and how could they be a blessing? Even though the exile would last another seventy years, God told his people to build houses, plant gardens, to take wives, give their children in marriage, and to seek the welfare of the city.

> Thus says the Lord of hosts, the God of Israel, to all the exiles whom I have sent into exile from Jerusalem to Babylon: Build houses and live in them; plant gardens and eat their produce. Take wives and have sons and daughters; take wives for your sons, and give your daughters in marriage, that they may bear sons and daughters; multiply there, and do not decrease. But seek the welfare of the city where I have sent you into exile, and pray to the Lord on its behalf, for in its welfare you will find your welfare (Jer 29: 4-7).

What could God have in mind with such a command? Certainly not turning Babylon into some kind of surrogate Jerusalem. Perhaps what was being accomplished was the shaping of a people more than the shaping of a city. In other words, God was building up his people in asking them to invest in and pray for Babylon.[6] The truth is, we are all exiles. Our citizenship is not of this world. God is more concerned with the redemption and shaping of his people than the formation of a problem free city. As noted above, in Jeremiah 29:7, God tells us exiles to "seek the peace and prosperity of the city" where we live. In other words, as God's new covenant people, the Church is to be a blessing to the context in which it finds itself. As distinguished by her gospel message, her sacred ordinances, her mission, and, above all, by her love for God, for one another, the Church should be a blessing to her immediate neighborhood.

Secondly, Goodman writes, "Where we live can either help or hinder our efforts to get to know people and build community."[7] It takes some intentionality to ensure contact with neighbors. For example, when considering where to live, most realtors and those well-meaning folks with sage advice will

---

5 Ibid.

6 *Sidewalks in the Kingdom*, 70-71.

7 "Where You Live Matters."

tell you to avoid living on a corner. They cite reasons such as less privacy, the likelihood of the school bus stop being in front of your home, and more yard than most urban dwellers want.[8] Yet these are the very things that ensure contact with your neighbors. The lack of privacy means you are not cut off from the neighborhood. The school bus stopping in front of your home lets you get to know the children in your neighborhood. What if you used this as an opportunity to provide a place for homework help for the latchkey kids who get off the bus in front of your home? And the yard? The possibilities are endless – from planting a community garden to hosting the occasional cookout.

When Jesus told us love our neighbors, he meant our actual neighbors—the people who live closest to us. Christians have long been making "neighbor" into a safe metaphor that allows us to believe we are carrying out the Lord's command when we show kindness to complete strangers. But when we insist we are neighbors with everybody, often we end up being neighbors with nobody. We must always bear in mind that we live and act as Christ's witnesses. For the wonder of Jesus' humanity reveals what God intends this person to be and to become. John 1:14 in *The Message* paraphrase of the Bible states that "the Word became flesh and blood and moved into the neighborhood." Intentionally moving into a neighborhood is to model what it would be like for our neighbors if they were to have a relationship with Him, not about showing non-believers how it looks for us to follow Christ. This is what Jesus did. He modeled for us what it is like to live in relationship to the Father over what it looked like for him.

So why not live in a house on a corner? Sure it may be a little noisy, you may have less privacy, and the school bus may stop in front of your home, but these are the very things that aid us in our efforts to love our neighbors, build community, and practice the radical hospitality demonstrated in the life of Jesus. God is a God of welcome, a God of hospitality. Receiving the grace of hospitality changes us into hospitable people. As we open our homes and tables to outsiders, we become people of welcome and children of God. As Earnest Goodman notes: "This requires us to give up our preferences. We may end up in a small apartment rather than a big house. We may not get the biggest bang for our buck. We may have to tutor our kids, develop new habits, and enter a new

---

8 Penzo, "21 Reasons Why Corner Lots Are For Suckers."

culture, but is not that what missionaries do?"[9] Stated another way, not only must we live where they live, but also live as they live.

The Art of Placemaking

One of the most important aspects of any city is its collective commons: the shared public spaces where people gather, be they streets, squares, parks, markets, playgrounds, coffee shops, bars, or something else. Yet, even in the heart of a city in neighborhoods like Argenta, the word that best describes the kind of lives many people are living today is isolation. More and more people are spending less and less time with one another. People no longer give time to civic participation, religious involvement, and neighborhood relationships. More often than not people spend much of their time alone. The deterioration of social connections in our neighborhoods should drive us to action. As followers of Jesus we know that we are created as relational beings. We know that God designed us to be in a deep, abiding relationship with him. But we also understand that we are also to be in live-giving relationships with one another. The idea of people sitting at home, dying relationally from lack of basic human connections should inspire us to bring about change. But what is a church plant in a gentrified neighborhood to do? Our answer: open a business that functions as our neighborhood's third place. In most church planting circles, that statement may sound unusual, even though we were not the first to think of it. Before I explain myself I need to define a "third place."

Sociologist Ray Oldenburg coined the phrase in his 1989 book *The Great Good Place: Cafes, Coffee Shops, Community Centers, Beauty Parlors, General Stores, Bars, Hangouts, and How They Get You Through the Day*. The subtitle says it all. According to Oldenburg, the first place is our home and the people with whom we live with. The second place is where we work and the place we spend most of our waking hours. A third place is a public setting that hosts regular, voluntary, and informal gatherings of people. Third places are where people hang out, relax, and have the opportunity to know and be known by others. At their core, they

---

9 "Where You Live Matters."

are places where people feel at home. They feel like they belong there, and typically have a sense of ownership.[10]

So why is it important for church plants in gentrified neighborhoods to create a third place? Because, as stated above, the vast majority of Americans are living isolated, relationally impoverished lives, and third places offer an opportunity for missional people to do life in proximity to others. Life without community has produced, for many, a lifestyle consisting mainly of a home-to-work-and-back-again shuttle. The trouble is, neither work nor family can by themselves possibly fill our need for novelty, for playful conversation with people whose thoughts are not already well-known to us, for talk that gives birth to new ideas, for undirected flowing chat that is not directed toward solving work and family goals. Neither work nor family can foster fledgling romances by offering places where young people can run into each other accidentally on purpose. Nor can they serve our need to escape from the limited roles that have been assigned to us in our day-to-day lives, whether these be "hipster" or "geek" or "jock" or "housewife" or "pastor." If we have no place to go to escape the strictures and confinements of companionship with people we might not have chosen, we may come to resent them.

Moreover, in neighborhoods like Argenta, the "great good places" gave way to the suburban flight. All those empty storefronts were once home to third places. They have always been an important way in which the community has developed and retained a sense of identity. For this reason, the Church needs to be at the forefront of enhancing opportunities for a richer public life. Our motivation should flow out the desire to see those who are relationally starved be drawn to a life-giving relationship not only with others, but ultimately with the giver of life himself. In addition, we need to recognize that people are not interested in church activities. The Church, as the missionary people of God, must realize that we must engage people on common ground—third places. It is so easy for us to withdraw to the comfortable confines of our Christian subculture. But that is not the example Jesus set. He crossed every conceivable demographic line. Think of it this way. Jesus did not hang out at synagogues. Jesus hung out at wells. Wells were more than just a place to draw water. Wells were natural gathering places in ancient culture. Jesus didn't expect people to

---

10 Oldenburg, *The Great Good Place*, 22-42.

come to him. He crossed cultural boundaries and went to them. Therefore, instead of building a traditional church building where people gather once a week, dig a well where people gather every day.

To do this, we are opening a coffee shop. A few bars and restaurants have opened in Argenta, but none function as a true third place. Third places are places to meet, socialize, relax, hang out, or work away from the office. Places to eat and drink without pressure to consume or move on. The third place is epitomized by the modern coffee house. Of course, in many ways a third place is a new name for the role that coffee houses have long performed in North American life. But the third place is not focused on the act of eating and drinking as in restaurants and bars. The food or drink one consumes is the entry fee, not the purpose. The third place is a living room, but not in someone's house; a workplace, but not in someone's office. I am not advocating that every new church plant open a coffee shop. That may be the worst thing to open and your neighborhood may already have many functioning third places. Taking the time to map the demographic, social, and religious aspects of where you live will help you in deciding when you need to create versus when you need to join, and when you need to do both. For us, by building a coffeehouse, we will be able to create a place where connections will happen week in and week out. We can only image how many people will walk into our coffee shop to get a cup of coffee and end up finding a relationship with Jesus and a church community. Our church building itself will become a welcoming public space for both sacred and secular functions.

Conclusion

The flight to the suburbs has left many neighborhoods in our cities plagued with problems. Yet people are moving back and revitalizing these once-forgotten places. The absence of the local church and the predominantly negative perception of the inner city is telling. Rather than seeing historical neighborhoods as places to live, work, and play, the Church views urban neighborhoods as places in which we do ministry *to* people instead of *with* people. But this will never facilitate the transformation of the city we all long for. Where we live matters. We cannot continue with the perception that we can do ministry in the neighborhoods of the city while living in our comfortable, landscaped, suburban utopias. Neighborhoods that once boasted home to the "great good places" that peppered Main Street have virtually been lost. In a time when people are relationally starved, who no longer see the church as an option, we must find ways to reveal the reign of God on residential streets, in commercial endeavors and local economies. This means entering into neighborhoods in which profound heartbreak, brokenness, and relational poverty prevail and offer the reconciliation and redemption all of humanity longs for.

Chapter 13

Church Planting in Gentrifying Neighborhoods
Part 2: Emmaus Church (Portland, OR)
Cole Brown

Alvin and Angela's sons grew up in the same neighborhood as their parents. As the boys entered their teenage years they were able to witness the rapid changes gentrification was bringing to their neighborhood. Beyond mere observation, they were also able to experience these changes on more occasions than they would like as police offers repeatedly pulled them over within two blocks of their residence. They had committed no traffic violations. Nor had they committed any crime when they were followed by a squad car as they walked home from school. Nor were they committing a crime when they were approached by a threatening officer wielding his nightstick as they walked up the steps to their own home. The only reason for their increasingly common encounters with the police is that certain officers believe black teenage boys no longer "fit" in their own neighborhood.

Duoshun has spent most of his 27 years in the neighborhood. As a food connoisseur it was only natural for Duoshun to gather his friends to celebrate his birthday at the brand new BBQ restaurant that entered the neighborhood on the waves of gentrification. It seemed to be just as natural, unfortunately, for the white server of the white-owned restaurant to greet her black guests with the words, "I know you all want ribs, but we're almost out." Being brand new to the neighborhood did not stop her from assuming that black people in the neighborhood only order ribs, nor did it stop her from assuming they could not afford any items of additional cost ("I don't think you want that, it's going to cost extra") or that they could not be trusted to leave a generous tip ("you guys never tip").

Dianne has owned her own home in the neighborhood for nearly 40 years. When she moved in she was one of many black residents on her block. She now owns the only two houses on the block occupied by non-whites. Every week Dianne receives unsolicited postcards from white individuals and families in Portland's surrounding suburbs. "We really want to move closer into Northeast Portland. Would you be willing to sell your house to us? We'll offer a nice sum." Needless to say, Dianne is the only homeowner on her block receiving such postcards because she is the final holdout of black homeowners who purchased homes on her block at rock-bottom prices (because no white people wanted to live there) that have since increased in value by more than 2,000 percent (because many white people want to live there).

These three stories all involve members of Emmaus, the multi-ethnic church I pastor. They are not uncommon. I chose them randomly from the many dozens of stories I have heard since we planted the church in Portland's lower Northeast section in 2006. In the decade since we planted the church the process of gentrification overtook the historically black neighborhood and resulted in 7,700 African-Americans being displaced.[1] That process has only continued into the current decade. While much has been written about the impact of gentrification on a city and its communities, much less has been written on the impact of gentrification on the local church. In this chapter I will review two ways that gentrification has impacted my congregation and others like it.

Cross-Cultural Relationships

It is sometimes stated that one of the positive effects of gentrification is that it moves multiple neighborhoods from a largely segregated state to a far more integrated state. This is seen as a positive because integrated neighborhoods provide improved services for minority populations and an opportunity for cross-cultural relationships in neighborhood schools, churches, businesses, and community organizations. While it is accurate to observe these effects of

---

1 Scott, "By the Grace of God," 52.

gentrification it is inaccurate to interpret these effects as necessarily positive. In my experience of pastoring people from both the "Old Neighborhood" (read: black) and "New Neighborhood" (read: white) these effects do not contribute to improving cross-cultural/cross-ethnic relationships. They more often contribute to even greater tension in cross-cultural/cross-ethnic relationships.

The more socially conscious in the New Neighborhood are initially excited about establishing diverse relationships for themselves and/or for their children in the integrated social spheres the gentrified neighborhood promises to provide. They are often subsequently disappointed to find that the Old Neighborhood is not equally excited about the opportunity to establish cross-cultural/cross-ethnic relationships with them. At the same time, many in the Old Neighborhood have difficulty believing that the new residents of their neighborhood truly desire equitable cross-cultural/cross-ethnic relationships. As a white man who has lived in the Old Neighborhood since long before gentrification began I find this to be a reasonable doubt based on reasonable questions. Such as,

If you really wanted to have relationships with us why did you avoid our neighborhood until it became gentrified? Why did you wait for it to become "your" neighborhood before you made any efforts to know us?

Now that you do live in our neighborhood why do you spend your time in the coffee shops, pubs, concert halls, and churches that serve the New Neighborhood? You say you want to be in relationship with us but you spend your free time and money in the places you are least likely to find the diverse relationships you say you want.

Why are you willing to sacrifice my entire community in order to meet your personal desires? In order for you to gain all the good things you wanted (such as cross-ethnic relationships) the people of my community had to lose many of the good things we had.

You say that gentrification provides positive benefits for minority populations because it improves schools, lessens crime, beautifies historic buildings, and raises property values. Why do you talk about these things as if they are positive instead of fighting against the unjust policies and practices that lead to these results? Do you really think it's a good thing that the only way for a community of color to experience these "benefits" is for white people to move into it? Why do you not acknowledge the terrible injustices that these truths reveal and you unintentionally perpetuate?

If you are so interested in building relationships with the Old Neighborhood why are incidents of subtle and outright racism only becoming more common with each phase of new residents and businesses?

Questions such as these only exist because of gentrification. The tension produced by the general failure of the New Neighborhood to acknowledge the presence (much less the validity) of these questions only exists because of gentrification. The stories that opened this chapter only exist because of gentrification. Thus, in my pastoral experience, gentrification tends to worsen cross-ethnic relationships rather than improve them.

The good news is that the Christian Church has the tools to confront this cross-ethnic tension and reconcile the two divided neighborhoods into one neighborhood through the message of the gospel.[2] The bad news is that in most gentrifying neighborhoods local churches are not making any attempt to narrow the divide. Instead, they are choosing to greatly widen the divide through planting churches by white people, of white people, for white people in the middle of historically black neighborhoods.

This is not to say that predominantly white churches entering into gentrifying neighborhoods want to contribute to the cross-ethnic division in the neighborhood. It is to say that they do contribute to this division in spite of the fact they do not want to. By building their church upon New Neighborhood leaders; by covering their facilities, website, and promo materials in New Neighborhood art; by filling their services with New Neighborhood music, preaching styles, and sermon topics; and by specifically targeting New Neighborhood residents these churches unintentionally become yet another emblem of the New Neighborhood and its utter disinterest in the communities, values, spirituality, and people of the Old Neighborhood. This leaves the Old Neighborhood with the perception that even white Christians do not really want the cross-ethnic relationships they say they do, nor do they really want the justice they say they do as they seem to be content with not only allowing gentrification to run its course but with participating in it.

All of the above leads us to conclude that gentrification is hurting local churches by multiplying cross-ethnic tensions (thereby hindering the

---

2 Ephesians 2:11-22.

proclamation of the gospel of reconciliation across ethnic lines) and by producing new segregated congregations even in ethnically diverse neighborhoods (thereby hindering the visibility of the gospel of reconciliation at work).

Community Discipleship & Community Benevolence

"Loneliness."

That is the word I hear most when asking African-Americans in my church to describe how gentrification affects them. Black men and women affected by gentrification often feel, in the words of my co-pastor D'Arcy, "like an alien in both neighborhoods."

They no longer fit in the neighborhood they grew up in. The community they used to be a part of is gone and the new community is not designed to serve them or welcome them. They also do not fit in the neighborhood they have had to relocate to due to gentrification. Since the black community has been scattered to various places outside of the city center they often discover they are the only African-Americans in their new neighborhood. Even when they are one of several new black residents in a neighborhood they remain without a single reflection of the unique culture that was a part of their everyday existence prior to gentrification. Their new neighborhood is without culturally appropriate food, beauty salons, or hair supply stores, without culturally relevant art, without culturally competent educators, and—most importantly—without culturally sensitive churches. Such changes cause people like Perry, a member of Emmaus, to lament, "I don't know where my community is anymore."

All of this impacts local churches in at least five ways.

First, because there is no longer a geographically discernible "African-American community" black Christians in my city no longer have the option of attending a neighborhood church.[3] They are left with three options, each of which is less desirable.

A) Commute anywhere from 20 to 120 minutes to one of the few remaining predominantly black churches in the Old Neighborhood. Many

---

3 "By the Grace of God," 55.

of these churches have died or are significantly declining in membership because of the long commute that is now required due to member displacement.

B) Attend a predominantly white church in their new neighborhood, of which only a minute number display even the smallest degree of cultural sensitivity or competency when ministering to African-Americans. This requires that in addition to the social discomfort of being one of very few persons of color in the congregation, the black Christian must also adapt to white cultural forms of preaching, worship, small groups, and community life.

C) Attend one of the predominantly black churches or multi-ethnic churches that have relocated outside of the city center due to gentrification. This allows for a culturally sensitive worship experience but, because the church community consists of people who are scattered throughout the suburban and outer-city landscape, community outside of Sunday mornings is very difficult to find.

None of these options does anything to heal the problem of loneliness that many black Portlanders experience as a result of gentrification.

Second, as neighborhood churches decline through gentrification so does church participation. Churches in the Old Neighborhood can attest that the longer the distance that one must travel to participate in church life the less frequently they will participate. For some, this is due to financial challenges. Each trip into the city center and back requires notable quantities of gas, which translates into notable sums of money. One can only travel into the city center and thus, to their church gatherings, as often as their finances permit. For others, the drop-off in church participation is due to scheduling challenges. Their work or family schedule will not allow them to spend 90 minutes on public transportation to get to the church gathering and 90 minutes more on public transportation to get home from the church gathering every time the church gathers. Yet this is exactly what is required of many who have been forced out of their church's neighborhood through gentrification. For still others, the decrease in church participation is due to social challenges. People are motivated to participate in church activities at least partially by the social connections they develop. As the physical distance between church members grows greater, the social connections tend to feel weaker. Through gentrification, church members begin to feel less connected to their church family. The less connected they feel, the less motivated and/or safe they feel traveling long distances to worship with them.

Third, as church participation declines, Christian discipleship is hindered. Jesus intends for discipleship to take place in community. It is difficult to read the Bible and imagine spiritual growth taking place in any other context. For example, one cannot even attempt to obey the vast majority of commands in the books of Ephesians, Philippians, or Colossians apart from active involvement in a local church community. One also cannot receive some of the much-needed grace that God offers apart from his chosen instrument of the local church.[4] Though Emmaus is a growing multi-ethnic church this remains one of our biggest challenges. Because of the effects of gentrification discussed above our members are unable to participate in community life to the degree that they desire and need. This affects their spiritual growth as Christians and our spiritual growth as a church. Therefore, beyond being an economic and political injustice, gentrification is also a spiritual injustice that distances minority Christians from their church communities and, consequently, robs the church of the contributions of its individual members and robs the individual members of the contributions of the church.

Fourth, as gentrification leaves many black Christians feeling disconnected from the communities they live in, and from the communities they worship in, evangelism suffers. A close reading of the Scriptures reveals that evangelism comes from communities and goes into communities.

Jesus' prayer in John 17:20-23 reveals that the gospel message is made more attractive and more believable by the unity of the Church that carries it. Likewise, Peter writes that it is through being built into a visible community that we as the Church declare the praises of Jesus.[5] By disconnecting many black Christians from their church communities (and their church communities from them) gentrification hinders the power of their evangelism in community. Gentrification also hinders their evangelism into communities. God moved to save us by becoming like us and coming to us in the person of Jesus.[6] When he

---

4 For example, see Galatians 6:2, Ephesians 4:11-13, Hebrews 13:1.

5 1 Peter 2:4-10.

6 John 1:9-14.

came to proclaim the gospel to the Jews he came as a Jew. The Apostle Paul took a similar approach.[7] Both made themselves "fit" into the communities they had been sent to in order to make the gospel intelligible. Yet, as explained above, many black Christians do not feel like they "fit" anywhere. They no longer fit in their old neighborhood. They certainly don't fit in their new neighborhood. And neither neighborhood seems to be very interested in welcoming them. This means that the people that black Christians can most effortlessly connect with on a human and cultural level are too far away—too scattered—to be evangelized as a community. Yet the people who are the closest—most geographically accessible—are those most difficult to connect with on a human and cultural level for many reasons, several of which were illustrated in the opening stories of this chapter. Again we see that gentrification produces spiritual problems as much as it does economic and political ones. It weakens churches.

Fifth, those who are most spiritually affected by gentrification are those who are most vulnerable. Consider who it is that has the greatest difficulty actively participating in church life after gentrification.

- It is the poor who cannot afford the money it costs to travel into the city center and back two or three times extra times per week.
- It is the single parent who cannot afford the time it costs to travel into the city center and back two or three extra times per week.
- It is the disabled or the aged who are not physically able to drive or walk to and from public transportation.
- It is the socially outcast who does not have relationships to depend on for transportation.
- It is the historically oppressed who find themselves displaced from their own communities to begin with.

Jesus has much concern for and mercy on such people.[8]

Gentrification does not.

But will the Church?

It goes beyond the scope of this chapter to list a number of specific practical ways the Church might respond. It also goes beyond necessity. We cannot

---

7 1 Corinthians 9:19-23.

8 Isaiah 58:6-9; Luke 14:12-14.

answer the "how local churches should respond" question until we answer the "will local churches respond" question. Will the Church respond to the ways gentrification is negatively affecting cross-ethnic relationships? Will the Church respond to the ways gentrification is leading many black Christians away from the blessing of community and into loneliness? Will the Church respond to the economic, political, and spiritual injustice that is gentrification? As a pastor of a church community that lives on all sides of the gentrification issue I pray we will all answer "yes" and then work on answering the "how" question together. And the only way we can answer the "how" question is to stop listening to white leaders such as myself and start listening to the stories of those who are directly impacted by gentrification.

I leave you in their far more competent hands.
May we listen well.

Chapter 14

Churches without Roots are not Plants
Springwater Community and Parish Collective (Portland, OR)
Brandon Rhodes

Preface: I write this chapter from a particular perspective in the church, in scholarship, and in creation. My perspective in the church is as a Neo-Anabaptist— that is, as one of those fools who is so prone to tweet quotes from John Howard Yoder and Stanley Hauerwas. It means I assume the nature of the church to be shared, embodied, peaceable, and above all Christ-centered. Or rather because of the latter the church is the first three.

I write within the place of scholarship of studying the ecclesial effects of automobility's historic ascent, present hegemony, and future decline.

I write from a particular perspective in creation as being rooted in Portland's eclectic Lents neighborhood. The halls of power have targeted us for uplift but we aren't currently approaching anything like gentrification. Being in Portland means I write as one crying out in the post-Christian wilderness, a reality which I believe will steadily continue to creep into the rest of USAmerican cultures. Thus, to be fully square with you, I write as one who believes "planting churches" may not be the wisest way to incite new ecclesial expressions in North America.

Church planters loved my neighborhood of Lents ... seventy years ago. Baptists planted in 1926, Church of Christ in 1930, Seventh Day Adventists in

1946, and the Roman tradition in 1957—all within two blocks of each other. At one point we had ten churches within our humble borders. Back then, Lents bustled with activity as the original gateway to southeast Portland. We were an outpost between farmland to the east and the Foster Boulevard Streetcar connecting us "Lentils" westward to Hawthorne and Powell. At that time mainline traditions saturated Portland's core with buildings in which to worship, leaving mostly evangelicals to saturate peripheral neighborhoods like us.

Not that evangelicals of that day would have wanted to plant in Portland's more urban nooks anyway. Fundamentalism's anti-urban sentiment was quickly re-staking the wide tent of evangelicalism far outside America's city centers. The city was akin to debauchery to the fundamentalist mind, and in Portland they were at least partly right. Our downtown had a grimy legacy of sex trafficking, opiate abuse, mob activity, racism, and drunkenness. Evangelicals could have remained near or retreated from such sin. Across Portland and most of USAmerica,[1] the rapture-minded chose retreat. Or rather: non-engagement. It is a deeper trend that you probably drive by in your own city, and which partially describes Lents' aging cluster of churches.

Lents' version of evangelical evacuation from city to suburb breaks the mould typified elsewhere in that we were more an annexed fringe town than post-war suburb. That new kind of development ascended in the 1950s countrywide and topped the priorities of many denominations. In most of 1950s USAmerica, churches were planted or replanted in the suburbs to provide worship communities for this new class of USAmericans. Such churches assumed a soft parish sentiment in which newly suburbanized Christians would continue the urban pedestrian practice of attending a church within walking distance.

That didn't happen. It didn't occur to many that suburbia's car-scaled dimensions discouraged walking and encouraged driving, which meant people were less likely to go to the church gathering closest to home (suburbia is quite unwalkable) and more likely to drive as far as they like to a preferred church (suburbia is quite driveable).

---

1 I use the term "USAmerica" to specify the United States. Using "America" in that place excludes our 576,000,000 brothers and sisters in Canada, Mexico, Central America, and South America.

Denominations planted throughout the suburbs with this assumption and oversight in tow. Mainlines were polite about it; evangelicals were competitive. And it was publicly named as a fight for the (monied) middle class; one mainline researcher argued that the historic Protestant denominations would disappear if they don't win suburbia. It was a scramble for who would secure suburban tithers. This car-enabled religious marketplace guided church history in the ensuing decades, and by 1980 evangelicals had arrived at certain victory in the suburbs—a hegemony they have retained ever since. The spoils of this victory were tithes from middle-income and white-collar Christians—tithes that may otherwise have gone to the mainline traditions.

Following tithe money out of cities underwrote evangelicalism's suburban success, and was the product of three happy accidents converging. First, the aforementioned anti-urban sentiment drove them to urban edges and suburbs. Zeal for purity from urban sins, not greed for money, defined their fuller tithe baskets. Second, evangelicals were simply more adaptable toward suburban religious preferences. They catered to middle class desires in a rapidly changing world more effectively than others. Third, evangelicalism was already disposed toward suburban culture's values with little reason to directly challenge them. Together, these chance fortunes were like Bilbo happening upon the magic ring in Gollum's cave.

That opening reflection may merit some explaining. I began with this extended backstory because I see teachable parallels between it and the topic of this book. The lessons of church planting in suburbia over the past seventy years shed light on church planting in gentrification-ready and gentrified neighborhoods today. I began with the story of Lents, too, because I hope to share some of the particular insights of being part of a church plant in a non-gentrified area. I'll unpack those insights later. For now let's consider the parallels between recent American church history and gentrification.

First, churches as *organizations* did not *cause* suburbia, and they won't be causing gentrification. Churches may have socially and theologically legitimized it, but they did not *cause* suburbia's development. Collusion between government and land developers in the form of sweetheart legislation, huge subsidies to developers, and other car-favoring dark magic were the primary fuels to suburbia's expansion. Churches, on the other hand, came a bit later to the game.

And as noted earlier, the shrewder churches proactively accommodated themselves to it.

The same thing seems to be happening with gentrification and newer churches. Gentrification has already been underway for decades in many cities, well ahead of the recent burst in urban church planting. Only in the past decade or so has it become fashionable and culturally safe for planting-savvy denominations and networks to again return to the city, and thus to areas primed for gentrification. Now, it's all the rage to see buzz-worded churches whose location and branding all draw on these neighborhoods. Neighborhoods, I suggest, which have only recently been re-legitimized for middle class and suburban Christians. The recent evangelical rapprochement with the city, then, coincides with the recent re-building and de-coloring of the city. It's a sort of white-flight in reverse.

Second, churches did not bring challenge or critique because they saw their new contexts as opportunities. Mainliners, evangelicals, and fundamentalists alike saw suburbia as a frontier to be conquered and properly churched. The suburban churches which succeeded were by and large those which properly produced a sense of identity and reinforcement of values among suburbanites. Thus suburban values increasingly became the values of suburban Christianity. The individualism, consumerism, isolation, fear, and racism that suburbia attracted and reinforced were rarely challenged by suburban churches. In their desperation to win market-share the churches failed to take responsibility for their new context's challenges.

I observe a similar trend in churches planting in gentrified neighborhoods or targeting stereotyped demographics of gentrification ("cultural creatives," etc). Planting networks target a neighborhood—say, Portland's Alberta district—and construct a ministry edifice contextualized to it. The music echoes Portland indie greats like Alela Diane or the Decembrists, yummy Stumptown coffee is offered for pre-service mingling, and pastors clad in tight pants and tattoos. They say they've contextualized, and that to me is problematic.

Of course, there is nothing wrong with contextualization within conversation. I'm all for it! But I don't think we're talking about that, any more than we can say that suburban churches contextualized themselves to suburbia. They *acquiesced through engagement-without-conversation*, which I see as distinct from healthy contextualization.

In my observation and practice, churches catering to gentrifying cultures and gentrified neighborhoods rarely do the full work of healthy contextualization. Too often this shallow contextualization is to a context-less culture. That is to say, it appeals to the aesthetics of an archetype (say, "hipster" or "urban yuppie") without any consideration of the particularities of the context(s) in which that archetype lives, works, and plays. Or still less what the particular people of that neighborhood are like. This is like contextualizing ministry from scanning a Pinterest board rather than from wading through conversations with particular people. Context-less contextualization can only ever be skin deep. It's like putting a bicycle on your church website but no bike parking outside the building. Such shallow accommodation eventually begins to feel more like slick marketing than sincerely missional. Full contextualization deals not only with broad cultural generalities but with the fine-grained particularities of a context's story, legacy, assets, existing relationships, and spiritual strongholds. What we have in the church's move to suburbia and to gentrified spaces is usually far from this.

What's behind this gap? Part of it stems from an incomplete view of culture. Though I think this is beginning to change, the evangelical tradition has historically lacked a robust theology of culture and so has not been able to exegete its context honestly. Our thin sense of culture only sees the *ephemeral and incidental*—such as different fashions or fads. No wonder we only let the Word put on skinny jeans instead of flesh. We're unable to take a full-orbed view of culture which includes the formative narratives, architecture, and everyday secular liturgies that form and inform a culture. In our thin reading of culture we are ill-equipped to critique our host culture. Because we are "targeting" it rather than indwelling it, we find ourselves unable to take responsibility for its legacy. Our desperation to "win" a culture for Jesus makes us unable to fully indwell it, to find ourselves at home in it. One commenter on the early church said that "Every foreign land is to them as their native country, and every land of their birth as a land of strangers." But I fear that we have taken the worst of both senses of that observation. We are so at home in our host culture that we struggle to understand the forces of gentrification; and as church planters we have been so well-groomed to play-act our way into a gentrification culture. Our posture in the world has thus neutered our ability to practice moral discourse about gentrification. This is not what it means to be in the world but not of it!

No wonder we embraced suburbia so uncritically, and no wonder church planters follow suit by uncritically chasing after gentrifiers.

But all of this is an aside to a deeper point that needs to be made. It is that contextualization is not the calling of the church: *incarnation* is. Contextualization begins with a universal sense of church and packages it to the particulars of a context. That is the wrong way around. The church is called to enact the gospel in the particularity of our neighborhoods and so point with our life together to the universality of the gospel. The Word takes on our flesh, not just our skinny jeans, and in doing so hedges against our inclination to reduce the living Christ to a culturally-pre-packaged commodity. Targeting a demographic chestnut (suburbanite, hipster, or whatever) in our hypermobile society, by contrast, draws us away from incarnation. Our churches and lives become what missiologist Michael Frost calls *excarnational.* That is, our ministerial practice resists corporate incarnation. Many suburban and gentrification-catering churches seem in this way to have accomplished the Christological heresy of Docetism (Jesus only appears to be human) applied to ecclesiology.

This book is about Bible-grounded responses gentrification, and so I should also add that seeking incarnation ahead of contextualization is consistent with Paul's strongly Christological vision of the church as the body of Christ. For Paul the church is the refracting locus of Christ's ongoing presence in the world. This being so, we can assume there are some deep parallels between Christology and ecclesiology. On this note I direct you to N.T. Wright's admonition about Christ's first incarnation:

> My proposal is not that we understand what the word "god" means and manage somehow to fit Jesus into that. Instead, I suggest that we think historically about a young Jew, possessed of a desperately risky, indeed apparently crazy, vocation, riding into Jerusalem in tears, denouncing the Temple, and dying on a Roman cross—and that we somehow allow our meaning for the word "god" to be recentered around that point.[2]

That's the logic of incarnation and revelation. So too, if we are to be incarnational with Christ's body, the church. We as church planters must not take an existing template or structure for ministry and cram our neighborhood's

---

2 Wright, "Jesus and the Identity of God."

culture into it. The weightier task of incarnational ministry is to somehow let our life together *embodied in our own neighborhood* be a faithful window into the true nature of Christ the Lord. Our particularity together points to the universality of God. Which makes excarnational church-by-template awfully difficult.

Beginning with incarnation doesn't just make things hard on church planters: it can quickly become bad news for the neighborhood. By not being incarnational, we leave the door wide open for gentrification to expand and persist. Excarnational suburban churches had little recourse for resisting that built environment's more insidious implications (individualism, consumerism, etc.). Today's planters chasing after gentrified areas risk the same failure: acquiescence to forces of systemic dehumanization and oppression like gentrification.

Which is why I don't accuse either group of cultic syncretism as much as opportunistic cultural syncretism. The move to the suburbs that clogged my neighborhood with church buildings and drained urban cores of so much ecclesial vitality involved a heavy accommodation to the new culture of suburbia for opportunistic purposes. And not entirely for bad reasons: when church planters have a denomination's burden to rapidly establish dependable, growing, and fiscally-independent churches, there may not be time for the careful work of incarnation. Hasty syncretism with the host culture became a necessity to outcompete others and retain a stronghold in the suburban frontier. The parallels to today's denominations pandering to gentrifiers is evident enough, no?

Church planters today don't care for Lents—or any neighborhood in Portland you haven't seen Fred Armisen and Carrie Bernstein spoof. The rest of my fair city is a compelling destination for church planters, and quite marketable for denominations and church-planting networks to strut their postmodern efficacy. What shows cultural engagement better than churches full of urban-dwelling, tattoo-adorned, fashionable young adults? It sends a powerful message of brand strength in untapped and emerging markets.

Twenty years ago, those same Portland neighborhoods were seen as an outpost of heathen desolation where no church can find purchase. Too few Portlanders were in the market for a church (still the case, actually), and evangelicals had some grudges against cities so awash in "secularism" and "new age" bugaboos. And in the shadow of Left Coast big hitters like Seattle and San

Francisco we weren't on anybody's cultural map. We weren't the best market for expanding one's franchise into.

Yet Portland today stands as a Mecca of quirky-cool with neighborhoods nationally-known for their manifold hipness. And we're a hotbed of church planters. What changed?

Three words: Imago Dei Community. This Baptist church plant was the first to find marked vitality in inner Portland in years. I wasn't around for their earliest years but by all accounts it was a formative place—and, to be fair, still is. God was and is up to something there. Things changed and Imago ballooned after one of their members, Donald Miller, wrote often about it in his wildly successful memoir *Blue Like Jazz*. What was already a quiet success story of church planting in Pagan City became a bestselling announcement that *you too can find ministry success in America's coolest town!*

Before long, everyone from Acts 29 to the Episcopal Church was sending church planters down the Oregon Trail to get in on the gold rush. When I moved back to Portland from college in 2005, you could pick out the fledgling pastors in any given coffee shop (the Celtic Trinity-knot tattoo gave them away). Some were explicitly commissioned to "plant the next Imago Dei." Yes, sir: we were up to our tall bikes in big-dreaming and quick-witted church planters after Don's book leaked Portland's newfound spiritual fertility.

Lents, though: *not so much*. While I love my neighborhood and while there is so much about it of which I'm proud, we aren't demographically an appealing place to set up the revival tent. The feds destroyed our town center by building I-205 and city hall didn't pave all of our roads until the 1980s. Our charm and comparative desirability languished until the name "Lents" was forgotten to many, becoming known only as Felony Flats. I don't want to overstate our legacy of neglect, but it suffices to say we're more the neighborhood that poverty and addiction ministries serve in than churches plant in.

This betokens a trend of church plant patterns following development and redevelopment patterns that I suspect is common across America and Canada. Historic urban cores were saturated with historic mainlines (First Pres, First UCC, etc.), post-war congregations migrated with suburban development, and recently have followed the mortgaged gentry back to neighborhoods undergoing gentrification. Fewer white neighborhoods and fewer monied neighborhoods underwent ecclesial activity from historically black denominations and the "urban ministries" of white churches.

More recently, it is the new monastic movement that has chosen to plant in less glitzy neighborhoods. These newcomers are an international lay movement of intentional communities, house churches, and the like seeking church renewal through shared spiritual disciplines within a particular neighborhood. It took on the name "new monasticism" by inverting the historic role of monastics choosing to live far from cities to preserve the faith, and instead choosing to live in urban areas to incite renewal. It's a diverse group, but one common practice, as outlined in the manifesto *School(s) of Conversion: 12 Marks of a New Monasticism*, is "relocation to the abandoned places of empire." That is, they ground themselves in poorer and neglected neighborhoods. As such they are one of the only ecclesial expressions happening these days that actively avoid gentrified areas.

And that, dear reader, is where I become part of this tale. In 2007 a core of us inspired by stories from new monastic communities such as The Simple Way in Philadelphia and Reba Place Fellowship near Chicago began sharing our hopes and fears of beginning a neighborhood-scaled church or intentional community. We held long, vivid conversations about Christocentric theology, mission, healthy evangelism, nonviolence, racial injustice, gardening, simplicity, shared spiritual formation disciplines, authority structures, commitment, and many other weighty matters.

By the spring of 2008 we had reviewed all of Portland's neighborhoods according to the demographics of their elementary schools, and found Lents to be an appealing place to begin experimenting with our new-monastic vision of church life.[3] Sixteen of us between 24 and 54 in age moved into one corner of Lents and lived within a five-minute walk of each other. We had a draft covenant to uphold the vision of the community for that first year, and took the

---

3 Looking back, leading with this settled sense of church practice before listening to the neighborhood was the wrong way to go about it. It was the cart-ahead-of-the-horse fallacy I had teased other church planters of earlier. Learning this mistake was one of the harder ones to diagnose for us as a young community. Some expected activism, others entrepreneurialism, others evangelism, and still others sought safe relationships. We were not all ready to love the neighborhood as our neighborhood, and live incarnationally according to its rhythms. But that is a story for another chapter in another book; I mention it here in a spirit of confession. I have not always practiced the lessons I now preach here. They were slowly learned.

name *Springwater* after the much-celebrated multi-use trail that weaves through our part of Lents.

We are fortunate to belong to a neighborhood partially composed of refugees from Portland's newest pockets of gentrification. Many of the historically black neighborhoods that today brim with MacBooks and fixie bikes have been dispersed across the city, and we meet them over our fences. They keep us sober to the deeper realities and stories of our city, that when city hall calls colorful communities "urban renewal" it often means "urban removal" of communities of color. We Lentils want uplift and vitality in Lents, but we don't want the kind that the world has thus far provided. We want life abundant, but one we all can share in. This has been no easy line to walk.

At times this specter of gentrification heightens our skepticism of anything that may lead down that road. It's like the anxieties that follow us into future relationships after a bad breakup; good opportunities can feel like traps. For example, Lents is a food desert. We don't have walkable access to affordable, healthy food. Corner stores offer you five flavors of Corn Nuts, but that's not a meal. Lents needs a grocery store. Whether as a neighbor, a bureaucrat, or an activist, we know what we need, and that's near the top of the list. Many Lentils have been slowly pooling resources to open a permanent grocery store.

Joining this effort for food access seems like something Springwater would get behind, right? To an extent we have: gardening and harvest block parties are becoming our specialty. But an enterprise effort has triggered our fears of gentrification. "Won't selling organic food cause gentrification?" The logic being: won't anything Portland-y be bad for Lents? What good can come from Hawthorne?

Well, more than we might think! I sympathize with this anxiety, but it misses how gentrification usually works. Gentrification, as I have only anecdotally observed it, begins when a wholly new and distinct culture creates businesses and public places that only it will enjoy—the handful of white artists opening a cafe in an historically black neighborhood is the easy archetype (or straw man?) of that. But it is possible to join common-good efforts in the neighborhood such as food access that don't do this. Organic food does not have to be a herald of gentrification. It's possible to eradicate food deserts without kicking out poor and working-class people.

We are discovering that as we incarnate in our neighborhood together with an awareness of how gentrification could exile many of us and our neighbors, we must nevertheless be driven by our hopes instead of our fears. Fear has lead us to avoid partnerships. Hope, I think, would help us better navigate toward renewal in Lents. Otherwise, if we the residents of Lents don't create something, we will only be keeping the door open for non-residents to gentrify all the more. But incarnation and non-colonial mission means we as a church of Lents joining God in the neighborhood and opening ourselves to the risks (including gentrification) that that may entail.

I am persuaded, in other words, that the best art of resistance against gentrification is hopeful and humble incarnation. Avoiding neighborhood engagement out of a fear of gentrification can lead to the same gossamer gospel I have seen at work among church plants unable to critique gentrification from within.

The future of the relationship between church planting and gentrification is open; we can become churches who seek a parish flourishing while resisting gentrification, or we can be complicit in structural injustices that cater to the privileged class and deepen race divisions in our city. We can colonize or we can inhabit. With this open future in mind I conclude my chapter by offerings a few actionable reflections for how to continue expanding the Body of Christ into every neighborhood with fresh expressions of church across America without contributing to gentrification.

I will begin these admonitions with the reminder that the church's primary duty is not to stop gentrification, nor to grow, nor to multiply, but to first and foremost *be* the church. That means somehow together being the locally worshipping body whose reconciled life together points to God's love, glory, and kingdom. If our primary goal is new churches, stopping gentrification, or even making new disciples, that goal can ultimately distract us from exploring our deeper identity together as God's covenant people. These good goals are secondary matters which flow out of being the church.

To Prospective Church Planters:

Begin with mission, and let church follow. It is much harder to gentrify when the people of the church have a stake in the health of the neighborhood. Churches planted as churches right out of the gate do not guarantee that all members will be stakeholders of what happens in the neighborhood. Planting a "missional expression" of neighbors instead of a church of commuters allows ecclesial life to emerge from shared local mission. This vigorously resists the benevolent colonialism that can so easily entangle generative mission.

Root together. When you are rooted and committed to your parish, you can see gentrification-creep happening. The canaries in the coalmine of boutique storefronts and the economic expulsion of indigenous neighbors is something you see every day. Seeing means you bear more responsibility for it. In your gatherings, name what you see happening in the neighborhood. Genesis 1 reminds us that words make worlds, and we "word" the world rightly when we name it truthfully. Naming gentrification as that, and prayerfully organizing against it, seems like a core function of the liturgy and everyday life of the truly local church.

Stop following the middle class. Dare to plant among the poor and working class. Don't merely gather on Sundays in a non-gentrified area; actually target a non-gentrifying demographic and live among them. There are already enough church planters fighting over the table scraps of the re-urbanized middle class. The world needs more apostolic leaders at the margins.

To Churches and Christians in Un-Gentrified Neighborhoods:

Let your "No" flow out of a deeper "Yes." One of a church's primary callings in a non-gentrified neighborhood is to seek humans flourishing there—not to oppose gentrification. That comes later. Remember, as we in Springwater are learning, to say Yes first to flourishing, and let any No to gentrification come out of that. For in Jesus we are called to say Yes to shalom, to peace and flourishing in our neighborhood.

212

Be proud of where you live. People take responsibility for and want to stick around in a neighborhood they're proud of. They awaken to their role as stakeholders in its future, and so possibly as folks who can help steer it from gentrification. Help create great memories in your parish; make it a place that people cherish. We in Springwater have at times succumbed to boasting about our neighborhood's challenges ... as if they are badges of righteousness. Learning to talk lovingly about the place where we belong to has opened up our hearts tremendously for a better witness and work in the neighborhood.

To Churches Living or Gathering in Gentrified Neighborhoods:

Speak the truth in love. One of the most important acts a church living amid gentrification can do is to tell the true story of that neighborhood. Systemic injustices like gentrification rest on false stories that try to erase the memory of what came before. Gentrifiers, for example, laud the new culture as a sort of conquest over perceived decay. The church is called to truthfully name the injustices happening to indigenous populations beneath that "civilizing conquest." Creatively practicing lament for what has been lost, for the stories ignored and the people exiled, is your burning prophetic task for Jesus.

Practice hospitality for indigenous residents. Stop hanging out and targeting gentrifiers. Join existing efforts to preserve space for the people who lived in your neighborhood before the cupcake shops and Macbooks crowded them out. Befriend and learn from them. Find ways for the neighborhood to be hospitable to its first tenants.

Be agents of reconciliation. New neighbors tend to either resent or sentimentalize indigenous neighbors. Indigenous neighbors tend to resent the new neighbors. Little wonder how easily bitterness engulfs a parish undergoing gentrification. God's saints there have a ministry of reconciliation between each group.

What I summon each group to, then, is simply faithfulness. I summon your congregations to indwell their identity as the those saints of a neighborhood (gentrified or not) gathering together under the Lordship of Christ.

Everything follows from that.

Chapter 15

Ministering to the Displaced
(Dearborn, MI)
Dave Arnold

Henry Ford did more for the city of Detroit than anyone else. Ford's entrepreneurial drive created the Motor City. As a result of the auto industry and the jobs it created, "Detroiters boasted for generations of having the highest percentage of homeownership of any big city,"[1] writes John Gallagher.

Detroit was the Mecca of the auto industry, creating thousands of jobs with good wages and benefits. A symbol of Ford's industry—the River Rouge Complex, more commonly called The Rouge—is located in the south end of Dearborn, rubbing shoulders with Detroit's south west. If you were to drive through it, you might think you had entered into Mordor from Tolkien's *Lord of The Rings* trilogy.

The Rouge is a massive factory that stretches almost two miles, Some of its buildings were created by the famous German architect Albert Khan. The factory reeks of auto fumes. Smoke billows into the air from its mighty towers, and the area around it is a seedy cauldron of strip clubs, bars, and back alleys and streets. It's not a place I like going through, especially at night.

But this factory stands as a symbol of Detroit's industrial strength; moreover, it was a magnet that drew hundreds—and eventually thousands—of immigrants from the Middle East. "Middle Easterners first came to the region

---

1 Gallagher, *Reimagining Detroit*, 24.

in the early 1900s, attracted to the U.S. by its industrialization and need for a greater workforce. Upon landing in America, many immigrants were not headed for Detroit, but changed their paths when they heard about Ford Motor Company's wage of $5 for a day's work."[2]

One of my Yemeni friends, in fact, told me his great grandfather immigrated from Yemen to come work at The Rouge. Eventually, after he assimilated well in the States, he in turn was able to bring the rest of his family over. That's how my friend came to Detroit. He now resides in East Dearborn.

An Arabic Enclave

Today, Dearborn is home to thousands of Arab-speakers, most of whom are Muslim, from about twenty-two different countries. Although California has more Arabic-speakers in totality, Dearborn is the largest concentrated area of Arabic-speakers in North America. The first immigrants, brought over by Ford himself, were mainly Lebanese Christians.[3] That eventually opened the doors for more people to immigrate from the Middle East. Eventually, the Christians—mostly from a Chaldean (i.e., Catholic) background—moved to the northern suburbs of Detroit, while the Muslims settled in Dearborn.

The local high school—Fordson High School—is about 95 percent Muslim. In 2011, Ramadan (the month where Muslims fast from sunrise to sundown), the coach of Fordson's football team (a devout Muslim) got permission to hold football practices at 10:00 at night after Ramadan so his players could fast all day.

Because of the school's heavy Muslim population, neither the school nor the parents had any problem with this.

---

2 Media.Ford.com, "Ford Motor Company Key Factor in Arab and Chaldean Migration to Metro Detroit."

3 Note: For more information, check out this link: http://www.alsintl.com/blog/arabic-in-dearborn-michigan/

Urban Village

In 2008, Alan Mallach, an urban planner out of New Jersey, led a team of people to Detroit to study the city. Their conclusion was that Detroit "was fragmenting and dissolving into a lumpy urban porridge ... Mallach used the term 'urban village' to describe the more vibrant districts of the city."[4]

The two main areas of Detroit's vibrancy are Midtown (where Wayne State University is located) and downtown, where there is a growing theater area and a lively sports community. These are the two main areas where the city is gentrifying. What's interesting, however, is to see is how gentrification has affected the city of Dearborn, an extension (in many people's opinion) of Detroit due to its proximity. In my opinion, Dearborn—although not a part of Detroit city proper—is an urban village. It's dense. It's vibrant. It's diverse.

The different people groups from the Middle East, for example, are very unique. The Iraqis, who live mostly in East Dearborn and on Detroit's west side, have a very different accent and different colloquialisms compared to the Lebanese.

The Yemeni accent, my Iraqi and Lebanese friends tell me, is so unique that they cannot even understand it—even though they all speak Arabic. And Yemeni food is quite different than other Middle Eastern cuisine, combining traditional Arabic food with a mixture of Indian and Pakistani spices.

All this to say, Dearborn is a very diverse urban village; and unlike a majority of neighborhoods in Detroit, save downtown and Midtown, Dearborn is vibrant and growing. An example of this is a new arts project that is currently underway in East Dearborn. The project includes living and working space for artists called Artspace,[5] a nonprofit, city initiative that will create for space for artists to live and work together. The initiative has been approved and now the city is looking for a good location.

A large part of Deaborn's vibrancy is the constant growth in the number of new immigrants to the area. Currently, the majority of these new immigrants are Iraqis who have been granted refugee status. However, I have met people from

4 *Reimagining Detroit*, 31.

5 For more information, check out Shine, "Art is in the Air in Dearborn."

Morocco, Iran, Turkey, Tunisia and other Arabic-speaking countries who come to Dearborn because it is known as the "hub" of Islamic culture in the States.

An Interesting Shift

East Dearborn, where I live, at one point was predominately Lebanese Shia (or Shi'ite) Muslim.[6] Now, however, as Iraqi refugees have been pouring into Dearborn consistently since 2007, and as the Yemeni community continues to expand, the cultures are more mixed than ever. At one point, the Yemenis all congregated in the south of Dearborn, the Lebanese in the eastern part, and the Iraqis in Detroit. That's all changed as many Yemenis and Iraqis have also now settled in East Dearborn.

Islamic expert and author Carl Medearis says, "Because of their strong familial identification, many Muslims will move to places where they can stay in their sub-groups. In Dearborn, Michigan, for instance, you'll find Arabs living together."[7] Due to the tumultuous situation in the Middle East, many different Arab groups—and even non-Arab groups such as Somalis and Afghans—are consistently moving either to Dearborn or the Detroit area.

This doesn't mean, however, these groups necessarily live "together." I was told that the Lebanese consider the Iraqis "dirty" and therefore unwanted by the Lebanese community. As a result of this—and more significantly as the auto industry in Detroit has changed dramatically and many Ford employees have moved away—Lebanese people are moving into the more "desirable" West Dearborn.

West Dearborn was once the home of Ford executives. The housing market was soaring. When the recession hit in 2008, prices went down dramatically and people relocated. Houses became affordable, which opened the door for immigrant families to move in.

---

6 There are two major sects of Islam: (1) Shia is the sect of Islam that believes the prophet Ali was the true successor to Prophet Muhammad (Islam's final prophet). Shi'ites are found mostly in Lebanon, Iraq and Iran. (2) Sunni is considered the majority or "orthodox" branch of Islam, and is found all over the Middle East (Saudi Arabia, Yemen, Egypt, etc.). Sunnis say the true successor to Muhammad was Abu Bakar.

7 Medearis, *Muslims, Christians, and Jesus*, 55.

Now, when you walk down Michigan Avenue—the main vein of West Dearborn—amid the cafes, cigar stores, and sushi places—you will see young Lebanese professionals strolling about. At one point Dearborn was almost two separate cities: East (predominately Arab and African-American) and West (predominately white, middle- to upper-class families). Now it's all mixed up.

So what should the church do to meet this challenge? How should missiologists and urban workers minister appropriately given the daunting task of reaching the displaced of our cities? Here are some thoughts to consider:

1. Immigration is Changing our Urban Landscape.

In 2011, according to World Relief Chicago, 80,000 refugees were resettled in the United States, the maximum amount the U.S. will take in one year. In spite of the troubled economy, in spite of fear and uncertainties, displaced people are coming to the States. And a majority of them come to urban centers.

According the United Nations High Commissioner for Refugees, "Worldwide, 42.5 million people ended 2011 either as refugees (15.2 million), internally displaced (26.4 million) or in the process of seeking asylum (895,000)."[8]

The Department of State has sent tens of thousands of Iraqi refugees to metro Detroit alone since the start of the Iraq War in 2003. Although Dearborn is the "hub" for Iraqi refugees to resettle to, cities across America are seeing growing Iraqi populations. I have been told that Nashville has become the epicenter for Iraqi Kurds to resettle to, and that there are more Somali refugees in Minneapolis than anywhere else in the States.

As a result, the "look" of our cities has changed. Gentrification, then, is an interesting phenomenon. On the one hand, in cities like New York and San Francisco more and more immigrants are finding it increasingly hard to remain in the city due to high living costs; on the other hand, cities like Detroit or Des Moines or Omaha provide new immigrants the chance to live in affordable housing and find decent jobs.

In Detroit, Arabic immigrants have an easier time assimilating. First and foremost, most of them have connections; secondly, housing is cheaper than in a

---

8 http://www.unhcr.org/4fd9e6266.html.

lot of other major cities and they are hopeful that one of their relatives can find them work.

I've personally met Arabic refugees and immigrants who were resettled in other cities but moved to Dearborn because they knew they could assimilate quicker and keep their cultural and religious identity. This, I find, is especially true for Muslims.

In Dearborn, there are Islamic schools for children and plenty of mosques that cater to both Sunni and Shia Muslims. Moreover, I have found that many newer immigrants from the Middle East are very open to the gospel—especially those who are younger, have been here less than six months, and are tired of the political coverage of Islam back in their home countries.

I can't help but think about what Paul said to the Athenians on Mars' Hill and how it relates to displaced people coming to our shores:

"From one man he [God] made every nation of men, that they should inhabit the whole earth; and he determined the times set for them and the *exact* places where they should live. God did this so that men would seek him and perhaps reach out to him and find him, though he is not far from each one of us" (Acts 17:26-27, NIV. Emphasis mine).

It's amazing to think that God leads people to the exact place where He wants them to live. Why? So they can hear His message of salvation. I see this firsthand in Dearborn as families in "closed" countries such as Yemen and Saudi Arabia are coming here where they have the chance to hear the gospel.

2. God's Heart is for the Displaced

There is a passage in Isaiah that I believe speaks directly to the issue of displacement.

"An oracle concerning Arabia: You caravans of Dedanites, who camp in the thickets of Arabia, bring water for the thirsty; you who live in Tema, bring food for the fugitives. They flee from the sword, from the drawn sword, from the bent bow and from the heat of battle" (Isaiah 21:13-15, NIV).

The context here is that Edomite refugees (the descendants of Esau; cf. Gen. 25:30) have fled to the Arabian Peninsula, "so that they may find refuge from the enemy from Mesopotamia."[9] These Edomite refugees are "exhausted, parched with thirst, and in need of food."[10]

God spoke directly to the Arabic tribes who have found safety in the wastelands not to ignore the tangible, felt needs of these refugees. Those who have food and water and shelter are thus called to provide it to those who do not.

Throughout Scripture, God's heart for the oppressed, the displaced, the stranger, and the poor is evident. And those who have are called to give to those who do not. James says, "Suppose a brother or sister is without clothes and daily food. If one of you says to him, 'Go, I wish you well; keep warm and well fed,' but does nothing about his physical needs, what good is it?" (James 2:15-16, NIV).

As the "middle class" becomes more and more a thing of the past, the gap widens between the rich and the poor. So many new immigrants in our cities (especially those who have been here less than four years) are forced to rely on government assistance such as food stamps and Medicaid. Many of them work, but their income is insufficient to meet their families' needs.

One Iraqi Christian man I met in Chicago who was having a terrible time finding a job and providing for his four children said to me, "I'd rather die quickly back in Iraq than slowly in America." Due to Chicago's high rent and low levels of welfare assistance, this poor guy was tempted to go back to Iraq and face potential death rather than to bring shame on his family by relying on the state.

That said, it's imperative for the body of Christ to get involved with the plight of the displaced. There are many great organizations such as World Relief and Lutheran Social Services, both evangelical, located around the country. I am currently volunteering with Lutheran Social Services in Dearborn to help Iraqi refugees learn how to type so they can apply for jobs that require proficiency in typing and computers.

Because the factory jobs are decreasing in our cities, new immigrants must learn to navigate the technological field, including how to type, use Microsoft, and social media. This is especially challenging for older immigrants.

---

9 Grogan, *Isaiah*, 137.

10 Ibid., 138.

So here are some practical ways to get involved with the displaced in your city:

- Find and volunteer at a local refugee resettlement agency. Most organizations are under-staffed and in desperate need of volunteers. You can tutor a family in English, help a child with homework, provide transportation to medical appointments, and more.
- Be a part of neighborhood gatherings and learn about the zoning laws, new developments, etc., that have the potential to push the poor out.
- Do tangible things to help people: bring a meal to a family, tutor children, help the elderly, clean up an abandoned lot, and so on.

The point is: get involved with the displaced. If God's heart is for the displaced, then so must ours. We have the opportunity to offer water to the thirsty, to comfort those who are victims of war and displacement. We are called to—as Shane Claiborne put it—to pitch "a tent with the people of struggle."[11]

3. The Displaced are Constantly on the Move

The word "displacement" suggests movement. It is characterized as those who have been forced to move out of their natural environment and live in an unnatural environment. And the truth is, immigrants are on the move. There are certain refugee populations, for example, such as the Somali people, who tend to migrate in groups to find cheaper housing and better jobs.

An example of this is an ABC News report that revealed 1,200 Somali refugees had moved to the small town of Lewiston, Maine, with a population 36,000. "'That a group from Africa would suddenly show up at our doorstep is really a surprise,' said Douglas Hodgkin, a political science professor at Bates College. 'It seems like a shot out of the blue.'"

Why did they move there? They wanted a safe environment for their children and a cheaper cost of living. "'Life in the big city is difficult,' said Musa Hussein, a Somali who now works as an English instructor in Lewiston. 'It's stressful. Access to services and employment is very difficult.'"[12]

---

11 Claiborne and Haw, *Jesus for President*, 35.

12 Claiborne, "Somali Refugees Settle in Maine Town,"

If the displaced are on the move, then we must be too. Jesus told His disciples to "go." Here in the West, we like to stay. We like our church buildings and programs. We like it when people come to us. But that doesn't work with immigrants. (Really, I wonder if it works for anyone. But that's not my topic.)

I'm not saying we need to pack up and move to where large pockets of displaced people live (unless that's what God calls you to do). I am saying we need to be willing to have the eyes of Jesus and see where the displaced are living in our communities, and then be willing to go to them with the love of Christ.

We need to embrace our new neighbors with the love of Christ and give them a sense of belonging. Really, isn't belonging what people need? To know they matter and that they are important?

Many refugees have been forced to be on the move for years. They don't feel like they belong anywhere. How wonderful would it be if God's people changed that? If we could say to them, "You belong here, you are my friend," it would change their lives!

It is my hope and prayer that we begin to see the displaced through the lens of Christ and His Kingdom. That we would embrace our new neighbors with open hearts and open arms. That we would fight for them in these tough economic times. Let us be a people of refuge who help the pushed-aside and the unwanted feel that they belong to the best family in the world – God's Kingdom.

Ministering to the Displaced

PART III
RESPONDING TO
GENTRIFICATION

After taking at look at some of the foundational elements of the gentrification conversation and then fleshing those out with stories and accounts of church planting and urban ministry in these settings, now comes a reflective response. We are transitioning from information and application to now reflection. What insight can be gleaned from these stories? One of the topics that surfaces is urban mission. What is urban mission? Or to put if differently, what is the mission of the urban church?

Urban mission is about the *missio Dei. Urban* is simply to descriptor of *where* the *missio Dei* is taking place in this conversation. Urban mission is not *our* mission, it is *God's.* We are participants, but ultimately mission originates in, with, and through God and we are humbly and simply the channel or conduit of his love mission of redemption and restoration.

What are churches to be about in gentrifying neighborhoods? Are they to boldly proclaim the Gospel in hopes of transforming lives and ultimately their neighborhood? Or are they to dive deep into social justice issues by advocating for the marginalized and the voiceless to stave off displacement and economic exclusion? Does urban mission necessitate one or the other or both?

The next section delves into this tension to straddle the line between Gospel proclamation and Gospel demonstration. As has been a theme throughout this book, it is fraught with tension and there are no easy answers. At times the discourse will sound as if we are speaking out of both sides of our mouths or contradicting ourselves. That is reflective of our own wrestlings as we attempt to set forth our best efforts in expressing our convictions and leanings.

Responding to gentrification is highly nuanced. There are no universal answers because there is no universal expression of this process in cities. While there are many overarching commonalities, they take particular shape in each neighborhood and district within the city. As a result, any particular response will be contextualized as well. That does not mean that we don't try to offer answers or solutions, but it is only by reflection and discernment through the Holy Spirit will we find the wisdom, insight, and understanding we need to be able to respond appropriately. The reality before us is that we at least need to do *something*, but what? How? When? Our hope is that this final section will help answer those questions.

Chapter 16

Introducing Urban Mission
Sean Benesh

If we're not careful, the storyline of our theological beliefs, as well as our thoughts and assumptions about such things as gentrification, urban mission, theology of the city and place, can become so rooted and localized that we lose sight of the larger picture. In terms of theology, this is what Craig Ott and Harold Netland attempt to communicate in their book *Globalizing Theology*. "Globalizing theology is theological reflection rooted in God's self-revelation in Scripture and informed by the historical legacy of the Christian community through the ages, the current realities in the world, and the diverse perspectives of Christian communities throughout the world, with a view to greater holiness in living and faithfulness in fulfilling God's mission in all the world through the church. Thus, theology is to be an ongoing process in which Christian communities throughout the world participate."[1]

On the one hand focusing on the local is healthy and normative; on the other hand we lose or miss out on the global perspective. For me to talk about gentrification I cannot only use my current city, Portland, as an example, a living laboratory and as a backdrop, but I also must keep an eye on how this process is shaped regionally, nationally, and globally. That is to say the conversation is *both* local *and* global. The temptation is to either focus on the local to the point of

---

1 Ott and Netland, *Globalizing Theology*, 30.

parochialism, or to make it so broad that is becomes generic to the point of irrelevance.

As I have pointed out thus far in this book, gentrification is sometimes a concept, process and reality that is difficult to pin down. It is tempting at times to point to something and say, "Aha! There it is!" Yet no two neighborhoods or districts going through gentrification will look the same. When we approach the conversation globally, then it becomes even more diverse with slum removal being the ever-present reality in some cities. The similar process of gentrification looks markedly different in Mumbai, Shanghai, Montreal, London, or Brooklyn. What is the church to do when it finds itself at the crossroads of a neighborhood on the verge of the gentrification process as opposed to one where the process is well on its way? Also, what do new church plants do as they come into a gentrifying neighborhood? Should they focus on the current residents who are being uprooted or on those moving in? Or should we reduce the scale to the individuals or families of those who identify as followers of Jesus? What are church planters to do as they live amidst and among the changes that are taking place? Who should they identify with? The established populace who are imbedded in the neighborhood or the new wave who will change the neighborhood for decades to come?

This brings us to the topic and discussion of urban mission, because our theological beliefs about urban mission will act as a rudder to guide and inform our thinking and avenues of engagement. As Roger Helland and Len Hjalmarson note, "This is where we accomplish vigorous theological work: in the ruins of an old world but with an active hope for a new world."[2]

So what is God's intent for us as his children in the city? Why were we placed in cities across the globe? Most of us, whether Reformed or Anabaptist, hold to the reality of God's sovereignty. Usually we end up haggling over what exactly it looks like, such as whether it's divine determinism or self-limiting. So when it comes to cities, what does God's sovereignty look like in such processes as urbanization, immigration, and so on? How should the church respond, especially in light of Tim Keller's assertion "that the cities of the world are

---

2 Helland and Hjalmarson, *Missional Spirituality*, 53.

grievously underserved by the church because, in general, the people of the world are moving into cities faster than churches are."[3]

As I daily pour over Scripture in my devotional times every now and then I come across a verse or passage that causes me to pause and reflect deeper. In Isaiah 45 God affirms and details his sovereignty over the earth and the nations. He specifically states how he raised up the Persian king Cyrus to accomplish his will. "'I made the earth and created man on it; it was my hands that stretched out the heavens, and I commanded all their host. I have stirred him [Cyrus] up in righteousness, and I will make all his ways level; he shall build my city and set my exiles free, not for price or reward,' says the Lord of hosts."[4] Here we see a clear picture of God intervening to guide the process for the (re)building of Jerusalem.

In Psalm 107 we find another example of God's sovereignty in relation to his guidance of the urbanization process. "Some wandered in desert wastes, finding no way to a city to dwell in; hungry and thirsty, their soul fainted within them. Then they cried to the Lord in their trouble, and he delivered them from their distress. He led them by a straight way till they reached a city to dwell in."[5] As our cities swell with immigrants and refugees, might we affirm that God is behind *at least* part of the process? How would that shape and affect how we treat immigrants (whether legal or illegal)? How does this affect our overall view of the city and urban mission?

Glaeser affirms that this process of urbanization is actually hopeful and helpful for people seeking to get a leg up in life. "What forces draw the poor to urban areas? Above all, they come for jobs. Urban density makes trade possible; it enable markets."[6] Brugmann echoes this thought: "Once settled in cities, even the most marginalized populations, under the most totalitarian regimes, can leverage urban density, scale, association, and extension to build their own economies, wealth, power, and political alliances."[7]

---

3 Keller, *Center Church*, 166.

4 Isaiah 45:12-13.

5 Psalm 107: 4-7.

6 Glaeser, *Triumph of the City*, 71.

7 Brugmann, *Welcome to the Urban Revolution*, 55.

Many would allow wiggle room in their theological system to assert that God in some way could be or is behind global urbanization, or is minimally a part of the process. To spin the conversation forward and bring it closer to home, then, is to ask whether the process of gentrification is simply a secular process. Wayne Gordon for one in *A Heart for the Community* claims, as I quoted him in an earlier chapter, it is: "In many ways gentrification is the secular response to dilapidated neighborhoods."[8] Or is this all part of God's sovereign plan? Or part of it? Or a small slice of it? Or none of it? I'm sure you're probably squirming right now since gentrification is most often associated with an evil (or secular) process right up there with genocide and teenage acne. I am not saying it is ... or isn't. But where we engage in urban mission is precisely in these neighborhoods and districts. This stirring of the cultural soil in the gentrification process creates ripe conditions for the church to engage with the Gospel both in proclamation and presence.

It is when where we're most open to spiritual things that we can feel the most pain and discomfort. Whether self-inflicted or sovereignly brought about by the Lord to test, refine, or discipline us, we oftentimes experience through trials and hardship the most gain and bear the most fruit. I wish it weren't so. Wayne Cordeiro in his sagely book *Sifted* writes, "God tested all the great patriarchs of the Old Testament at one time or another, allowing them to experience difficult circumstances to try their faith, leading them to greater reliance on him. When something challenging is happening to us, we shouldn't spend too much time trying to figure out who is causing it. The choice we face is simple: will we trust God and look to him throughout the difficulty we face, regardless of the cause, or not?"[9]

Is it the same for a neighborhood in transition? "A neighborhood's renaissance can lead to a spiritual reformation. As these old communities revitalize there is vibrancy that returns, creating a buzz, and even momentum. Pretty soon this movement takes a life of its own where urban renewal is widespread as it reaches a tipping point. Could this be one of the triggers that

---

8 Gordon, "Gentrification," 40.

9 Cordeiro, *Sifted*, 30.

leads to a spiritual reformation, where people's hearts are open to spiritual issues?"[10]

I remember one of the desert wildflowers common in the Sonoran Desert that had a unique start to its life. The desert landscape would appear to be a dry and brown wasteland with little color or vegetation. After some heavy spring rains the desert would explode with color as if an artist's palette had been poured out across the desert floor. The seeds would often lie dormant for years waiting for the rain. You see, they would only germinate under the right circumstances. Usually it would entail flash floods during which the seeds were tossed, tumbled, and thoroughly roughed up. That is exactly what was needed to shock the seed into a growth mode where it would then germinate and sprout. Could it be the same for urban neighborhoods where the path to renaissance is first one of pain, hardship, and conflict? Could this actually be the right circumstances for the seed of the Gospel to germinate and grow, spilling life-saving and life-giving color from God the master artist?

It is my intention in the first part of this chapter to raise more questions than answers. I also want to poke around theology and missiology in the urban petri dish. It is easy to either fully embrace gentrification or simply be dismissive of it, but the tension lies in the middle. And it is in this tension where we need to construct a framework for urban mission in gentrifying neighborhoods.

Urban Mission

What then is urban mission? Or maybe we should instead ask, *what is the mission of the church in urban gentrifying neighborhoods?* Conn and Ortiz poignantly ask, "If Christ is the urban answer, what are the questions?"[11] Let us construct a theology of mission, then, for the urban context, in gentrifying neighborhoods in particular.

In a chaptered entitled "Constructing a theology for mission for the city," Charles Van Engen notes, "God's initiatives in sending mission messengers to the city is evident. The Gospels mention Jerusalem's mixed (mostly negative) response to God's love. But the dominant image is one of pained, loving, salvific

---

10 Benesh, *Metrospiritual*, 48.

11 Conn and Ortiz, *Urban Ministry*, 33.

tenderness: a hen clucking furiously to gather her wayward chicks under her wings."[12] Van Engen goes on to ask three pertinent questions when approaching the city: Why construct a theology of mission for the city? What is a theology of mission for the city? How may we construct a theology of mission for the city?[13] On the other side of the world, Andrew Davey echoes this sentiment when he writes, "The world is now an urban place. This new situation means that, more than ever, theological reflection is needed on cities and the future of urban life."[14]

In this theologizing or theological reflection, the end game is not to *know* about urban mission but to *do* or *engage* in urban mission. Theology is our foundation, framework, and reference point. "A commitment to engage with the reality of life in urban areas at the beginning of the twenty-first century demands a new set of tools for social analysis and for theological engagement."[15]

The first thing we need to keep in mind is that mission, or *urban* mission, belongs to God and God alone. Canadian missiologists Gary Nelson, Gordon King, and Terry Smith "argue that ultimately, mission belongs to God and that the actors play their parts as servants whose passion and skills are offered first to God and then to the common task of mission."[16] Later in the same chapter ("Whose Mission Is It Anyway?") they drive home their thesis:

> Missio Dei helps clarify that God's mission in the world–rescuing the world, saving it, redeeming it, restoring it—is not something we define. It defines us. It tells us who we are; what our mission is; how we were to do ministry, worship, and evangelism. No aspect of the Christian life, thought, or ministry is not connected with God's mission to the world. That mission continues today in he worldwide witness of churches in every culture to the gospel of Jesus Christ. That mission moves toward the promised consummation of God's salvation in the eschaton ("last" or "final day").[17]

---

12 Van Engen, "Constructing a theology of mission for the city," 242.

13 Ibid., 243.

14 Davey, *Urban Christianity and Global Order*, 7.

15 Ibid., 9.

16 Nelson et al, *Going Global*, 41.

17 Ibid., 53.

First and foremost, urban mission is God's mission. We are simply and humbly ambassadors of reconciliation, as well as sons and daughters of the King living out the in-breaking reality of the Kingdom of God. We follow in the footsteps of Jesus as we live incarnationally as witnesses of the living God. Canadian professor Stephen R. Harper writes, "The incarnation is therefore arguably the most important theological concept in the whole Bible. It is here that God not only communicates how He is going to reconcile humanity and all of creation with Himself, but also provide us with the example of how we are to continue Jesus' work after His ascension."[18]

Such is the dual work of God's mission in the world in both urban and rural contexts. *Urban* simply addresses the specific *where* of this mission. Contextually, mission looks different in urban settings versus suburban versus exurban versus rural. That is to say, not different missions or *mission*, but the same *missio Dei* being played out and embodied by the church globally in various settings. The duality (or two sides of the same coin) of this mission indicates a redemption and reconciliation of both the spiritual and the physical. Ray Bakke famously states, "Does God care only about people, or does he also care about places, including cities? And if the Holy Spirit of Christ is in us, should we also care for both urban people and urban places?"[19]

If the *missio Dei* is larger than we may have previously assumed, then what does it mean in urban contexts, especially gentrifying neighborhoods? Again, Bakke points us towards the tension of desiring the redemption of both urban places and urban people. "God's kingdom agenda seeks the personal salvation of all persons *and* the social transformation of all places."[20] Jon Kuhrt, working for the West London Mission, contributes a chapter in the book *Crossover City* entitled "What Does Salvation Mean in the Urban Context?" As a seasoned urban ministry veteran, he poignantly asserts, "Too often our use of the world 'salvation' and associated phrases like 'being saved' become religious jargon, flowing easily from the pages of liturgy or within internal church discussion. But those engaged in Christian ministry and mission in the urban context need to reflect carefully on what we mean when we talk about salvation. Are we

18 Harper, *They're Just Not That Into You*, 29.

19 Bakke, *A Theology as Big as the City*, 61.

20 Ibid., 66.

declaring a whole gospel? Are we guilty, like many of the false prophets in Israel's history, of telling 'our people' only what they are comfortable hearing? (Micah 3.5, Amos 7.10-17, Jeremiah 6.13-15)."[21]

Putting these seemingly disparate pieces together we begin to see that salvation, the Kingdom of God, and the *missio Dei* are about holistic transformation. That the physical realm has repercussions in the spiritual, and that the evidence of the spiritual is played out in the physical. In other words, to divorce the spiritual from the physical in regards to urban mission relegates our ministry to a 21st-century version of Gnosticism. Therefore, urban ministry in gentrifying (or gentrified) neighborhoods must be both physical *and* spiritual knowing that in reality they are one and the same. "Loving and serving the city not only shows love and compassion; doing so also strengthens the hands of the people of God, who bear the message of the gospel to the world."[22]

Recently on Netflix there was a documentary available to watch called *Urbanized* by Gary Hustwit. "*Urbanized* is a feature-length documentary about the design of cities, which looks at the issues and strategies behind urban design and features some of the world's foremost architects, planners, policymakers, builders, and thinkers."[23] One of the interesting features that jumped out to me was how urban design actually proves to either promote or decrease crime. It cites a South African city and how a well-lit pedestrian walkway through a slum area featuring parks, play areas, and "safe zones" which were clusters of buildings, *reduced* crime by 40 percent. Yes, 40 percent. What this shows is that it is possible to remedy a spiritual problem (i.e., crime and violence) with a physical solution (a new pedestrian walkway). As pastors, church planters, urban ministry workers, and so on, we're most often seeking to apply spiritual remedies to physical problems. We usually default to "let's get them saved" as the cure-all for everything that ails and plagues a city. Indeed that is important and is not to be minimized, but what the documentary revealed was that good urban design can actually help shape and transform a city. In addressing the issue of crime and violence in that particular city and district, most of us would look to strong evangelistic outreaches, Bible studies, and prayer vigils. Again, instrumental and

---

21 Davey, *Crossover City*, 74.

22 *Center Church*, 143.

23 Urbanized, "About the Film."

foundational. But what does it tell us that at times we can address social, spiritual, and relational problems by taking action of a physical nature? It tells us the problem is not the physical at the expense of the spiritual, but instead how they are ultimately one and the same. Where we get into trouble is when we divorce the two.

Glenn Smith, director of Christian Direction in Montréal, writes, "If we accept that the Scriptures call the people of God to take all dimensions of life seriously, then we can take the necessary steps to a more holistic notion of transformation. A framework that points to the best of a human future for our city-regions can then be rooted in the reign of God."[24] Urban mission necessitates holism in terms of our framework and approach to the city. This is precisely what is needed when we tackle the process of gentrification and the resultant effects on the inhabitants of gentrifying neighborhoods. If our remedy is to *only* prayer-walk, hold Bible studies, and counsel people then we have failed them and the neighborhood. That is not to minimize such things as we know that throughout Scripture God often employs methods, modes, strategies, and tactics that are mind-boggling on the human level. In adopting an incarnational posture we love people, pray for (and with) them, *and* we serve them physically and tangibly.

> Following Jesus in the city means getting serious about issues like good schools, responsible government, sanitation and clean streets, fairness in the marketplace and justice in the courts. It means working to eliminate squalor slums and every depressing condition that dishonours God by degrading human life. Once urban disciples see the big picture of what it means to be citizens of the Kingdom in the cities as they are, they begin to work from a new and enlarged perspective. Obedience to King Jesus takes them to every nook and cranny of city life. They find the challenges innumerable and the cost often high. But they know that while the dark powers are awesome, God's rule is greater and its advance is worth every sacrifice.[25]

In Jon Kuhrt's chapter "What Does Salvation Mean in the Urban Context," he displays a diagram that does a remarkable job of detailing the causes and effect of original sin as well as how the Gospel address those affects. The big "A-

---

24 Smith, "Key Indicators of a Transformed City," 15.

25 Ibid., 21

ha!" moment for me was when I saw how he tied together the social (including environmental) with the personal (including spiritual). He showed there's a symbiotic relationship between the two. One affects the other. He also demonstrates how sin impacted both. Sin devastated humanity's spiritual life, but it also wrecked havoc on the earth and the physical world. In the same way, the impact of the Gospel sets into motion the redemption of both. Christ's death is more than only dying for sinners, but his death, burial, and resurrection put in motion the redemption of humanity as well as all of creation.

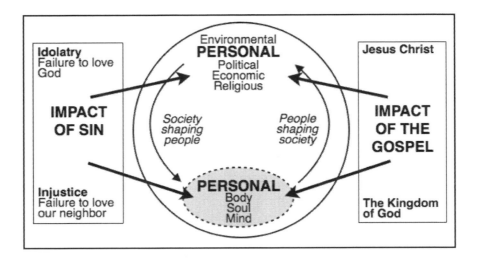

The outworking of Kuhrt's diagram reveals that the scope of the Gospel includes the physical and the spiritual, and that in reality they are one. We cannot afford to divorce the two. This is impactful in regards to urban mission and gentrification in that the church's role and responsibility is to proclaim and embody the Gospel in order to bring about spiritual and physical renewal. It can't be simply about populating heaven nor can it only be about physical changes on earth. We live in the tension of doing both. Extending both arms of grace ... saving grace and common grace.

I spent time in *View From the Urban Loft* exploring this concept in terms of the city in the chapter called "Parameters of City-Reaching."[26] "City-reaching

---

26 I continue to give credit to others such as Ray Bakke, Glenn Smith, and Ron Boyce as influential in my thinking about this.

then can be defined as *extending both saving and common grace to the city.*"[27] In our attempts to love the city as well as create strategies to impact and influence the people who live in them, both arms are needed. This is especially true in the conversation on gentrification. To simply offer spiritual answers to a community divided and writhing in pain is almost like withholding food from a starving child while we "give them Jesus." At the same time, to only focus on advocacy, policy changes, the built environment, and equitable gentrification also fails to hold the eternal in perspective. That is akin to refusing to throw a life-preserver to a drowning swimmer.

So what is urban mission? What does it look like in gentrifying neighborhoods in particular? It is about seeking the redemption and renewal of both urban *people* and urban *places*. Redemption and renewal carry both physical and soteriological dimensions. Again, we cannot divorce the two. For an individual to come to a saving faith in Christ is much more than getting a one-way ticket to heaven punched. A groundswell of redemption or "saving" continues for a lifetime. The spiritual has physical implications ... because a man's marriage has been saved, he no longer finds the need to use porn and abuse alcohol, he becomes more ethical in his business dealings, his crusty shell softens, he is reconciled with his father, he owns up to his previous affair, forgives, seeks forgiveness, and so forth. Remember Zacchaeus? After he had an encounter with Jesus, he says, "Behold, Lord, the half of my goods I give to the poor. And if I have defrauded anyone of anything, I restore it fourfold."[28] His transformation had social, financial, and physical outworkings.

This is our calling as individual followers of Jesus as well as the church, to proclaim and embody the Gospel ... the Good News that the Kingdom of God is *here*. We are living in the here-and-now of the *missio Dei* and our role is to live it out in gentrifying neighborhoods.

---

27 Benesh, *View From the Urban Loft*, 23.

28 Luke 19:8.

Introducing Urban Mission

Chapter 17

Presence and Proclamation
Sean Benesh

Living as we do in an action-oriented society we are prone to continuously stay in motion. This is especially true of those in church planting and urban ministry circles. Everyday becomes a routine of moving forward as we follow timelines, deadlines, checklists, to-do lists, goals, and objectives. We get frustrated if we are not seeing daily, let alone weekly, progress. Swept up in the tyranny of the urgent we become like programmed automatons lurching forward, feeling squeezed by the pressure to perform and make a difference.

For most of us our identity is framed by our performance; this is inescapable whether we are a skinny junior higher, church planter, business professional, urban ministry worker, or athlete. Performance is what we allow to define us. Our worth is relegated to what we do. As a result our self-worth, whether self-imposed or administered by others, is unequivocally derived from our movement forward and our results ... or lack thereof.

Os Guinness asserts that "nothing short of God's call can ground and fulfill the truest human desire for purpose."[1] He goes on to do a masterful job of tying this sense of calling to our identity. Our identity becomes rooted in our calling which challenges the modern framework of identity which derives its worth from performance and appearance. "The notion of calling, or vocation, is vital to

---

1 Guinness, *The Call*, 4.

each of us because it touches on the modern search for a basis for individual identity and an understanding of humanness itself."[2]

Not only that, but the relationship between calling and identity is done in the deep recesses of our being. Greg Ogden picks up on this theme. "Much of the will of God for us is 'written' in us. God has created us to live lives that are complete only when directed by his purposes. Yet in our evangelical subculture, we are often programmed to seek God's will in the outward circumstances of our lives. We tend to equate God's will with the discovery of the right marriage partner or with a career. But the will of God is a far more dynamic, lifelong process of being a steward of our inner design in the context of the specific demands of the various spheres of our call."[3]

This conversation becomes a pivotal feature in the way we live out the urban mission in gentrifying neighborhoods. It takes a strong sense of identity (based upon our calling) and a grounding in knowing who we are in Christ as well as how he has formed and shaped us. To fail at this point most often means we run wildly in a myriad of directions. Oftentimes we notice and track what others, whether contemporaries or predecessors, are doing in living out the *missio Dei* in urban neighborhoods. If they have found movement and some semblance of success we strive to emulate them all the while betraying our own inward callings and identities that God himself is carving out within us.

This was pointedly true for us while we served in Canada. Knowing how God has wired and formed us we decided that taking the conventional route in church planting was not for us. Most often, the conventional approach in church planting entails gathering a core group of interested Christians, casting the vision of how a new church can and will impact a neighborhood, and plans are made towards the launching of public worship services. Almost everything is directed towards the public launch to the point that life and ministry begin revolving around that event and ensuing weekly events. While many may chafe at this assessment, there is also little the many church planters are doing to step away from this template. I'm not arguing the merits of whether that is a warranted approach or not because I am an advocate of *more* churches of various *kinds*. This way of church planting is still viable, helpful, and hopeful.

---

2 Ibid., 20.

3 Ogden, *Unfinished Business*, 260.

As a family we decided to simply be missionaries ... and thus we began calling ourselves *urban missionaries*. We kept asking ourselves, "If we were missionaries in Dubai, Paris, Mumbai, or Moscow, what would we do?" It should come as no surprise that the default answer was *not* to focus on the launching of a public worship service immediately where we would attempt to entice unchurched people to become churched. Living in one of the most multicultural neighborhoods in the world meant that many were unchurched not because of disinterest or apathy, but because they simply did not know much of anything about Jesus. Therefore, we had to distance ourselves from the conventional templates that circulate in the church-planting world and to head in a different direction.

I would be remiss if I didn't admit that caused some tension, or that few people even understood it. But we knew who God had made us to be, we knew the dynamics of our neighborhood, and what we needed to attempt to do. As a result we jettisoned the notion of "starting with a core group of believers" because we honestly did not know of very many believers in our neighborhood. The very few we did know were already involved in a church. On a weekly and daily basis we humbly tried to live and act like missionaries which meant we started by laying a different foundation. The first thing we began to do was to simply establish a presence and daily rhythms in the neighborhood.

The daily activity of us trying to establish a presence leads into the conversation of holding together presence and proclamation in regards to living out the *missio Dei* in gentrifying neighborhoods. We all run in various circles and networks. Holding this tension of presence and proclamation in balance is daunting. We can rattle off groups who are skilled and bold about proclamation in terms of verbally presenting the Gospel. Their Achilles' heel is they have an underdeveloped theology of place and thus fail to be rooted. As a result their work is focused on *out there* rather than *here*. They do little to focus on establishing a presence where the rhythms of the Gospel are lived out for all to see. On the other hand, we all know of groups who have the presence thing down. They create urban gardens, have a deep introspective spirituality, serve the needs of the broken, but seem to never get around to proclaiming (or presenting) the Gospel. This is their Achilles' heel. What if we simply did both?

Through the remainder of this chapter I will attempt to hold together the balance between Gospel presence and Gospel proclamation. I believe that by default we tend to lean to one side more than the other which is healthy and normative. Also, we recognize that individually we do not possess all of the skills, gifts, and capabilities to do both adequately. However, within a body of local believers lies the latent potential to do both, and do it well. I will try to flesh out what it means to embody and proclaim the good news in gentrifying urban neighborhoods.

Presence and Place

In his book *Rethinking A Lot: The Design and Culture of Parking*, Eran Ben-Joseph, Professor of Landscape Architecture and Planning at MIT, shares a vision of the future of parking lots. He believes they are ripe for transformation, and can be recreated and revamped to become instrumental in reshaping public spaces and for use by pedestrians.

> It is no surprise that parking lots and the cars they service raise strong feelings and opinions about their use, importance, and impact on our society. For some, they are the ultimate symbol of a car-based culture that is destroying our world. For others, they provide a vital apparatus, crucial for maintaining economic vitality. Regardless of which view one concurs with, the space used for parking, whether occupied or not, provides a perfect stage for articulation of any view. Like streets and civic plazas, parking lots are spaces that allow for commentary and expression.[4]

Ben-Joseph walks the reader through the development of the parking lot as well as creative ways to revamp and use them beyond seas of endless concrete. It is a call to a creative reclamation of space, a call to redefine the *presence* of pedestrians in relation to cars.

Last year I attended a lecture and presentation at Portland State University by Denver Igarta. As a transportation planner for the City of Portland, he received a grant to explore bicycling and street life in four different European cities (Munich, Rotterdam, Malmo, and Copenhagen). I was thoroughly intrigued by what Igarta (who I now call my friend) had to share, especially his conclusions. His whirlwind trip across Europe impacted him so much that he is

---

4 Ben-Joseph, *Rethinking A Lot*, 117.

now applying the principles he observed and learned there in his job here in Portland.

Most notable is this concept of "complete streets." As a follower of Jesus, Igarta's desire for better planning transcends simply aesthetics; there's a spiritual component as well that has been influenced by the Kingdom of God. The concept behind complete streets is to make residential streets more livable. According to the *National Complete Streets Coalition* website, here is how the term is utilized: "Complete Streets are streets for everyone. They are designed and operated to enable safe access for all users. Pedestrians, bicyclists, motorists and transit riders of all ages and abilities must be able to safely move along and across a complete street. Complete Streets make it easy to cross the street, walk to shops, and bicycle to work. They allow buses to run on time and make it safe for people to walk to and from train stations."[5]

One of the roles of street usage that Igarta promoted was the "sojourn function." In other words, streets are more than routes to get from Point A to Point B. Instead, they are is for people to "stay, linger, abide ..."[6] Interestingly, a recent article on *BikePortland's* website offers a new twist on this sojourn function. Restaurants are reclaiming out-front parking spots and turning them into outdoor seating called "street seats." "Directly in front of their location on SE Division at 31st, Wafu has installed a large wooden deck with three tables and seats for 18 customers in a space of about two on-street auto parking spots. According to head chef Trent Pierce, they finished constructing the deck on Saturday and opened it for business for the evening dinner crowd last night. 'It's awesome,' said Pierce, 'It was packed out there last night.'"[7]

This notion of place, a return to becoming more rooted and established, with a heightened sense of localism, is certainly not a conversation exclusive to the church world as we have just seen. In fact, as with many pertinent conversations we often arrive late. Not "late" in the sense that we turned an apathetic or disinterested ear, but because I believe we continue to have an underdeveloped theology of place, a theology of the built environment, and a theology of the city.

---

5 Smart Growth America, "What are Complete Streets?"

6 Igarta, "Livable Streets."

7 Maus, "Spotted."

While it is obvious that the world has indeed truly become urban, we're still struggling to make sense of this phenomenon.

"It is both interesting and disconcerting to reflect on the relatively minor attention paid by theologians to the study of 'space' or 'sense of place' and its role in the expression of our humanity–the search for identity and meaning–and to the mission of the church, particularly when compared with the effort invested by scholars in the social sciences,"[8] says William McAlpine, Associate Professor of Practical Theology at Ambrose University College in Calgary, Alberta, in his book *Sacred Space for the Missional Church*. He goes on, "If the intent of the Western church was to extend the redemptive message of the gospel to humanity in a holistic manner, attention must be given to the pivotal role place plays in the human experience, particularly human spirituality. To excuse our apparent lack of intentional concern for 'places' and 'sense of place' on the grounds that such endeavors are less than spiritual is demonstrative more of a postmodern version of Gnosticism rather than a commitment to biblical truth."[9]

As noted earlier, while we as evangelicals have been zealous about populating heaven, it is the whole "rest of our lives" on earth that we were not too sure to do with, especially when it comes to the supposed sacred/secular dichotomy which in reality does not exist. Os Guinness states, "If all a believer does grows out of faith and is done for the glory of God, then all dualistic distinctions are demolished. There is no higher/lower, sacred/secular, perfect/permitted, contemplative/active or first class/second class. Calling is the premise of Christian existence itself. Calling means that everyone, everywhere, and in everything fulfills his or her (secondary) calling in response to God's (primary) calling."[10]

As wave after wave of change sweep across the urban landscape, we are forced to continue to theologize since what confronts us does not always fit into the nice, tidy boxes of modern systematic theological tomes. As individuals and businesses across the nation, poignantly so in cities like Portland, recapture localism and a heightened sense of place, this forces those of us in the church to construct and reconstruct a theological framework. We are simply trying to fit

---

8 McAlpine, *Sacred Space for the Missional Church*, 107.

9 Ibid., 129.

10 Guinness, *The Call*, 34.

the pieces together with what we know while identifying new or unchartered territory to explore.

This all ties into the concept of place and presence. In the city, especially in gentrifying neighborhoods, there has never been a better time than now to embody the presence of the Gospel. Not only do we proclaim the Gospel, but we also live it out in our homes, in the streets, in the cafes, at the pubs, and so on. The first step towards presence is simply to listen.

In his recent book *Thin Places: 6 Postures for Creating and Practicing Missional Community*, Jon Huckins writes, "As a missional community seeking to engage our local contexts with the good news of Jesus, we choose to view our neighborhoods and our cities as our classrooms. If we are to be good news, we need to listen to the needs and dreams of our surrounding contexts."[11] Huckins also says, "Listening requires humility and trust in the Spirit, but it is also an act of honoring those we come alongside with the good news of Jesus. The *missio Dei* requires us to ask, *Where is God at work, and how can I be part of what he is already doing?*"[12]

Practicing establishing a presence means embodying the Gospel in all of society's cracks and crevices. It is easy to simply hang out with other Christians and not ever really venture "out there" emotionally and experientially. Sure, we may meet friends at coffee shops or pubs but that doesn't mean we're establishing a presence. Huckins lays out six postures for embodying the Gospel that form the backbone of the covenant community of NieuCommunities.

Listening: We desire to be attuned to God, to self, and to our neighborhood.
Submerging: We desire to embody Jesus in our neighborhood while participating in an apprenticing program.
Inviting: We desire to grasp the depth of God's invitation to kingdom life and to become more inviting and invited people while welcoming our neighbors into God's redemptive story.
Contending: We desire to confront the things that hinder the full expression of the kingdom of God, both spiritual and natural, in our community, among our friends and neighbors, and in our city.
Imagining: We desire to discern God's intent on our lives and help shape transformational faith communities.

---

11 Huckins, *Thin Places*, 32.

12 Ibid., 34.

Entrusting: We desire to entrust people to God and to others, celebrate our deeper understanding of God's call on our lives, and lean confidently into our future.[13]

As I alluded earlier, this concept of localism is something the church is rediscovering, based upon the prevailing winds of our North American culture. To say we are late to the conversation also suggests that the church continues to be adaptable. As a result, my goal is not to deride the church but to humbly affirm our desire to be indigenous. In his groundbreaking book *Indigenous Church Planting*, Charles Brock asserts, "Excess baggage can be a major problem in church planting. It may include concepts and programs, as well as the use of material things. To carry things beyond the essentials will tend to be excess baggage."[14] We do indeed carry a lot of baggage into our work in ministering and church planting in gentrifying neighborhoods. Much of it revolves around our preoccupation with techniques, forms, and functions. As a result we do not give ourselves permission to theologize and push the envelope in search of new approaches as well as adapt to the changing landscape of the urban frontier.

From the first century onward the church has adapted to culture. We continue to do so which results in a good deal of tension within the church today as it has throughout history. How much adapting to the culture is too much? How will we know if we've gone too far? Or not enough? Many of our theological formulas and creeds were the result of the church responding and reacting to the cultural milieu and heresies of the day. For example, the postures that Huckins details are derived from the truths and concepts in the church practices of yesteryear, in this case the Celtic Christian lifestyle and missional posture of Patrick in Ireland nearly 1,600 years ago.

George Hunter in his book *The Celtic Way of Evangelism* writes, "There is no shortcut to understanding the people. When you understand the people, you often know what to say and do and how. When the people know that Christians understand them, they infer that maybe Christianity's High God understands

---

13 Ibid., 28.

14 Brock, *Indigenous Church Planting*, 29.

them too."[15] Hunter goes on to explain how Patrick's approach to proclamation (of the Gospel) first entailed establishing a presence:

> Patrick's apostolic band would have included a dozen or so people, including priests, seminarians, laymen, and laywomen. Upon arrival at a tribal settlement, Patrick would engage the king and other opinion leaders, hoping for their conversion or at least their clearance to camp near the people and form into a community of faith adjacent to the tribal settlement. The apostolic team would meet the people, engage them in conversation and in ministry, and look for people who appeared receptive. They would pray for sick people and for possessed people, and they would counsel people and mediate conflicts. On at least one occasion, Patrick blessed a river and prayed for the people to catch more fish. They would engage in some open-air speaking, probably employing parable, story, poetry, song, visual symbols, visual arts, and perhaps drama to engage the Celtic people's remarkable imaginations.[16]

First, in significant contrast to contemporary church planting techniques or urban ministry ventures, Patrick's posture was one of listening and establishing a presence. This is foundational in proclamation. Presence does not negate proclamation, instead it empowers it. Presence gives proclamation legs to stand on. By becoming rooted and established in place we earn the right and the credibility to be heard.

Again, tension ensued on all fronts as Patrick's approach was a decisive and strategic shift from the conventional Roman Church paradigm for starting new missions or churches. It was a radical break from the norm. Urban ministry workers or church planters in gentrifying neighborhoods may feel this tension as well because of their propensity to run hard and try to move fast. If that is you, I implore you to rest in God, trust the Spirit's movement in the neighborhood and people's lives, and move forward in patient listening and trust. God is the One who transforms hearts and lives, not us.

What was once normative for the church in Patrick's time eventually faded away only to be rediscovered again and again and again. Usually what has taken place throughout history is some massive cultural change that creates dissonance and forces us again to theologize. Not only theologize, but to live out the

---

15 Hunter, *The Celtic Way of Evangelism*, 8.

16 Ibid., 10.

rhythms of the Gospel in new (but old) creative and culturally indigenous ways. As our globalized culture refocuses on the concept of localism this has implications for the church today.

Localism is not only about recalibrating our economy; it has drastically altered the way the church in North America approaches the city and establishes a presence. Localism is bringing much attention back to the neighborhood level whether in public art, shared space, businesses, or overall culture. Many who move into gentrifying neighborhoods do so because of the cultural vibe and appeal and they certainly do not want to see it spoiled. As the twenty-first century moves forward the church is continuing to rediscover its role in place, especially after it had abandoned many church buildings and neighborhoods over the past forty to fifty years. Will we make the same mistake again? Or will we again truly become rooted and established in place?

Tim Keller does a remarkable job in balancing this notion of Gospel presence with Gospel proclamation when he writes:

> We evangelize, telling people about the gospel and preparing them for the judgment. We also help the poor and work for justice, because we know that this is God's will and [this] that? he will ultimately overcome all oppression. We teach Christians to integrate their faith and their work so they can be culture makers, working for human flourishing—the common good. The "already but not yet" of the kingdom keeps us from utopian, triumphalistic visions of cultural takeover on the one hand, and from pessimism or withdrawal from society on the other.[17]

---

17 Keller, *Center Church*, 47.

Chapter 18

My Neighborhood is Gentrifying! Where on Earth Does Urban Ministry Need to Go?
Glenn Smith

Two events in my life as an urban practitioner shape this article on social and economic upgrading in neighbourhoods and missional theology. I invite the reader into those situations as we reflect on the task of the church within the confines of God's urban mission, specifically when a neighborhood goes upscale.

In 1992, I had just completed my doctoral studies[1] and was anxious to further my reflections on the differences between Canadian and American cities. Most urban geographers blur the distinctions in North America. Then I sought a better understanding of primate cities in the Two-Thirds World, especially Haïti. An internship I did in Haïti during my doctorate only whetted my appetite to learn more about urban realities in that country and the southern hemisphere. I stumbled onto the writings of David Ley, the Canadian urban geographer who

---

1 Glenn Smith, "Towards A Contextual Praxis For The Urban French World: A Case Study To Engage Christian Direction, Inc. with Montreal, Quebec." (DMin diss., Northern Baptist Theological Seminary, 1991).

subsequently has had an enormous influence on my thinking on this subject of social and economic upgrading of neighborhoods.[2]

He made a comment that was to shape my practice for the next 20 years. He wrote, "In the quest to understand society, things are not always as they appear; causes and consequences may be concealed; subtle explanations may on the surface seem implausible. A recent personal example makes the point. I met the mayor of Toronto in the course of my inner city research, a civic leader knowledgeable on housing matters. I mentioned that some analysis had shown that the best indicator of gentrification in the inner city housing market was the amount of office space built in the metropolitan area. To my surprise, the well-informed mayor had not made the connection in his mind between housing markets and labour markets. *For him the cause was concealed from the consequence.*"[3] That set me on the journey to understand better these dynamics in my city, Montreal.

Fast forward to 2011 for the second event to affect my thinking. My wife is a community development organizer in Hochelaga-Maisonneuve. This area has continuously been the poorest borough in Canada going back to the 1871 census![4] Our ecumenical roundtable has become quite active in the neighborhood after many years where the churches were significantly marginalized (and themselves marginalized) from public life. We were attending a community meeting called an *Operation populaire d'amenagement.* (An OPA is a community initiative to take local action. It is actually a play on words in French to mean a hostile takeover!) Citizens were doing a form of transect studies to observe firsthand the needs and opportunities in each quadrant of the neighborhood. One could not miss the "social engineering" going on in the borough. Several housing projects had been approved in the past five years where

---

2 In spite of the vast and excellent literature on Canadian urban issues that exists today (Ley, 1996; Bunting and Filion, 2000, 2006; Lorinc, 2005), unfortunately very little has been written to document the experience of Christian ecclesial reflection and practice in our census metropolitan areas. Even less has been written on gentrification. Over the past two decades very few significant articles have appeared. David Ley, professor of urban geography at the University of British Columbia has written three fine, accessible pieces about faith in the Canadian city (Ley, 1992, 1993, 2000).

3 Ley, "Christian Faith and the Social Sciences in a Postmodern Age," 281-282. Italics mine.

4 Ley, "The Inner City," 196.

developers build a combination of condominiums, apartments and low-cost housing, all in the same city block.

Located only seven metro stops from the central business district of Montréal, this neighborhood fits the classic residential model of a Canadian (but not American) inner city.[5] This mixed housing development model goes back to thirty years of gentrification in Montréal, where "the best predictor of revitalization was the proximity of a census tract to an existing elite area."[6] At this OPA public gathering tempers were high. Anger flowed among the poorer residents, who are renters, when the question of condominiums came up. They were not welcome in the borough and their owners were not welcome in the room. I smiled and thought back to David Ley's comments from 1991 that "the best indicator of gentrification in the inner city housing market was the amount of office space built in the metropolitan area." Young professionals can buy a small condo close to the downtown sector, gentrifying this neighborhood. If mayors don't understand the causes, how are populations ever going to understand? *The cause was concealed from the consequence.*

Setting the Framework for Understanding Cities and What is Driving Gentrification

My own personal education over the past twenty years forced me to see how social context and our Christian traditions (meaning the study of the narratives of Scripture, history and missiology) intersect. I was forced to move beyond understanding urban growth and urbanization to grapple with the forces shaping our city/regions. I began to see that we need to move beyond a theology of the city and a practice called urban ministry. We need a true understanding and practice of missional theology for the global city.

Gentrification is one of those forces shaping our city/regions. Like other forces it is part of what we call urbanism. This is the philosophy of how a city culture affects the behavior of the greater population of its nation and the world. It is closely linked with globalization and the forces that are at work in the

5 Ibid., 274-302.

6 Ibid., 288.

democratization of information, the expansion of global capitalism, and the extension of homogeneous expressions of culture and styles. The process of gentrification dates from the 1960s. In fact the word first appears in the literature in 1964. It relates to the restructuration of cities as they moved from manufacturing and industry to "post-industrial" milieu. The economies of the former were dominated by the factory horn and clock. Office towers dominate the landscape today. The move to the service sector has coincided with the downtown boom of the past 50 years ... however delocalized some downtowns have become. A relationship was born between the growth and evolution of those emerging labor markets and the rise of the bourgeoning middle class and the social and economic upgrading of inner-city neighborhoods.

Roland Robertson understands *globalization* as the compression of the world and the intensification of consciousness of the world as a whole. It is a multidimensional set of processes that is transforming our present social contexts, is weakening national conditions and is experienced through advances in communication technologies, neoliberal capitalism, realignments in political movements, and dramatic cultural shifts. Robert Schreiter states that these developments represent the extension of the effects of modernity on the entire world and the compression of time and space, all occurring at the same time.[7]

For reasons that defy logic, metropolitan areas continue to be home to the emerging informational technologies. In the age of digitization, high-speed Internet, and 24-hour investment, why do large cities need to be home to the sector? One can just as easily "practice globalization" from Chibougamau, Quebec, as from the new technopole and the world centers for aerospatial, pharmaceutical, telecommunications research and development, and cinematic animation that are all literally in downtown Montréal! Now the compression is truly urban. Admittedly, there is no theory that helps us explain globalization and urbanization. But it goes a long way to explain gentrification.

Max Stackhouse, however, helps us to grasp the complexities of this compression by showing how globality manifests itself in different spheres of

---

7 There is an abundant literature of this subject. See Robertson, "Globalization and the Future of 'Traditional Religion,'" In *God and Globalization*, edited by Max Stackhouse and Peter Paris, 53-68. London: T &T Clark, 2000. Also, Schreiter, Robert. *The New Catholicity: Globalization and Contextuality.* Maryknoll: Orbis, 1997. Taylor, Charles. "Defining Globalization." In *The Gospel and the Urban World*, 5th edition, edited by Glenn Smith, 9-15. Montréal: Christian Direction, 2007.

social life. These spheres are the channels for the moral and spiritual life which drive the structures of human life in all societies. One finds certain specific "channels" all the time. When one thinks about the city in a functional manner rather than a geographical one, these include: the demographic, social, cultural, economic, political and technological functions, as well as the media. The compression and intensification is all-pervasive in our major cities.

This emerging social condition, coupled with massive societal secularity is a perfect context to understand what is central to gentrification: the public/private distinction. Jeff Weintraub develops a fine typology to help us weave through this issue, explaining four ways in which this distinction is often used.[8] First, in the classic Roman distinction, there is the *res publica* or the category of citizenship governed by the sovereign state. This is public life. Second, it is used in making a distinction between public administration and the market economy of private enterprise sometimes referred to as the second sphere. Third, a distinction is made between the private domain of the family and the larger economic and political "public" orders. These aspects are not under consideration in this chapter. However, there is a fourth way to understand the public/private distinction. There is the fluid, "public" realm of social life and the cultural ways that we sustain it. We talk here of public space. This is the realm most under pressure with the onslaught of hyper-individuality in most major urban centers. With the compression of time and space, the immanent world dominates. We control everything *on our own*. There is little sense of the transcendent in daily life. The lives of human beings in cities are increasingly split between a private and a public sphere, between secret and public behaviors.

This distinction has existed for decades. Personal, intimate, intense life was lived out in the family, with friends and a primary group. Public space in the boulevards, the gardens, the squares, and festivals provided the place for strangers to meet. Increasingly, this public sociability has suffered decline, and friendship and the family (in particular) cannot bear the weight of emotional expectations.[9]

---

8 See his chapter, "The Theory and Politics of the Public/Private Distinction," In *Public and Private in Thought and Practice*, edited by Jeff Weintraub and Kristan Kamur. Chicago: The Chicago University Press, 1997.

9 The most significant contribution to this thinking is Sennett, Richard. *The Fall of Public Man: On the Social Psychology of Capitalism.* New York: Vintage, 1978.

The consequences of the decline of sociability also affect the very nature of our urban understanding. John Mercer has illustrated at length the fundamental differences in Canadian and American cities on a private/public (city) continuum.[10] Whereas public cities prioritize the corporate life, the common good, belief and trust in government, and active urban planning, private cities look to autonomy in municipal affairs, special purpose districts, individual rights and extensive use of user fees. It is not merely a question of government intervention, regardless of the level of intervention. The continuum reflects the result of the nature of the intervention. Sam Bas Warner did the classical work on the issues in his historical study of Philadelphia.[11] However, over the course of the past 20 years, Montréal, where I live, is increasingly becoming a "private city" as evidenced by the significant percentage of people who live alone – now close to 40 percent of the population on the island of Montréal.[12] In fact, there are now boroughs in Montréal where over 50 percent of the population lives alone. This movement to a private city will only be accentuated in the days ahead. With the monumental infrastructure challenges that cities like Montréal face, the polarized social landscape rooted in educational and economical polarities and the marginalization of institutional life this privatization will only get larger. This is the cultural context within which gentrification is taking place in my city. The social forces at work have direct consequences on the housing market and must be understood, especially by urban ministry practitioners.

Through those two events and the ongoing reflections of the 20 years in between, I was forced to rethink God's urban mission. Some people may study gentrification and ask the question, *"Where is the Church?"* and then rush to critique the Church's lack of significant involvement in the complexities of the community. In the midst of the competing pluralities that a practitioner runs into on a weekly basis, I would rather ask the questions, *"What will the Church*

10 Goldberg and Mercer initially articulated this thesis in *The Myth of the North American City*. Vancouver: UBC Press, 1986. Mercer pursued it further in "The Canadian City in Continental Context." In *Canadian Cities in Transition*, 3rd edition, edited by Trudi Bunting and Pierre Fortin, 24-39. Toronto: Oxford University Press, 2006.

11 Warner, Sam Bass. *The Private City*. Philadelphia: University of Pennsylvania Press, 1968. Eric Jacobsen uses similar nomenclature in his interesting text, *Sidewalks in the Kingdom*, 49-56, 157-159. However, it applies the idea primarily to the Church.

12 Germain and Rose, *Montréal*, 193-197. Charbonneau, Johanne, et al. *Habiter seul: un nouveau mode de vie?*. Québec: Les Presses de l'Université Laval, 2009.

look like?" "How will the Church reflect biblically about the city, How will she pursue relevant mission in her context in the years ahead?" We are not taking the time to think biblically so as to act contextually.

To come to grips with a missional theology and practice in the context of gentrification, let's begin by defining some terms. In the next section, I will propose some criteria to do missional theology. In the third section, I want to propose a model on how improvisation is a motif to do missional theology in our milieu. Finally, let's look at what transformation in gentrifying neighbourhoods might look like.

Applying Missiology to the City Today – Some Critical Notions

The basic purpose of theological reflection has never really changed. It is the reflection of the people of God upon God's project in human history in light of their own circumstances. Theology is *God in dialogue with his people in all their thousands of different situations.* Yet how does a journey through a global city/ region and into gentrifying neighbourhoods help us to articulate and live a missional theology in the context of social and economic upgrading within those contexts?

In the context of this chapter, what do I mean by missional theology? When we talk about a novel, we refer to it as "fictional literature." The noun, "fiction" becomes the adjective, "fictional." It is same thing with the wonderful word "mission." When it is used as an adjective, we say "missional," as in a church which is dedicated to mission.

But *missional* is an accordion word—the more air you pump into it, the more noise it makes! At the core, in spite of all the noise, there are four key ideas:

- First, we are affirming that God is *missionary* in his character—God's Being in action. Mission is first and foremost about God through Jesus as being active in His creation by the work of His Spirit. Yes, God is love, just, holy ... he is also missionary!
- When we use the word *missional*, we are reaffirming the Gospel – Jesus is LORD. A king has a kingdom; the Good News is about the

LORDSHIP of Jesus over all His creation, in our lives, in his Church, and over our cities!

- When we use the word *missional*, we are admitting that we live in a new period in our history. Some people call this "Post-Christendom"—a period where Christianity and the Church are no longer at the centre of our culture. We may grieve our loss, but we also need to think and act in fresh ways.

- When we use the word *missional*, we are affirming that the Church is a group of people sent into our neighbourhoods and cities to live out the implications of the Gospel.

Missiology is the exegetical, theological, historical and cultural study of the mission of God in the world and the ensuing tasks of the Church. For that reason it is often defined as an inter-disciplinary field of reflection and action.[13] When we shape this discussion contextually and pursue this reflection for a city/region, we are seeking to create dialogue between urban geography and mission. The former analyzes the reasons for the spatial differences of human activity in urban areas. Gentrification is an essential part of the reflection. Missiology seeks a more adequate understanding of the apostolic mission of the Church while remaining faithful to the exegetical task of understanding the mind of the biblical writers. But this "fusion of horizons" is fraught with danger. As Paul Minear reminds us, "When, therefore, the exegete deals with the apostle Paul, and when missiology accepts Paul's apostolic work as normative for the continuing mission of the Church, then these two aims coalesce."[14] It is rarely an easy fusion.

Missiology is a fertile field today for a battle over the definition of three terms—mission, evangelization and contextualization.

Mission is the embodiment by the whole community of the followers of Jesus of the whole task of God in their specific context for the sake of the whole world. "Mission is the Church sent into the world to love, to serve, to preach, to

---

13 Missiology refers to the inter-disciplinary reflection and actions by the people of God about Christian witness and the mission of God in the world in light of their proper circumstances. It begins on the exegetical level (Christian faith is a missionary faith rooted in Jesus' practices, the hope of the rule of God, and his justice) and follows with historical, theological and practical reflection and initiatives. It is inter-disciplinary because it takes into account cultural studies, holistic community transformational development theory and practice, a critique of the past, contextualization, and strategies that move the people of God in their local situation forward.

14 Minear, "Gratitude and Missions in the Epistle to the Romans," 41.

heal, to liberate."[15] This embodiment cannot be separated from Christian spirituality. This means living fully in the world in union with Jesus Christ and his people and growing in conformity to his person. It is a grateful and heartfelt yes to God expressed both in act and attitude—the follower of Jesus lives in obedience and imitation of Jesus Christ and walks in the disciplined and maturing pattern of love for God. Spirituality is the process of developing a deep relationship with God. It is a process of being conformed to the image of Christ for the sake of others.

It is also about how Christians live their faith in the world. Spirituality cannot be divorced from the struggle for justice and care for the poor and the oppressed. The people of God have something to say about gentrification! Gentrification inevitability results in displacing the resident population, the poor, the marginalized: those who cannot afford to live in the neighborhood when it goes upscale.

The comprehensiveness of the mission of the Church in the city requires the proclamation of the gospel, the planting and nurture of congregations, and the application of the principles of Christ's lordship to all areas of community life, especially when social upgrading happens. It means concern for all that is "city," even for the cosmos above and beneath the city, from the quality of the air people breathe to the purity of the water in the rivers and canals.

Following Jesus in the city means getting serious about issues like good schools, responsible government, sanitation and clean streets, fairness in the housing market, and justice in the courts. It means working to eliminate squalor slums and every depressing condition that dishonors God by degrading human life. Once urban disciples see the big picture of what it means to be citizens of the Kingdom in the cities as they are, they begin to work from a new and enlarged perspective. Obedience to King Jesus takes them to every nook and cranny of city life. They find the challenges innumerable and the cost often high. But they know that while the dark powers are awesome, God's rule is greater and its advance is worth every sacrifice.

Evangelization is that set of contextual, intentional initiatives of the community of followers of Jesus to demonstrate in word and deed the offer that

15 Bosch, *Transforming Mission*, 412.

God gives to everyone to change one's way of living and follow Jesus in every area of life as Lord.

Contextualization means a "weaving together." For our purposes, it implies the interweaving of the Scriptural teaching about the city and the Church with a particular human situation, called a context. The very word focuses the attention on the role of the context in the theological enterprise. In a very real sense, all doctrinal reflection from the Scriptures is related in one way or another to the situation from which it was born while addressing the aspirations, concerns, priorities, and needs of the local group of Christians who are presently doing the reflection.

The task of contextualization is the essence of theological reflection. The challenge is to remain faithful to God's revelation and the historic texts of Scripture while being mindful of today's realities. An interpretative bridge is built between the Bible and its context to the circumstances of the local body of believers. The first step of the hermeneutic exercise involves establishing what the text meant at the time it was written: what it meant "then." The second step involves studying the local context and creating the bridge to understanding the text in meaningful terms for the interpreters today: what it means "now." The final step is to determine the meaning and application for those who will receive the message in their particular circumstances as the present-day interpreters become ambassadors of the Good News: what it means "here". *Contextualization is not just for the one communicating, nor about the content that will be passed along. It is always concerned about what happens once we have communicated; about the ultimate impact of the message on the audience.*[16]

Paul Hiebert uses the term *critical contextualization*; first, to help the practitioner exegete the culture, second, to exegete the Scripture and, third, to effectively evaluate the responses of the past and the future. Finally, new contextualized practices are formulated. At no point does such an order of approach put into question the authority of the Scriptures. To the contrary, Hiebert writes, "... *critical contextualization* takes the Bible seriously as the rule of faith and life. Contextualized practices, like contextualized theologies, must be biblically based. This may seem obvious, but we must constantly remind

---

16 R. Daniel Shaw pursues this very point in a recent article in *IBMR. Beyond Contextualization: Toward a twenty-first-Century Model for Enabling Mission* 34(4) 208-215.

ourselves that the standards against which all practices are measured is biblical revelation."[17]

Each of these terms forces the local congregation to engage their contexts. But how does Scripture relate?

The Unchanging Story of the Lord of the City

We are very accustomed in Protestant circles to studying the history of theology or to reading theological texts. In other words, we want to see the results of other people's reflections. As Douglas Hall has pointed out, because clergy and professors have done so little to alter the situation, laypersons tend to think of theology as a more or less fixed set of beliefs, contained in embryo in the Bible, codified in various historical creeds, confessions and faith statements, refined in forbidding volumes of doctrine and relayed to congregations in simplified form through sermon, catechetical instruction, and (for a few) college classes in religious knowledge.

In contrast to that approach, the urban practitioner first needs to reflect upon the meaning of the Bible in its original context. Then the local congregation can contextualize that message in all the spheres of her life – including the neighborhood when it undergoes social and economic upgrading. In this manner, the community can communicate the relevance of the Scriptures in situations very different from Bible times.

This means that the Church will need some very clear criteria as she goes about this process. Without wanting to be either exhaustive or too theoretical, let me briefly suggest five principles that will guide the process of contextualizing the Gospel.

First, this reflection is rooted in an inductive study of the Bible. It sees God's revelation as progressive. This exegetical study examines closely how the Bible illustrates the process of making God's word Word? relevant to the recipients of the message. By understanding the principle of historical progression in the biblical record from creation through the tragic fall, into the redemption offered in Christ and the future consummation of the celestial city, the Church sees how the Bible seeks biblical justice in a diversity of contexts. At

---

17 Hiebert, "Critical Contextualization," 110.

the same time, it upholds the fundamental unity of God's revelation in time and place.

Second, this reflection and resulting strategies that respond to the needs of the local situation is a community enterprise. No one individual can write a theology on one's own. It is communal in the sense that applying the principles of Scripture in a specific cultural context is not only left up to professionals, or the highly trained.

Third, doing theology in context will mean that we will listen to the cries of the vulnerable and the call of the Scriptures on this subject. The theme of God's justice is found in over 400 texts in the Bible. Any reflection for the modern world, therefore, will need to include this component, having a clear prophetic dimension in its action.

Fourth, as we have already pointed out, this attempt at a local theology will be contextually practical and relevant to both the people implementing the action and the group that will receive the Good News. We are not just trying to systematize what the Bible teaches on the subject. We are trusting God to transform the situation through the collective efforts of the Church. Scripture speaks clearly that the development of "sound doctrine" is not just the cerebral acquisition of knowledge; it is the development of true Christ-like character. For that reason, the Great Commission call to make disciples of the nations, who in turn will reproduce this command, is found throughout the Bible.

Finally, this reflection and action will be "place specific." God's concern for people includes a deep love for the situation in which they live. God used particular places to speak to individuals such as Nineveh in the case of Jonah or Rome in the case of Onesimus. The same principle was at work for the people of God when the Lord used, for example, the city of Babylon to speak to the children of Israel who were in exile there in 587 BCE.

This principle forces the interpreters of the Bible to wrestle with what is transferable from one culture to another. God reveals Himself in specific contexts; the Good News is not merely a general memo addressed in impersonal terms. Therefore, each situation must strive to make the eternal purpose of God appropriate to the context.

In the light of these principles, what does the biblical story say about God and the city?[18]

The biblical account of human history begins in a garden "toward the East in a place called Eden." This creation was good. That account culminates in a city, one that was made ready by God. This city carries the very glory of God, with no need of the sun, the moon, or even a place of worship. This city is God's final gift to humanity.

There are some 1,200 references in Scripture to urban life, with references to 119 different cities. In fact, the story of Scripture is a "tale of two cities," the city of man, *civitas mundi* and the city of God, or *Civitas Dei*. *Civitas mundi* graphically summarizes the evolution from the city that Cain built in Genesis 6 to *Civitas Dei*, the city that God is building in Revelation 21.

In 1,090 different passages, the Older Testament portrays the city (the Hebrew word *ir*)[19] as fortified (*misbar* "that which cuts off abruptly"). Interestingly enough, the city in the Older Testament was never regarded primarily as the centre of culture or the sphere of civic or legal government. Security was the hallmark of the city in the Older Testament. The Hebrew term includes the sense of a fixed settlement that is rendered inaccessible to assailants by a wall and/or other defense works.

Therefore, it was foremost a place of refuge (Joshua 20:1-6). Lewis Mumford describes this phenomenon under the theme of city as "sanctuary."[20] It was also the centre of worship (Psalm 123:3f) and the residence of the Levites (Joshua 21). In Psalm 107, the city becomes the desired place of settlement (4-9) and in Jeremiah 29, God encourages his people to view the city as a context for life, prayer and peace, even in exile.

It is also true that the city was a place of sin. Genesis 11, Micah 6:9-10, Ezekiel 7:23 paint the spiritual pollution of the urban context. Therefore, they are places of paradox, capable of great depravity and evil (i.e., Sodom and

---

18 The best new work on the city in the biblical texts is *The City in Biblical Perspective*. London: Equinox, 2009. For an interesting overview of urban issues through a theological lens, see the articles in *Interpretation* 54:1.

19 Beaudry, "Où demeures-tu?" 31-51.

20 Mumford, *The City in History*, 48.

Gomorrah) yet centres where God will enact his cosmic plan (i.e., Nineveh and the story of Jonah).

Yet no portrayal of the city in the Older Testament is complete without reference to the New Jerusalem depicted in Isaiah 65 and especially in Zechariah 8. In that chapter, the city of Truth celebrates its senior citizens (8:4) and its youth (8:5). They share the public square. The city celebrates ethnicity (8:7, 23), prosperity (8:9-13), justice (8:14-17) and spirituality (8:18-22). Written after the humiliating Babylonian destruction of Jerusalem in 587 BCE, the prophet is surfacing images of what *Civitas Dei* will look like in reconstruction.

The New Testament city (*polis*, used about 160 times) is in some places a continuation of the Older Testament idea of the fortified centre (Mark 5:56; Luke 10:1). But we now see the Greek idea of *polis* as "state" and the centre of culture. They become the magnets that draw large numbers of people for economic and social enterprises. The typical urban centre had a diversity of traditions, peoples and economic factors. The city was becoming truly cosmopolitan.

Despite the rural imagery surrounding certain dimensions of Jesus' ministry, he was born in a city (Luke 2:11) and his ministry focused on Palestinian cities (Matt. 9:35). As portrayed through a parable, he is the Lord of the City (Luke 19:11-27). Under the influences of the powerful and religious leadership of the urban establishment, he was crucified (John 18:1-20).

Lucan literature depicts this emphasis in a unique way. Thirty references to the city are found in this Gospel. Even though specific names are not mentioned, Luke sees the city as the scene and the scope of mission of our Lord. In the Acts of the Apostles, this strategy continues. Philip "preached the gospel in all the cities" (8:40). James said that Moses had "been preached in every city from the earliest times" (15:21). Stephen is stoned outside the city (14:13).

When we place the Lucan record in the context of Sjoberg's description of classical peasant society as a set of villages tied socially to pre-industrial cities, then Jesus' commission (Luke 10:1) and His parable preaching (Luke 8:4) take on a new meaning. Instead of a rural Jesus and an urban Paul, we find Jesus' earthly ministry as focused in the streets and to the people of the cities of first-century Palestine.

The apostle Paul was born in a city, Tarsus (Acts 22:23), experienced his conversion in the city (Acts 9:6), was commissioned by a well-known urban church (Acts 13) and followed the Roman roads to the major centers of the empire. Paul moved from city to city. His teaching and model of diverse mission strategy marked the Church for decades to come.

It is important to note two passages that underscore the urban imagery of the New Testament. Philippians 3:20 sets our heavenly citizenship while on earth in urban imagery. Hebrews 11:10 and 12:22 both point to Abraham's example, who "was looking for the city ... whose architect and builder was God" to define our future hope.

Since "discovering" cities in the Bible, I learned that no one text would ever inform all that is the mission of God in a community. One of my dear friends and doctoral mentors, Harvey Conn taught me well. I remember him commenting:

> Picking one biblical text to sum up my view of urban ministry is an assignment too awesome and dangerous for me. Too awesome, because wherever I turn in my Bible it shouts 'urban' to me. Too dangerous, because the text I select could leave out a piece of the picture too crucial in another text and distort the whole. We need a hermeneutic serious enough to link Genesis to Revelation in the unending story of Jesus as an urban lover and the Church as God's copycat.

I realized that I needed to keep studying the biblical texts!

Therefore, we can summarize the biblical data of the urban place by not merely studying particular cities in the biblical record or by examining certain individuals involved in urban mission. We can survey the landscape through a biblical theology that centres on the history of special revelation. Through the six themes of this revelation - Creation, sin and the fall, Israel, re-creation in the person and work of Jesus of Nazareth, the era of the Church and its consummation - we get a clearer picture of God's strategy in the city. The first cities recorded in Genesis are a natural extension of the cultural mandate given to Adam. Through reproduction come the populations that will lead to urban centers. This Creator-monarch who acknowledges no other power equal to his own is the sovereign Lord. The heavens and all that is of the earth are his dwelling place by this creative act (Psalm 24). In creating, God provided cities as an evidence of his common grace to humanity.

But we must readily admit that the city is undeniably tainted by sin. The city that Cain built (Genesis 4), the work of Nimrod at the Tower of Babel (Genesis 10 and 11) and Sodom and Gomorrah all underscore what was to come. Yet, God has chosen a city, Jerusalem, as his celestial place (Psalm 132). It carries his name (Deuteronomy 12:11) and it exists for the worship of his glory (Psalm 24). This city was to stand as a reminder to all the urban places of the earth of the unity and the *shalom* that is possible under God's redemptive covenant (Psalm 122:6-9). We see then that God has chosen cities to accomplish his cosmic plan. Places like the cities of refuge, Babylon for the Jewish exiles, and the Roman cities for the advancement of the Gospel, bear this out. Nowhere is this image of the "new City" more profoundly presented than in the consummation image of John's vision in Revelation 21. This creative work of God is his sovereign dwelling place, the symbol of love and care. As many an urban pastor has said, "What God began in a garden will be consummated in a city."

Invited into the Story - The Improvisation of Cosmic Salvation

All of life is a narrative and individual actions are an essential component of that unfolding story. How do we find our place in God's story for human history? Furthermore, what is the place of "city" in the unfolding drama of God's love affair with his creation? If we follow the principles of biblical theologizing that we just articulated in the previous section, I believe we have a fruitful field in which to think about both of these questions. We are looking at the progressive revelation of God's plan, seeking to see how he contextualized his message for different people at different moments in their social situations while unfolding his intentions to establish his rule in the cosmos.

At the heart of our reflections as Christians lies an understanding of God's intentions for human history. These intentions read like a narrative, the unending story. Numerous writers have attempted to summarize it.[21] My best effort would read like this:

> Reality as we know, see and experience is the result of a Creator who made the world and fashioned creatures in his image to live in harmony, well-being and peace (*shalom*). These creatures were given a series of mandates to pursue so that one day all of creation should be flooded with the Creator's life, in a way for which it was prepared from the very beginning of the human story. By tragic irony the creature rebelled against these intentions. The rebellion brought dissonance at every level of creation. But the Creator acted astoundingly and solved the problem in principle in an entirely appropriate manner—through Israel and ultimately through Jesus—to rescue creatures/creation from the plight of the rebellion. The full scope of this rescue is not yet apparent but the story continues with the Creator acting by his Spirit within the world to bring it to that purpose originally foreseen. To this end, the Creator has created a new community of witnesses to this story. While waiting, this community is called to speak, to serve, to live in loving obedience to Jesus Christ and to be a sign of God's peaceful purposes for the world and to dialogue to subvert other ways of telling stories of the world. One does this in patient attendance to the grand finalé of his story.

We cannot do this essential dimension of contextualization as mere outside observers. How can we proceed with the art of relating the Bible to these two questions? How do we find our place in God's story for human history? And what is the place of "*city*" in the unfolding drama of God's love affair with his creation? I would suggest that we must do this in a manner that does justice to the individual texts within their own horizon and in a way that informs us as learners in our own particular cities. One of the fundamental problems that urban ministry practitioners face is that the Bible is seen as merely a religious

---

21 In the past decade many Christian authors have attempted to summarize God's project in human history in a succinct paragraph. Wright, *The New Testament and the People of God*, 41, 97-98, 132, and Hays, *The Moral Vision of the New Testament*, 193, employed the most recent insights in narrative theology, while maintaining a historical focus on the faith, helping the Church understand God's Story in fresh ways in theology and ethics. McLaren, *The Story we Find Ourselves In* applied the method in an all-together different literary genre that he calls creative nonfiction. He employs it for the broader theme of the authentic mission encounter of the Church with our culture that has been explored by many authors since Lesslie Newbigin first published *Foolishness to the Greeks*. Grad Rapids: William B. Eerdmans, 1987. One fascinating summary of the Christian story is found in the Montréal novelist, Yan Martel's famous novel, *Life of Pi*, Chapter 17. The film captures a part of the incident.

book or worse, one that is irrelevant to their concerns in their contexts. As long as we treat it as an ancient text about things gone by, it will only stand as a "philosophical/theological" authority for us, but unable to deal with today's urban complexities.

In a very real sense, this is the problem that biblical proof-texting has created for the Church. Because we treat the canon as a theological repository of verses to be correlated to specific themes, we have lost the notion that God has a project and that he has invited us to be partners with him in his strategy and that there are texts in the canon that drive even Christians to ignore God's rule over certain areas of their lives. We need a way to read the Text as a story that gives its Author the proper authority to speak to our work.[22]

The Bible itself does not present a story of a people blindly trying to figure out what God is up to in their situation. For example, during Paul and Barnabas' first missionary journey, they were invited to address the synagogue in Pisidian Antioch (Acts 13:13-41). After recounting the history of Israel from the prosperous days in Egypt through to the story of Jesus (vs. 16-24), Paul personalizes the message. He states, "...it is to us that this message has been sent" (v. 26, 32). It is as if he is asking his listeners to live in the story! We read a similar thing during Moses' second rendition of the Ten Commandments in Deut. 5:1-4. There he states, "It was not with our fathers that Yahweh made this covenant, **but with us, with all of us who are alive here today.**" It is almost as if Moses ignored the initial audience who received this revelation and sees its real application for his hearers, one generation later.

Rather than glossing over this, I believe this opens a door to understanding what God is up to. As Paul and Moses invited their hearers to live the story, we, too, can change our way of reading the text of Scripture. Our conception of the authority of the Bible is also challenged. God constantly invites his people into the story! The Bible then is not just a theological library to be analyzed but also an unfolding love affair with his creation. And, I believe the city is at the heart of the love affair.

---

22 Lesslie Newbigin offers a very stimulating reflection on this very point inspired by his reading of Polanyi, See *Truth to Tell*, 41-50.

Innovating with proposals that several writers have suggested on this subject over the past decade,[23] I think we can conceive of God's story as a jazz sextet.[24] This motif has great potential because improvisation, an essential element of good jazz, is also present within the stories. They are a key indicator of the social imaginaries of the Bible, which is primarily narrative. The authority is now found in the God of story, not in a theological dictionary or a philosophical principle of a particular dogma. This God has revealed a story, centered in history, beginning in Creation and focused subsequently in the story of the Jew, Jesus of Nazareth, and the people he is forming by his Spirit. But it still needs completion. We are invited to improvise today! At this juncture, one could look closely at God's sextet and use exegesis along the way so that we can find our place in God's story and the place that cities played in his plan.

What would this drama look like if we applied the framework of the previous section? Let me make the following suggestion.

Instrument One – the violin ...

Scene i - God is creative and breathes life into the world. He gives humanity demographic, ecological and cultural mandates in Genesis 1-2. He sets into motion the populations for the great settlements to come.

Scene ii - God is good, and desires *shalom* for the order he has established.

Scene iii - God is just and governs this creation in justice. This carries the very notion of right standing and right behavior in the public square effecting people, things, relationships, judges, and politicians with public and individual implications.

Instrument Two – the bass violin ...

Scene i - Evil spoils God's design of the cosmos. Sin breaks shalom with the Creator, systems, others and ourselves. It displeases God and deserves blame. We are guilty.

---

23 The writings of Brian Walsh, Richard Middleton and Tom Wright have been most helpful to me.

24 As a lover of Jazz and improvisation, I find it a fitting metaphor to describe God's narrative. One only needs to spend time in Montréal during the International Jazz Festival of Montréal to understand why I opt for this metaphor. Jazz is an Afro-American music created at the end of the 19th century rooted in improvisation, an original treatment of the musical score with an emphasis on rhythm.

Scene ii - Cities are undeniably polluted by sin. The expansion of cities is affected by these realities.

Instrument three – the clarinet ...

Scene i - God chooses one ethnic group, living in a holy land and He gives them his Torah. He even allows them to build a permanent structure where he chooses to live on earth. Yet they constantly betray him and eventually find themselves in exile.

Scene ii - But God still loves the city and chooses "place" for his own benevolent purposes. One city becomes his holy dwelling.

Instrument four – the trumpet ...

God redeems the plan of creation in Jesus. Life and ministry is centered in the cities of Palestine. In restating the message of creation in the language of the reign of God, Jesus looks beyond Temple, Torah, land and race.

Instrument five – the drums ...

Scene i - God invites us, the Church, to partner with him as witnesses and servants of this new reign over all that God has made. The first Church implements God's strategy for human history. The great cities of the Roman world are the scene of the initial action.

Scene ii - Gratefully, God sends his Spirit so that his project for the cosmos and the kingdom can be realized.

Scene iii - Following Jesus means we are committed to take the whole message of the reign of God to the whole city, structures and people. This means that mature learners must be developed. We are dependent on the Holy Spirit to use us in God's project.

Scene iv - The story goes quiet here. It would almost appear that something is missing. God did not totally complete the play. Rather than seeing this as a problem, or as an invitation to just proceed with studying what we received up to now, the art of contextualization invites the practitioner to live in the story in a way that does justice to what God has revealed and to contribute to the unfolding of the drama today. We are partners in the story, as God intended Creation.

Instrument six – the saxophone ...

God is creating a new city. We want to work towards its accomplishment fully realizing it will only happen at God's return. As local congregations discover the social and economic upgrading taking place in their neighborhoods, it is time to both listen to the biblical narrative afresh for texts about contextual change and learn by the Spirit how to improvise locally.

Contextualization and Transformation

For what purpose does the practitioner pursue contextualization when gentrification takes place? Why listen to both the present context and Christian tradition, including our study of the Scriptures, Church history and theology? Increasingly, we hear the use of the word *transformation* as a term that encompasses all that the Church does as followers of Jesus in God's mission in the city. But what does this mean? What does it entail? Inspired by the reflections of the South African missiologist, John de Gruchy, I suggest that a transformed place is that kind of community that pursues fundamental changes, a stable future, and the sustaining and enhancing of all of life rooted in a vision bigger than mere urban politics. He adds that "it is an open-ended multi-layered process, *at once social and personal*, that is energized by hope, yet rooted in the struggles of the present."[25]

Because our purpose is to look at how transformation might take root in a Canadian community, we will need some subjective indicators rooted in the social imaginary of Canadians. I would like to propose a model from community faith-based initiatives, rooted in the biblical notions of peace and well-being (See figure below).[26] The model comes from the work of Christian Direction, the urban ministry I lead in Montréal, Québec.

---

25 Gruchy, *Christianity, Art and Transformation*, 3.

26 For more information and to view a larger graphic go to www.direction.ca.

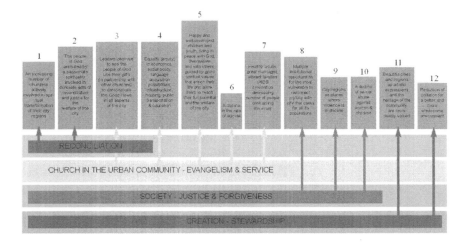

Transformation means that the community is moving with increasing awareness and intentionality towards the vision of peace and well-being represented in the diagram. In light of contextual realities, we at Christian Direction have adopted the following schema and the twelve indicators as a vision of what the transformed city (in our case, Montréal) would look like. These indicators are rooted in four tracks underneath the cityscape. They represent God's concern for all of life, beginning with the congregation that embodies *shalom* and reconciliation. These communities then demonstrate the Good News in their neighbourhoods in word and deed. They are deeply concerned about justice and forgiveness in society. But as stewards they are also concerned for the whole created order. To measure the vision realistically, we have articulated twelve indicators of the type of transformation congregations are pursuing.[27] These address contextual concerns in our city. Accompanying these indicators are baselines rooted in research on the state of life in the city. Congregations work together to pursue the welfare of the city.

This vision seeks to help congregations participate in the transformation of the city, particularly in an era of broken relationships and the holistic understanding of poverty. Unfortunately, poverty is often viewed and portrayed in economic terms. Essentially, poverty is about relationships, not just about

27 These have been inspired by the eight United Nations Millennium Objectives, although this schema lacks the rigour of the Millennium Development Goals (MDGs) eighteen targets and thirty-two indicators.

economics. Poverty is a broad concept including economic, social, emotional, physical, and spiritual realities. It is often intergenerational. It affects people's identity (social exclusion, absence of harmony in life and well-being) and their vocation (deprivation at every level of life including the ability to participate in the welfare of the community). The causes of poverty can be traced to *inadequacies in the social imaginary*. These inadequacies are in fact a web of lies beyond the mere cognitive level of deception. This intricate web leads people to believe that their poverty or social status is somehow divinely sanctioned or a factor of fate. People sense that they have no choices. The social imaginary is a powerful instrument in perpetuating chronic poverty.

To measure these territorial social indicators, we employ objective measures from primary field surveys and from secondary census-based data sets. For example, Indicators 4, 5, and 6 in the diagram above can be measured by a blend of documentation from both sources. However, they also include subjective social indicators that describe the way people perceive and evaluate conditions around them. Indicators 7, 8, and 12 are highly dependent on an individual's perceptions and aspirations of the context in relationship to the indicator. As the reader will see, social imaginary indicators rooted in the religious, spiritual and transcendent experiences of congregations are included in the presentation. Indicators 1, 2, 3, 5, 7, and 11 touch on these aspects of "the community in the mind"—the subjective views people have about their neighborhood.

Where the Rubber Hits the Road

In 2006, Christian Direction, in conjunction with Roman Catholic parishes and Protestant congregations, published a 45-page study of the east end of Montréal—Hochelaga/Maisonneuve. Numerous initiatives have been launched as a result of that study. Together we created the *Regroupement œcuménique de Hochelaga/Maisonneuve*. To address the 53 percent high school drop-out in the neighbourhood, in collaboration with another social service agency, we started a centre to work with adolescents, their families and the local schools to promote school success. Together with others in the borough, we advocate with local businesses so they do not employ kids during the school day. To address the relational poverty, there are four events each year to break the deep solitude people experience. To break the cycle of intergenerational poverty, three "financial capability" projects[28] have been started for young people and their families. In a short time, all three were generating income. To address the social upgrading we have begun to engage these new populations as partners in the social and spiritual transformation of the borough. This same experience is now being repeated in four other boroughs on the island of Montréal and four other cities in Québec. Research can *and must* inform transformational strategies.

---

28 http://www.entreados.ca.

Chapter 19

Localism and Gentrification
Nieu Communities (San Diego, CA)
Jon Huckins and Jon Hall

The reality and implications of gentrification have been something we have spent less time studying on an academic level and much more of something we observe, experience, and to some degree participate in within our neighborhood of Golden Hill. There is a unique tension in forming a Christian response to gentrification when we own up to the fact that—based on many traditional definitions—we unintentionally find ourselves as being part of the "problem" rather than the solution. Not only is identifying our complicity with gentrification the first step in approaching it, it is the only place we can begin to enter the conversation with humility and a constructive posture that resembles that of Jesus towards our neighbors.

It is here that we must offer the framing problem: *gentrification is both good and bad.*

As inhabitants of gentrified or gentrifying neighborhoods, we must ask ourselves a series of questions:

- Are these competing values inherently incompatible or is there a way to embrace the reality of both?
- Whichever the answer, how should Christians respond?
- Is there a theological and biblical foundation on which to build such a response?

Our Context

Before moving forward it is important to note that this is written through the lens of a couple guys who are living in, and seeking the good of, our neighborhood. As we continually dive deep into the reality of our place, we are continually evaluating how to define what "good" truly means for us and our neighbors. It is not something we can assume to know the answer to before fully submitting ourselves to the common good of our place. To know what is good for our neighborhood requires us to have enough "skin in the game" to feel both the benefits and the pain of the presence or absence of good. It is to live not *independent* of, but *interdependent* with our neighbors and the neighborhood we live in.

Not only have both of us chosen to raise our young families in Golden Hill, we have hopes of fully immersing ourselves in the common rhythms of this place, as well as seeing the Kingdom come to Golden Hill. Jon Hall is raising his family in Golden Hill and owns/operates two businesses in the neighborhood. I help manage our neighborhood farmer's market and sit on the board of our neighborhood council, as well as participate in a local community of faith. Most of our neighbors don't know us as pastors or churchgoers, but as business partners and neighbors committed to living, loving and leading in the unique soil of this place.

I offer this background not as a way to share all the great things we are doing, but in the hopes of showing that people who deeply desire to be good news in a place still have to be subject to the realities of gentrification that may be coming about despite our good intentions. As followers of Jesus, we take seriously our vocation to be representatives of God's restorative work in the world. We seek to be a presence of reconciliation rather than division. We hope to bring about unity rather than discord. Ultimately, because we know that the Kingdom of God is best reflected in its diversity, we hope to be participants with God in cultivating places in our neighborhood where unity is found through diversity rather than in the enclave of any ethnic or socio-economic grouping.

So, what is the role of a community of faith in a gentrified or gentrifying neighborhood? Is what we may see as good actually good for the whole population of a neighborhood? How do we become aware of those issues? How do we promote a common good of both the haves and have not's?

Living Well In The Tension

In developing a biblical framework for the reality of gentrification, there are two themes that we see helpful in highlighting. First, how we enter a place is as significant as how we end up living in a place. In other words, we can move into a neighborhood or city in the posture of the colonizing hero, or we can enter it with humility and a willingness to embrace the already established ethos. Second, we are to live in neighborhoods as advocates of the Kingdom of God and with the hope of God's reign being made manifest in this place. That requires we hold the first theme in radical tension.

So how do we enter a place with humility as a learner, while still advocating for a hope found in the reality of the Kingdom of God that was inaugurated in Jesus?

As the physical place where all three monotheistic religions share a common history, Hebron is one of the most volatile cities in the Middle East today. Home to the Tomb of the Patriarchs, Jews, Christians, and Muslims alike are able to trace their roots back to their father, Abraham. Today, there is a daily struggle for the acquisition of more land and better access to the cities' religious sites to the point that land is being stolen from one another. Rather than working with one another in common respect for the land, there is a posture of domination and acquisition that trumps their ability to celebrate a common bloodline.

The irony of today's struggle is that their father, Abraham, gives us one of the most important insights into how we are to enter into a neighborhood that is already inhabited. After his wife Sarah died at the beginning of Genesis 23, Abraham enters a time of mourning and preparation for her burial in Hebron, which at the time was inhabited by the Hittites. Having a significant reputation among the people, Abraham could have easily taken land for Sarah's burial or assumed that it would be given to him. Instead, he says, "I am a foreigner and stranger among you. Sell me some property for a burial site here so I can bury my dead" (23:4). Over the course of the narrative, he is offered the land multiple times for free, but Abraham insists on honoring the inhabitants by paying a fair price for the land.

Living as Reflections of Unorthodox Hope

At a later point in Israel's story, God's people find themselves in exile under the heavy hand of Babylon. They no longer inhabit their neighborhood and their understanding of a rightly ordered world is a distant dream. Yet, despite it all, the prophet Jeremiah shares the word of Yahweh to his people in exile:

> Build houses and live in them; plant gardens and eat their produce. Take wives and have sons and daughters; take wives for your sons, and give your daughters in marriage, that they may bear sons and daughters; multiply there, and do not decrease. But seek the welfare of the city where I have sent you into exile, and pray to the Lord on its behalf, for in its welfare you will find your welfare.[1]

It is here that we get a picture affirming our second theme that we are to be advocates and participants in the in-breaking of God's Kingdom in the places we inhabit. No matter how we land in our neighborhood, city or suburb, we are to seek the good of our place. We are to embody and advocate for the reality of God's reign because the good of our place will equal the good of our family.

After hundreds of years, exile had become Israel's primary reality when Jesus, their deliverer, finally arrives. For Israel, the Messiah was to bring about three realities: 1. Restoration of the Davidic throne through military conquest, 2. Rebuilding of the Temple, and 3. Reoccupation of the Holy Land. While Jesus comes bringing a message of hope in announcing the reality of the Kingdom of God, such hope wasn't always realized in the way they would have anticipated. In fact, because Jesus didn't bring about any of these three realities in the way Israel expected, the majority of God's people considered Jesus a failed Messiah. He had moved into the neighborhood of humanity with the hope of the Kingdom of God, but rather than establishing God's reign through military conquest, he established it through suffering and selfless sacrifice. For Jesus, the common

---

1 Jeremiah 29:7.

good of the human neighborhood required that he make himself last in order for others to be first.

While Jesus was viewed as a failed Messiah by the standards of the Jewish community of his day, we know that his upside-down approach was actually the means through which the Kingdom was made manifest. Jesus did have some "short term" wins throughout his ministry, but there was a longer-term impact he came to bring about that wasn't as easy to see or measure.

As we faithfully inhabit our neighborhoods with the hope of the Kingdom of God inaugurated in Jesus, maybe our goal isn't to fix everything right now, but to seek a longer-term good. In fact, what might look like failure in the short term could be the sowing of seeds that lead toward a long-term good. Maybe just being with the people in a neighborhood can offer a long-term good that transcends some of the short-term realities of gentrification. Maybe moving towards a common good with our neighbors out of the tangible hope of God's Kingdom reign will redeem some of our apparent short-term "failures."

If there is anything we have learned, it is that transformation is slow and often comes about in ways we would never have expected. Such is the life of Jesus, and such is life as a follower of Jesus. While committing to find our hope in Jesus' enthronement as King of the Kingdom, we live, love, and lead in our neighborhoods with curiosity, humility, and a listening ear that leads us towards a common heart and life in our neighbors.

Having explored some of the theological realities of gentrification through the exploration of the biblical narrative, let's turn to what this might look like fleshed out in real time and place. How do we live well in this tension of being the humble listener and the hopeful advocate of God's Kingdom reign in our neighborhoods? With that, allow me to turn it over to my friend and community mate, Jon Hall as he invites us into this tension lived out in the everyday realities of our neighborhood, Golden Hill.

Good for the Neighborhood, Yes. But for Who in the Neighborhood?

It was another gorgeous Saturday afternoon when I heard a knock at the door. My front door is what you might call "rickety," maladjusted, with drafty gaps that seem to shift weekly with every settling movement of the old foundation of this house. A good hard knock, or even a stiff gust of wind could blow it open. Opening the door, I was greeted by two policemen, one of whom I recognized from a few days earlier. Police activity is fairly common on my street, and he had been out front a few days prior, responding to yet another problem two doors up. As I often do at such times, I went out front to see what's what, and ended up talking to him.

On this day, he and his partner were coming to me, seeking my help. The property two doors up from mine has been what some neighbors, and the police, would consider a nuisance for as long as anyone could remember. It's a collection of small single-unit residences. Some are burned-out, most are uninhabitable, and could easily qualify in the eyes of many as urban blight, ready-made for a bulldozer. It's also been a magnet for gang and drug-dealing activity, with at least four shootings (that I know of) since we moved in a few years ago. Today, the police officer was seeking my help in having the property declared uninhabitable and a nuisance, which would be the first step in evicting all who live there, and forcing the apparently negligent owner to sell or give up the property. The officer was asking me to lead a neighborhood effort on our street to get a petition signed, which could be the first step in running them out of the neighborhood.

I could see the developers lining up now, ready to build a multi-unit complex that could turn a nice profit. Golden Hill is one of those neighborhoods in transition, a place some refer to as a land of "in-between." Higher-income folks looking for a more edgy neighborhood on the verge of becoming cool, and profit-seekers buying old properties to renovate and flip would be at the ready, cash in hand. Homeowners on our street would likely celebrate, as it would surely raise property values and, some would hope, rid the problem neighbors from our street.

I understood where the policeman was coming from, and appreciated his trust in coming to me with a plan. He explained that the police can only be reactionary, only getting involved after there's a call of a problem. He expressed to me that he felt it would require a neighbor, someone who lived here and cared about the neighborhood, to take proactive steps and lead this effort. With formal complaints filed and a petition signed, he then could be authorized to take further action. It seemed so simple the way he explained it, but I'd been here long enough to know there's more to this picture.

Just a few days earlier I was walking down the sidewalk on our street and stopped to talk with a young man and his little girl. We chatted for a moment, I pointed to where I lived, and he pointed to his place, one of the little run-down places at the *casa de urban blight*.

"Have you lived there long?" I asked.

"A few months," he said. Looking up at the poor condition of the property, he went on, "At 250 bucks a month, it's the only place we can afford." He said this with what I interpreted as equal parts sobering reality and gratefulness.

We talked a few more minutes, as his energetic little girl, who looked all of four or five years old, skipped circles around her dad. As they walked to their home, the weight of the policeman's request sat on my shoulders like a pile of concrete blocks. Running out the "bad element" of our neighborhood would also run out this man and his daughter. And in a city where a studio apartment typically rents for $850 a month or more, where would he go? Would they end up on the street, with the 12,000 other homeless in our city? And what of the drug dealers and gangbangers, where would they go, and whose problem would they become? Bulldozing this property, I knew all too well, wouldn't fix anything, but simply move the "problem" on to another neighborhood, on to the street.

My kids sit safe at night in our home, doing homework on the computer, maybe playing one of their video games, reading a book, then crawling into a warm bed at night, without a concern that it all may not be there tomorrow. Yet two doors down from us was a very different reality, where neighbors of mine battled drug addiction, gang violence, poverty and now, quite possibly, eviction.

As I wondered what role I should take in all this, the wheels of progress continued rolling. The property was recently purchased by a group of developers, residents were evicted, and the property is currently undergoing a complete refurbishing. What happened to the father and his little girl? I'll likely never know. To some, this is good news. To others, it could be tragic. So is the tension of gentrification.

Gentrification: Better, or Just Different?

Chris Yanov was a college student living in Golden Hill at a time when Golden Hill looked a bit different than it does today. Over breakfast one

279

morning at Tobey's, a small local cafe, he told me, "Today when you see someone running down the street in Golden Hill, you can be pretty sure they're getting exercise," he said. "Back when I first moved here eleven years ago, if you saw someone running, there was usually someone else chasing them."

Chris was a college student then, living in Golden Hill. He wanted to help out in the community, so he volunteered with the youth group at one of the local churches. He said he realized that after a few months, and being stabbed through the hand, he wasn't making much a difference in the lives of these kids.

"The gang members would show up and bring their friends," he said, "and I'd find myself simply entertaining gang members. No life change was really occurring."

It was after this that he started Reality Changers, an after-school educational program that went on to realize amazing success in turning the lives of gang youth around through education. To date, Reality Changers has sent over 400 kids to college, raising over $25 million in scholarships along the way.

Chris is a guy who has seen what works and what doesn't in a neighborhood like Golden Hill, so I asked him about the issue of gentrification, and the shifting landscape of Golden Hill.

"It's better today than it was back then," I said, making more a statement than asking a question.

"Well, I don't know about *better*. It is *different*," he replied.

Chris acknowledged that yes, you can now usually walk most of the streets of Golden Hill without fear of getting shot or robbed. But he also told me about the types of families he works with, and how they are often the victims in the reality of gentrification.

"There aren't many cheaper places for these families to go to in San Diego, after getting priced out of Golden Hill," he said. "They go to the street, or maybe to Tijuana. Neither are usually good options though."

The reality of gentrification in our neighborhood, like many neighborhoods, is complicated. And what is good for one neighborhood may well not be for another. It all left me wondering, can "good" be defined and lived out in a way that's good for all? Who gets to define what is good? And what role does a community of faith play in defining it?

Cultural Movements within the Neighborhood

While the perception of gentrification is most often seen in changing physical space and socio-economic realities, the effects of change in the neighborhood often occur on many different levels. Yes, we're seeing change occur in older properties being made into newer properties,

In neighborhoods like Golden Hill, other, more subtle changes and movements are often occurring. Being aware of these is vital to those hoping to both understand and be part of the neighborhood on a deeper level, and often requires heightened awareness. In our neighborhood, like some others around the world, these have included cultural shifts in food, consumption, the arts, and transportation. And they don't always affect all ethic, age and socio-economic groups the same. Some movements are good, some not so good, and others are simply different. Some movements favor certain groups, disfavor others, and leave yet others untouched. In a neighborhood as diverse as Golden Hill, understanding these dynamics, and how they impact the lives of people, requires continued effort. In short, it requires we listen well and often.

These and other experiences leave us asking ourselves the question, "What is good for the neighborhood?" It's not always an easy question to answer, one that requires constant exploration, experimentation, listening, and submersion into the realities of our neighborhood. This gets lived out as a constant rhythm of listening, then doing, then listening, then doing, and so on.

Listen Well

It was the spring of 2008, six or seven months before moving to Golden Hill, that I began walking its streets. Living about 90 miles away at the time, I occasionally had meetings in the San Diego area, and would often make time to stop by Golden Hill for lunch or dinner, or to work in one of the local coffee houses. Sometimes I simply walked the neighborhood. Thus began my process of listening to the neighborhood. Five years later, I'm still walking the neighborhood and listening every day.

Listening is an attentive task, experiential as well as visceral. While I won't dive deep here into all the elements of good listening, there are a number of practices that are critical to beginning to grasp to the realities truly at work in a neighborhood, realities that are critical to individuals or groups to understand, if they are to respond well to a neighborhood, and the realities surrounding gentrification. These may include cultural, political, religious, and socio-economic realities. To understand a neighborhood, we must understand these well, both within our neighborhood, the city or region we're in, and the larger cultural cousins the neighborhood may share identities with.

Listening to our Neighborhood's History

What's the local history, and how does that inform the neighborhood's current reality?

Golden Hill's history dates back some 10,000 years to the first inhabitants who arrived here after crossing the Bering Strait. "Discovery" by Europeans in the 16th century, religious conversion and conquest by the Spanish in the 18th century, and white settlers who arrived in the 19th century, the San Diego/Tijuana region's history is thick with the story of newcomers displacing those already here. Our neighborhood of Golden Hill went through times of change, transition, and displacement as well, from its first wealthy residents in the mid-19th century, mostly businessmen working downtown, through days of working-class residents, giving way to the crime-ridden, gang-inhabited and drug-dealing days during the 80s and 90s when it was known as "Heroin Hill." This regional and local history speaks volumes about the place and its people, and plays a big part in understanding its current reality.

Listening to Neighborhood Boundaries

What are the actual boundaries that define our neighborhood, and what influences those boundaries?

Much like the boroughs of New York City, the downtown/midtown region of San Diego is largely a collection of neighborhoods. The boundaries of Golden Hill are generally defined today as the 5 Freeway to the west, the 94 Freeway to the south, A Street to the north, and about 32nd Street to the east, a roughly a 7-block-by-14-block area. This is important, as it speaks to the identity of those who live and work here. South Park to the north, East Village to the west,

Sherman Heights and Grant Hill to the south, and City Heights to the east are all unique neighborhoods, with distinct identities and ideas of belonging. To understand well these boundaries is to understand many of the dynamics of the neighborhood, including ideas of belonging, needs, and opportunities.

Natural and manmade barriers can powerfully impact neighborhood boundaries for better or for worse. Many cities have faced these challenges, often resulting in issues of haves and have-nots, class separation, and socio-economic differences. While neighborhood boundaries can help create a sense of identity, they can also separate people and cultures in ways that break down community. At one time, the neighborhood of Golden Hill extended a number of blocks further south, but the construction of the 94 Freeway in the 1960s created a formidable physical barrier that separated a large segment of the neighborhood. Today, class barriers are more clearly separating Golden Hill from South Park, its northern neighbor. Old-timers consider much of South Park as Golden Hill, though a rapid and pronounced increase in gentrification of the neighborhood north of A Street has more clearly defined that as South Park, with many residents there openly desiring not to be considered living in Golden Hill, preferring a South Park identity instead.

Some people, though, recognize these divisions, and are choosing to do something about it. A local architect/developer who lives and works in Golden Hill is opening a new mixed-use development on 25th Street, just north of the 94 Freeway. Called *You Are Here*, this property mixes retail, residential, and commercials spaces in what used to be an abandoned gas station. In the new design, the architect managed to retain the original gas station, a testament to Golden Hill's past, and constructed *You Are Here* specifically as a gateway to the neighborhoods to the south. It's a practical expression of creating a "bridge" of sorts between our neighborhoods, as well as creating a much-needed gathering and retail space the neighborhood so desperately needs.

Listening Outside the Neighborhood.

What do the areas and neighborhood surrounding your neighborhood have to say? How are their identities informed, or respond to, that of your neighborhood? What about your city or region as a whole? ... What is it saying culturally, politically, religiously and socio-economically, and how might that be impacting your neighborhood? Lastly, what do similar neighborhoods, even those outside your region (or country) have to say, and how might that inform the realities of your neighborhood?

Geographically, Golden Hill sits in the heart of the city of San Diego. As a result, it is both influenced by surrounding neighborhoods, and has opportunities (and obligations) to work alongside its neighboring communities. We're also part of a city that exerts influences and presents opportunities for our neighborhood. In order to understand our role in the neighborhood and its future, it's critical we understand our place in this reality.

And more than just our city and region, an increasingly global reality means that we may indeed share identities with, and can learn a great deal, from neighborhoods in other parts of the country (or the world), places that may be, in terms of culture and identity, our cousins. Many who are familiar with the boroughs of New York City have likened the neighborhoods of San Diego to that reality. And Golden Hill, along with other San Diego neighborhoods, share cultural similarities with some of the boroughs of Brooklyn, such as Park Slope, Fort Greene, and Williamsburg. We can learn much about our present and future by understanding the cultural and especially the gentrification realities of these places. In many ways, Golden Hill shares far more in common with these neighborhoods 3,000 miles away, than with the suburban neighborhoods just 15 miles to the north.

Listening to our Neighborhood at Work and at Play

Where and how do the people in your neighborhood gather to work and play? Do they travel outside the neighborhood or work here? Where do they gather for play? Where are the third places and neutral spaces?

While Golden Hill is dominated by a residential reality, it is sprinkled with small markets, *panaderias*, restaurants, a few bars, and coffee houses. Many are locally owned and operated, and provide at least a few jobs to local residents. Our neighborhood has historically lacked gathering spaces, though a few have sprung up over the last few years, including a couple of coffee houses and bars. These have become vibrant places to see at least some of our neighborhood residents, though the type of place largely dictates who you'll see there. The local bars and coffee houses are magnets for a younger, often hipster set, with the

Latino residents almost completely absent from these places. Going to the Golden Hill Park or 28th Street Park, you'll often find Latino families picnicking or playing soccer on the weekends.

Some of our community of faith folks who were soccer players began hanging out in these places, joining pickup games, and getting to know these folks who aren't likely to go to the local pub or buy a latté at one of the local coffee houses. Eventually they started their own league, occasionally grilling dinner together after the games.

Jon Huckins, a writer, speaker, and staff member within a local missional community of faith called NieuCommunities, supplements his income by working at our local Golden Hill Farmer's Market. There he serves a practical need by managing the market, participates in an important and viable commerce side of our neighborhood, while getting to know folks. He also serves on the board that guides our neighborhood.

My wife and I, both with a strong creative bent and business background, began connecting with local artisans and makers, eventually hosting gatherings in our house where they (and we) could sell locally handcrafted items, art, and home goods. These events grew bigger and more frequent, and eventually led to the opening of a retail store, where we sell handmade and up-cycled goods by artisans in San Diego and Tijuana.

Others in our community of faith spend time each week with folks at a local halfway house in the neighborhood. They take walks with residents there, share meals, and offer friendship and guidance, when needed. Some took up the cause of getting a much-needed playground built at a local park. And a soccer-playing group within our community of faith started playing at a local park with local Latino residents. This resulted in an informal league of play at night, opening a door into a cross-cultural experience few others in the neighborhood have bridged.

For all of us, the act of listening took on an element of active, not just passive, participation. As we play or work or gather, we're also trying to listen and respond. We find often that God tends to speak loudly through these places and these people. And as we do this, we're better understanding the needs of our neighborhood, the realities of work and play, who gathers where and who doesn't, who is included and excluded, and what it looks like to bridge gaps and span boundaries. We see up-close and personal who the haves and have-nots are, as we step into spaces and realities that we might not normally step into. We see hints of who the displaced are, who's on the edge of displacement, who is taking their place, and why. And through all of this, we hear the voice of God and see his fingerprints, his promptings, and his invitation to join him where he's already at work in our neighborhood.

Interdependence and the need to Iterate

Part of the covenant of NieuCommunities is that participants live within a ten-minute walk of one another, and within the boundaries of the neighborhood. This physical act puts participants *in* the neighborhood, not always an easy task with increasing rent and few available properties. But even after those hurdles are cleared and participants find themselves living *in* the neighborhood, that doesn't make them *of* the neighborhood. And the reality of being a community that values shared life, regularly gathering, sharing meals and lives, makes the gravitational pull toward inwardness not insignificant. It is in fact a frequent challenge of Christian gatherings.

When first moving to Golden Hill, I found a welcome comfort and familiarity in the regular gatherings of our community of faith. It felt good to grow closer to those in my community of faith, to know and be known, to share the realities of living in a neighborhood like ours. One of the challenges of this exclusive intimacy, though, is the potential of widening the Us and Them gap. Overcoming this gap requires a regular, intentional outward effort.

Seeking Interdependence

In a culture that puts a high value on independence, seeking interdependence can feel counter-intuitive. Missional faith communities can be a great step toward interdependence with community members. But if we're to truly seek becoming part of the fabric of the neighborhood, not just living in the neighborhood, we've found we need to seek an interdependent relationship with others.

Interdependent relationships can feel risky and uncertain, and they can require giving up some degree of control and giving ourselves to those we're in relationship with. Some within NieuCommunities have taken steps toward interdependent relationships by joining local planning groups, working for local businesses, and participating in community events and planning. Some have pursued long-term relationships with local centers that provide rehabilitation and substance abuse treatment, building friendships and partnerships through that process. And a few soccer enthusiasts created an informal league with Latino *futbol* players in our community, playing every week and often sharing a meal afterward.

When my wife and I opened our retail store here, we knew its success and long-term sustainability would depend on an interdependent relationship with people in and around our neighborhood, as well as our vendors and suppliers. We made the choice to sell only locally made merchandise (from the San Diego/ Tijuana region), hire employees living in the neighborhood, and participate in community—and city-related events. Now a few years into this venture, we've grown to deeply appreciate the realities of what it means to enter into interdependent relationships with our customers, our artisan/vendors, and our employees. We've found it to be filled with as many unexpected opportunities as uncertainties, and it has allowed us to become part of the fabric of the neighborhood in ways nothing else could.

Interdependent relationships require a certain element of risk. We're putting ourselves in the hands of others, staking at least part of our success on them, and theirs on us. I've found few other methods that embed us into the fabric of a community as well, or as deeply.

Iterative Experimentation.

In the fields of science, engineering, and software development, an iterative approach to experimentation, development and creation has been around for some time. The idea is simple: Try small experiments, learn from them, then try again (based on your learning). The iterative process favors agility, speed, and small efforts, always with an eye to learn what's working and what's not.

Even after we've listened and learned well to our neighborhood, and perhaps have a sense of where, how, and through whom we sense God may be at work, acting on those findings can be daunting. This is where an iterative approach can be more than helpful.

The process of moving from an interest in the creative subculture of San Diego to opening a retail store was an iterative process. We took small but deliberate steps. Our first step was seeking creative events, art and music gatherings, and people. Accepting invitations to join others in what they were already doing came next. Collaborating with a handful of local folks from the neighborhood to begin creating something new followed. We tried to embrace a comfortable (but deliberate and consistent) rhythm. Along the way we made mistakes, we tried things that didn't work or were ill-fitting. We also found a few things that seemed right, met some amazing people, and said yes to invitations. Opportunities presented themselves, doors opened, and we walked through.

Small iterative experiments also mean small risks. When something didn't work out as we expected, it was rarely a tragedy. As things have grown, some risks have indeed increased, but we continue to iterate, test, measure, and try new things, letting go of what doesn't work well and looking for that which does.

Chapter 20

The Church's Response to Gentrification
Caleb Crider

The cycle of gentrification affects all the citizens of a neighborhood, including churches. How should the church respond to gentrification? What is a Christ-like posture for a local church on either side of the demographic shift? To begin, let's consider how the typical church fares in the gentrification cycle:

Birth, Change, Flight, Repeat

The development of an urban center has almost always included a house of worship. In the "Christian" West, typical architectural cues make this particularly clear: the center of every village, town, and city is marked with the steeples of church buildings. It makes sense, if you think about it, that sacred buildings would be designed in such a way as to communicate their purpose. They aren't just buildings, they're statements: a spire communicates the presence of religious people in the community.

Historically, as people moved into burgeoning cities, they tended to look for communities of faith that resembled those they came from. In its early days, San Francisco (a city named for the Catholic mission that started it) had many churches. First United Methodist downtown was a draw to all the Methodists arriving in the city. This was especially true of immigrant groups, where German, Dutch, and Scandinavian churches became the centers of community life for newcomers of those nationalities. Increased attendance usually meant increased giving, and churches tended to build newer, larger buildings to accommodate their growing numbers.

After a few generations of life, urban churches tended to benefit from their community's population explosion. But, as it approaches the end of its life-cycle, a once-thriving city center begins to suffer the side-effects of dense population: more traffic and crime, higher costs of living, fewer jobs. More people are coming to church, but things become crowded and less personal. Urban churches are caught off-guard as unexpected diversity threatens their unity.

Then comes the flight. Those who can afford to leave (businessmen, property owners, politicians) begin to move out into the suburbs where they can buy larger houses and live in planned neighborhoods that feel comfortable and safe. The departure of community leaders and business owners speeds the rate of decline in the inner city. Those who make decisions for the city now live a comfortable distance from it.

Churches lose their best tithers to suburban church plants. Those who stay connected to the church commute as far as fifty miles each Sunday. Having a non-resident membership drastically affects the mindset of the church. As the demographics of the church's surrounding neighborhoods change, church members begin to view the inner city as hostile. Now-valuable property is sold off to generate enough revenue to keep the lights on. The church's footprint shrinks, along with its influence, involvement, and presence in the community.

But then, as we see in cities around the world, comes the return. Starting with the most creative, adventurous, and open-minded, the children of those who fled the city centers begin to return to the city center. Having more money and education, the urban immigrants begin to move back into the city, buying what is now depressed property, opening a business, and displacing the inner-city-dwellers. This is the beginning of gentrification, and churches haven't done a very good job of navigating it.

As bohemians move into the depressed neighborhoods, they encounter churches that are all but dead. Remaining church members rarely show interest in the sort of revitalization desired by the gentrifiers. Having failed to demonstrate their relevance, churches tend to be marginalized in the process. Oftentimes the only interaction between the new urban creative class and a local church is when the church rejects the artisan's offer to buy the church's property.

Eventually old churches die out, and new churches are planted among the new, upwardly-mobile urban residents. The cycle begins again by destroying the fabric of the old neighborhood and rebuilding it with homogeneous neo-urban tribes. Transplants from the suburbs make a go of being an urban church until they retreat again to the safety and convenience of suburban life.

Two Steps Behind

As we see, the church's typical response to the life cycle of a community is to react slowly to the change. Always two (or more!) steps behind, a local congregation ends up struggling for survival instead of proactively leading their neighbors through the change. Catching up with the community is made all the more difficult due to some of the "baggage" churches end up carrying. When a church orients its life around unnecessary things that distract it from its identity in Christ, these things become every bit an idol for the church as carved stone statues may be for a pagan temple.

Consider, for example, the Western Church's tendency to own property and build houses of worship. Church buildings, of course, are not inherently bad. For hundreds of years, God has led His people to gather in buildings dedicated to the work of the church. But has "nesting" in buildings negatively affected the church's understanding of how it is to relate to the world?

Take the typical American urban church; in most cases, the building, located in the city center, is only used for worship services on Sundays and sits empty during the rest of the week. The parishioners of most American churches drive to church, with requires parking lots and bus "ministries." As a result, the geographic, financial, and environmental footprint of a church can be tremendous. Congregations outlive local businesses and social organizations that could never afford to operate this way. Temporarily isolated from the economic effects of urban change, churches become disconnected from the realities of their contexts.

As the demographics of the neighborhood surrounding the church property change, churches tend to be slow to respond. Some start schools and social ministries or begin to allow other groups to use the facility. This is why many churches share or lease their space to ethnic congregations, Alcoholics

Anonymous meetings, preschools, and the like. But these efforts at outreach and community involvement often have a negative affect on how church members view their neighbors.

Use by non-church members during the week results in heavy wear on the building and equipment. The founding members come to resent seeing the facilities they paid for fall into disrepair. "Those people" just don't respect "God's house." Of course, a building in distress invites vandalism, break-ins, and further misuse. Maintenance costs go up, while income in the form of tithes and offerings go down. The occasional church grounds "work day" isn't sufficient anymore. The building that once seemed to be such a blessing now seems like a burden.

As the makeup of a church diversifies and devolves with the community, many members leave to join churches in the suburbs. There is an allure to worshiping closer to home with people "more like us." Christians justify such moves as being "best for their families"; suburban churches offer programs for children, students, and families. In many cases, these churches were started by splinter groups from the city-center churches. They are comfortable, professional, and offer a variety of worship times and styles to suit their preference and convenience.

Left behind at the downtown location, then, are the older people (who may feel that they have invested too much to leave), minority groups, lower-income people, the marginalized, and those who began to attend as a result of the social ministries and ethnic outreach. The makeup of the church changes, and resources are depleted. Churches are left with dilapidated grounds that require costly renovations to meet the building codes required for occupancy permits or lease contracts. Unable to maintain the services and facilities, the urban congregation finally dies out. The building sits empty until gentrification changes the demographic once again and the property regains value.

Now typically, this is when speculators and entrepreneurs move in. The former church building is bought by other groups and turned into a New Age center, a mosque, a nightclub, a pub. At some point it's used as a real estate office, an insurance agency, and a daycare center. Developers see potential in the location and petition for rezoning and remodeling for use as urban lofts or commercial space. If the building is beyond repair, it's bulldozed and turned into a strip mall.

In the end, the neighborhood is left with no Christian presence. God's people have retreated to the suburbs. Remaining church buildings stand as monuments to a failed religion.

Certainly the church has more "baggage" than just its buildings. Things like money, programs, tax status—even the freedom to gather—all impact a church's behavior and cloud our perspective of who the Church is supposed to be in the world. Despite the Lord's admonition that we remain "unencumbered," the stuff we own weighs us down, keeping us two steps behind the communities in which we live.

A Better Response to Gentrification

Gentrification is part of the natural ebb and flow of urban context. It is one side of the life cycle of a city. On the one hand, gentrification is a natural phenomenon. Cities are living, dynamic things, so demographic change may well be an inevitability. But God's people must work to minimize the negative effects of the cycle. We must seek the "prosperity and peace of the city" (Jeremiah 29:7). This requires that we rethink our theology, philosophy, and practice as they relate to our dynamic, ever-changing communities.

Theology of Place

First and foremost, the Church must develop a better understanding of why it matters where we live. A theology of place, as Tim Keller calls it, provides us a framework upon which to build a local expression of church. When we begin to recognize the importance of our sent-ness– the value of being where we are– we can move ourselves into the social center of our communities, tying our welfare to that of those around us. In this way, we can be salt and light. We can rejoice with those who rejoice and mourn with those who mourn. This is incarnation, and it is the posture and attitude every church should take.

Buildings

Most city churches meet in a dedicated building/space for worship. During a time of transition in the community, the value of that property will change. To meet the needs of church members and the surrounding neighborhood, the use of the property should change as well. But with no real sense of location, and no theology of "place," most churches default to an isolationist mentality–defending the church's property against those who may not consider it sacred. This is why churches across the United States fall into conflict over things like pews vs. chairs or determining what is appropriate use of the fellowship hall.

When a church is in tune with its community, it knows when change is coming. When the neighborhood reaches the (inevitable?) end of its life cycle, it becomes depressed, unsafe, and hostile. Living there can become difficult. But rather than fleeing a struggling community, a church has a choice: respond as others have by moving to more stable places, or stay and react to the changes with love, grace, and hard work.

Every time I visited a church in a major city, I see the same thing: bars on the windows. It usually begins with a break-in—local youth stealing some sound equipment in the middle of the night. The church feels violated, and installs some form of security against local thieves. In one sense, this makes good sense—good stewardship calls for the protection of our property. But what does it communicate to the neighborhood when a church barricades itself against it? Inner-city churches don't need to put bars on the windows of their buildings. The alternative, of course, may be to suffer theft and vandalism, but what would that say to the community (which is also likely to be victimized by theft and vandalism)? Every choice a church makes can communicate either solidarity with or animosity toward its neighborhood.

Values

Ask most Christians how they decided where to live, and you're likely to get an answer that sounds very similar to prevailing secular wisdom: low crime, good schools, best value. But are these criteria—safety, comfort, and storing up treasures here on earth—consistent with the life Christ calls us to? As God's people, we cannot live our lives according to the values of society. This includes how and where we choose to live. A good theology of place would seek to use Kingdom values for determining our lifestyles.

This may mean that church members deliberately move into economically depressed neighborhoods in order to be a redemptive force there. It may mean enrolling our children in public schools even though the alternatives may be safer and more academically challenging. It might mean learning a new sport, belonging to an out-of-date gym, or shopping at a rundown grocery store. When the people of God apply Kingdom values to the decisions that shape their lives, they become deeply integrated into their communities.

The Gathering is Both Sacred and Redemptive

When I was a kid, an elderly man in our church, Mr. Wall, took it upon himself to police the congregation and protect the sacredness of the church building. He confronted anyone who wore shorts or ball caps into the auditorium (or sanctuary, as he preferred to call it). He didn't allow open-eyed prayer, chewing gum, or running in the halls. I'm sure he was a good and godly man, but the only thing I remember about him was being sorely afraid of him.

What Mr. Wall failed to understand was that it was the gathering, not the building, that was sacred. When a church gathers, the Most High God is there among them. The very soil beneath them is holy ground. If they truly understand this, a church can begin to break out of their dependence on a specific location and begin to recognize their role as priests in their communities. A theology of place recognizes the redemptive power of the gathering itself.

When our small church in Portland, OR, met in the neighborhood pub for our summer study of the Book of Romans, we weren't just trying to "be a witness" by reading our Bibles in public. We were cognizant of the fact that our presence as a church was both challenging and healing to the neighbors who frequented that place. We knew that ungodly things were sometimes celebrated there in that establishment—just a few days prior tone of our studies, the pub hosted a meeting of the Wiccan Society—and that was part of the reason why we met there. We were also aware that the pub was a center of social activity in the neighborhood. Families ate dinner there, friends got together there, book clubs met there. A church can be part of its community by meeting in that community. By serving it, caring for it, and investing in it.

Sentness

In Christ, we are all sent. We identify with the Sent One, and our salvation seals our citizenship in God's kingdom. Jesus adopts us into His family, making us outsiders. But human culture doesn't leave us the option of objectivity—it would be impossible to talk or think about God without culture's lens of language, history, and worldview. So we don't have the option of leaving culture, but we can't simply be passive participants in it, either. No, the Christian life is one of motion and momentum. Christ-followers aren't where they are by accident. You were sent to where you are.

Because we are sent, we must learn to think and act like missionaries. Doing so requires a different perspective on things. We must use a different set of criteria to make decisions about things like where to live, what job to take, or how to manage our money. Instead of comfort, education, security, and material things, our criteria are calling/obedience, opportunity, community (church/team decisions), need, incarnation, sacrifice. When we recognize our identity as sent-ones, we see our schools, streets, and places of business as our mission fields. We work to understand the people in our cities and to get to know them. So when gentrification comes, we are there to help the community navigate the change. This is our responsibility because we have been sent here for this very reason.

Leading Through Change

So how, then, can a local church lead a community as it weathers the process of gentrification?

We must start by knowing our neighbors. When the people in our communities are nameless strangers to us, it can be very difficult to feel compassion for their hopeless states outside of Christ. Too many churches view their neighbors as statistics and demographics rather than as people. Consequently, we tend to carry a distorted view of those around us.

In order to truly get to know our neighbors, we must take the initiative to meet and interact with them. Fortunately, there is no shortage of opportunity to do just that. A quick perusal of meeting sites such as meetup.com or the online classified ads site craigslist.com reveal a long list of possibilities for personal interaction. Social tribes of every sort are actively looking for new members. Love trying a new restaurant every weekend? There's a restaurant club looking for new foodies. Interested in learning to fly-fish? The Stream Anglers Society is now recruiting.

These social gatherings and events are open invitations to real relationships, and they are excellent opportunities to get to know the people who live in your city. When you are dealing with real people you know and care about, your response to gentrification is likely to be very different than if you simply see people as projects and numbers.

Insure Indigeneity

Another way the church can prepare for urban change is to insure its indigeneity.

As a foundational principle, a local church should reflect the soil in which it's planted. Too often, churches look nothing like the communities in which they live. Indigeneity is the result of a contextualized approach to church life. When someone from the neighborhood walks into an indigenous church, they aren't leaving their own culture for some transplanted "Christian" culture, but rather moving into a redemptive version of the culture they move in every day.

Indigeneity begins with the rhythms of the local church. Traditions tend to be established very early in the life of a church. Things like when the group meets and where are often decided without much thought. Though these things may seem inconsequential, they dramatically affect the culture gap between the church and its community.

Take, for example, the built environment of the neighborhood. How do the design, layout, and architecture of an area affect how church is done there? Does walking onto the ground of the church feel like leaving the neighborhood, or does it give the visitor the impression of entering into the epitome of the community? How does transportation factor into how you do things? In *The Bikeable Church*, Sean Benesh highlights the importance of adapting our church models to the transportation modes used in our communities. This is the kind of thing that differentiates an indigenous church from an imported one.

As the face of the community changes, the makeup of a church should reflect that change. As younger people move in, churches need to move them into leadership. As the creative class settles, their contribution should be incorporated into the expression of church. Every step of the way, the church assumes a new outward appearance in keeping with the renewal of the neighborhood.

Of course, the goal here is not to "get ahead" of the gentrification curve. It would be foolish and reckless to dismiss the existing leadership of a church simply because they represent the "old neighborhood." Here, the church acts as a bridge between what was and what is coming. It won't do to fight for the old neighborhood- that would estrange us from the new. Likewise, it would be destructive and irresponsible to abandon the legacy of local residents.

Protecting indigeneity takes constant effort. It can be especially difficult as a community weathers gentrifying change. But the church, in order to be salt and light, has no other choice but to adapt to its environment. Again, the goal of indigeneity is to model God's Kingdom in this place. The church cannot mimic the culture in a half-hearted effort to stay relevant. No, it must truly be a redeemed version of the local culture. In order to do this, we must keep in mind Kingdom values such as the wisdom of experience and the innocence of youth. The proper place of the church in culture is to be deep in the middle of it. Only from the vantage point of willful immersion can we discern between the positive and negative aspects of gentrification.

Promote the Good, Fight the Bad

The key to leading a community though change is to go through it with them. It is promoting the good, which, in the case of gentrification, may include greater resources, lower crime, better schools, and higher property values, and actively resisting the bad, namely displacement, segregation, classism, and racism.

Gentrification can have very positive effects on a neighborhood. As creative, connected, and educated people move in, new businesses are opened, resources stream in, and community involvement increases. Tying its well-being to that of the community, a church should promote these positive changes by connecting newer residents with higher levels of free time and disposable income to those areas of the community that could use more time and money. It should become involved in the conversation around urban revitalization and renewal, and offer ideas for moving into the future.

On the other hand, however, is the negative impact of gentrification. The church should do what it can to stand in the way of the exploitation, division, and marginalization that often accompany such change. One common effect of gentrification is globalization and the "generickification" that accompanies it. Local restaurants are replaced with national chains that are more familiar to those who are moving in to the neighborhood. Big-box home improvement stores open to serve homeowners and developers remodeling homes and businesses. Before too long, every shopping district is the same: chain restaurants, global coffee shops, international banks, and massive discount retailers. These threats to the welfare of the local businesses and culture should be resisted by local churches.

Churches As Agents Of Change

Ultimately, the local church is to be an agent of change. Our mission is to make disciples, to teach them to obey all that Christ has taught us. This makes us agents of change. We want to see people come to Christ, but we also want to see families restored, relationships reconciled, and people moved into community. Gentrification is change. The role of the Church is to identify with their communities and minister to them through that change, and to make the change as positive as possible.

Afterword

Sean Benesh

Perspective is everything. The way that is true in terms of this book and Portland particularly is that the *where* determines the *how* of the conversation on gentrification. Since most of my life revolves around life in central city and downtown Portland I am affected by this geographic reality. In other words, when talking about gentrification in a hipster coffee shop full of white hipsters it taints and flavors the conversation and framework a bit. Conversely, writing today from NE 82nd Avenue in a McDonalds that is sandwiched between strip clubs and where right now all the patrons of this fast food eatery are Hispanic or Asian also affects the conversation and framework. With no hip coffee shops or brew pubs in sight the discourse on gentrification certainly is cast in a different light.

Several things have transpired since the genesis of this book two years ago. First of all, we have continued to settle into the life and rhythms of Portland. We have finally and fully made the transition from an immigrant and refugee neighborhood to life in the central city of Portland. This is home and we have grown to love this city as we did Vancouver, albeit in a much different way. Both cities, while regionally are somewhat neighbors, are still culturally distinct in many ways. I feel like an "insider" now here in Portland especially given my love and passion for all-thing bicycling.

Secondly, what has impacted much of my thinking has been my continued journey in higher education. In 2010 I graduated with my Doctor of Ministry from Bakke Graduate University. It was (and still is) a life-changing experience for me as I learned to think theologically and biblically about the city more than ever before. Three weeks after arriving in Portland in 2011 I transitioned to begin work on a PhD in Urban Studies at Portland State University. It was a quick and abrupt change from seminary education to state university education. While I am still a long ways off from completing my degree (at least it feels that way) I have learned much and have continued to be impacted and transformed by these experiences and educational opportunities regardless if I finish or not.

I bring this up because my education is directly tied to this book and our approach and framework for responding to the topic of gentrification. Throughout the book I have made it my goal to present the importance of Gospel proclamation and Gospel demonstration. I hope that I communicated the need to view that the supposed dichotomy between the spiritual and the physical is merely a self-imposed philosophical construct. In realty everything is spiritual but with physical implications while everything physical has spiritual implications. I have read much on the topic of gentrification over the past few years, most of which (almost all) was from the academic community. I am deeply appreciative of the numerous attempts to study, research, and understand all of the nuances associated with gentrification. It has been humbling to read scholar after scholar crying out for an equitable gentrification and for the least and the last to be given a voice and preferential treatment. This is near and dear to God's heart.

But what I have also seen is that every attempt to address and rectify gentrification without acknowledging the spiritual falls short. We have broken families, broken neighborhoods, and broken cities because of the spiritual reality of sin and the resultant alienation from God, from one another, and from creation (including cities). In addressing gentrification I am all-in on economic development, a better and more vibrant built environment, social mixing, equity in housing, better schools, and so forth, but it cannot and should never be divorced from the Gospel presentation. The movement from Genesis to Revelation is Creation, Fall, Redemption, and Restoration. The Gospel is the Good News of a God *who came* to set right what was wrecked by original sin.

When we enter into the gentrification debates we should do so armed with these truths and these realities. We are inherently spiritual and within everyone is stamped the *imago Dei*. Let us seek the welfare of our cities in humility and grace.

Appendix

Table 1 Sample Demographics N = 2023

	Frequency	*Percent (%)*	*M*	*SD*
Sex				
Male	929	45.9		
Female	1094	54.1		
Age			47.7	17.35
18 to 24	184	9.1		
25 to 34	347	17.2		
35 to 44	379	18.8		
45 to 54	414	20.6		
55 to 64	314	15.6		
65 to 74	208	10.3		
75 / older	167	8.3		
Missing from system	10	.5		

Race		
White	1545	76.8
Black	280	13.9
American Indian	27	1.3
Asian/Pacific Islander	70	3.5
Hispanic	83	4.1
Other race	7	.3
Missing from system	11	.5
Religion		
Protestant	1040	51.6
Catholic	470	23.3
Other Christian	78	3.9
Jewish	39	1.9
None	332	16.5
Eastern/ Islam	38	1.6
Other	17	.8
Missing from system	9	.4

Table 2 Cross-tabulation Recoded Religion * Recoded Age

			Recoded Age							
			18 to 24	25 to 34	35 to 44	45 to 54	55 to 64	65 to 74	75 and older	Total
Recoded Religion	Protestant	Count	73	139	166	235	186	130	107	1036
		% within Recoded Age	39.7%	40.2%	44.3%	57.0%	59.4%	62.5%	64.5%	51.7%
	Catholic	Count	43	82	99	79	71	47	44	465
		% within Recoded Age	23.4%	23.7%	26.4%	19.2%	22.7%	22.6%	26.5%	23.2%
	Other Christian	Count	8	16	21	16	11	3	3	78
		% within Recoded Age	4.3%	4.6%	5.6%	3.9%	3.5%	1.4%	1.8%	3.9%
	Jewish	Count	4	7	8	6	5	6	3	39
		% within Recoded Age	2.2%	2.0%	2.1%	1.5%	1.6%	2.9%	1.8%	1.9%
	None	Count	52	89	63	67	33	19	8	331
		% within Recoded Age	28.3%	25.7%	16.8%	16.3%	10.5%	9.1%	4.8%	16.5%
	Eastern/ Islam	Count	2	8	16	4	5	2	1	38
		% within Recoded Age	1.1%	2.3%	4.3%	1.0%	1.6%	1.0%	.6%	1.9%
	Other	Count	2	5	2	5	2	1	0	17
		% within Recoded Age	1.1%	1.4%	.5%	1.2%	.6%	.5%	.0%	.8%
Total		Count	184	346	375	412	313	208	166	2004
		% within Recoded Age	100.0%	100.0%	100.0%	100.0%	100.0%	100.0%	100.0%	100.0%

305

Figure 1: Sex and Recoded Religion

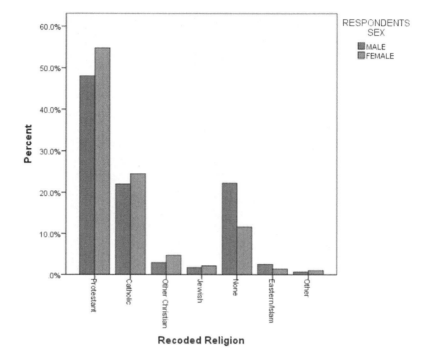

Figure 2: Recoded Age and Recoded Religion

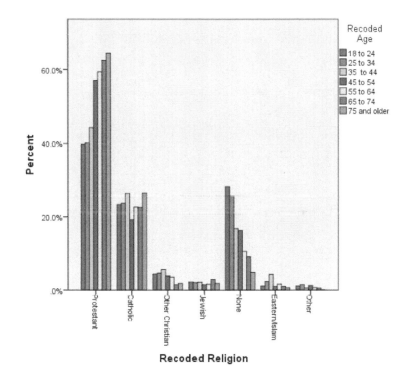

Figure 3: Recoded Race and Recoded Religion

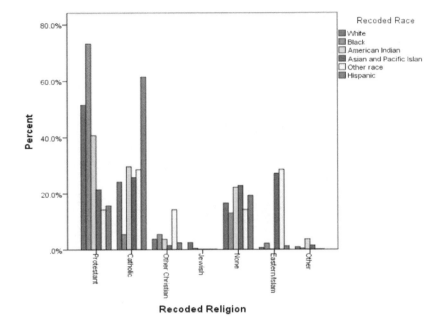

Bibliography

Alonso, William. "Location Theory." In *Regional Development and Planning: A Reader*, edited by John Friedmann and William Alonso, 35-63. Cambridge: The MIT Press, 1964.

Argenta Community Development Corporation. "About Us." Online: http://www.argentacdc .org/about.shtml.

Atkinson, Rowland and Gary Bridge. "Globalisation and the New Urban Colonialism." In *The Gentrification Debates*, edited by Japonica Brown-Saracino, 51-61. New York: Routledge, 2010.

Baker, Linda. "Developers Cater to Two-Wheeled Traffic in Portland, Ore." *New York Times*, September 20, 2011. Online: http://www.nytimes.com/2011/09/21/business/portland-ore-developments-cater-to-bicycle-riders.html?pagewanted=all&_r=1&.

Bakke, Raymond J. *A Theology as Big as the City*. Downers Grove: IVP Academic, 1997.

Barcelona Field Studies Centre. "GCSE Industry Glossary." Online: http://geographyfieldwork.com/GeographyVocabularyGCSEIndustry.htm.

Barnes, Kendall, et al. "Community and Nostalgia in Urban Revitalization: A Critique of Urban Village and Creative Class Strategies as Remedies for Social 'Problems.'" *Australian Geographer* 37:3 (2006) 335-354.

Beaudry, M. "Où demeures-tu?" In *L'urbanization à l'époque du Fer*, edited by J. Charron, 31-51. Montréal : Fidès, 1994.

Ben-Joseph, Eran. *Rethinking A Lot: The Design and Culture of Parking*. Cambridge: The MIT Press, 2012.

Benesh, Sean. *Metrospiritual: The Geography of Church Planting*. Eugene: Resource, 2011.

_____. *View From the Urban Loft: Developing a Theological Framework for Understanding the City*. Eugene: Resource, 2011.

_____. *The Multi-Nucleated Church: Towards a Theoretical Framework for Church Planting in High-Density Cities*. Portland: Urban Loft, 2012.

_____. "When Gentrification is a Good Thing." *The Urban Loft*. Blog site no longer active.

Bereitschaft, Bradley. "Midlands Voices: Omaha's quality of living appeals to 'Creative Class.'" *The Omaha World Herald*, March 10, 2013. Online: http://www.omaha.com/article/20130310/NEWS0802/703109955.

Bletterman, Linda. "Who are the gentrifiers in new-build gentrification?: A study on the 'Kop van Zuid'-developments in Rotterdam, the Netherlands." Masters thesis, University of Utrecht, 2010.

Bonilla-Silva, Eduardo. *Racism Without Racists: Color-Blind Racism and the Persistence of Racial Inequality in the United States*. Rowman & Littlefield, 2006.

Bosch, David J. *Transforming Mission: Paradigm Shifts in Theology of Mission*. Maryknoll: Orbis, 1991.

Brock, Charles. *Indigenous Church Planting: A Practical Journey*. Neosho: Church Growth International, 1991.

Brown-Saracino, Japonica "Social Preservationists and the Quest for Authentic Community." In *The Gentrification Debates*, edited by Japonica Brown-Saracino, 261-275. New York: Routledge, 2010.

Brugmann, Jeb. *Welcome to the Urban Revolution: How Cities are Changing the World*. Toronto: Viking Canada, 2009.

Bunnell, T., et al. "Kuala Lumpur metropolitan area: A globalizing city–region." *Cities* 19:5 (2002) 357–370.

Butler, Tim. "Consumption and Culture." In *The Gentrification Debates*, edited by Japonica Brown-Saracino, 235-260. New York: Routledge, 2010.

Cassidy, Sarah. "'Super-gentrifers' ruin integration." *The Independent*, September 1, 2006. Online: http://www.independent.co.uk/news/uk/politics/supergentrifiers-ruin-integration-414219.html.

Chapman, Keith and David Walker. *Industrial Location: Principles and Policy*. London: Basil Blackwell, 1991.

Charbonneau, Johanne, et al. *Habiter seul: un nouveau mode de vie?* Québec: Les Presses de l'Université Laval, 2009.

Chong, Emma. "The Gentrification of KL - Around Town." *Timoeut KL*, July 24, 2012. Online: http://www.timeoutkl.com/aroundtown/articles/The-gentrification-of-KL.

City Club of Portland. "Case Study: North Williams Avenue." Online: http://pdxcityclub.org/2013/Report/Portland-Bicycle-Transit/2013/Report/Case-Study-North-Williams-Avenue.

Claiborne, Ron. "Somali Refugees Settle in Maine Town." *ABC News*. Online: http://abcnews.go.com/WNT/story?id=130098&page=1.

Claiborne, Shane and Chris Haw. *Jesus for President: Politics for Ordinary Radicals*. Grand Rapids: Zondervan, 2008.

Conn, Harvie M. and Manuel Ortiz. *Urban Ministry: The Kingdom, the City, & the People of God*. Downers Grove: InterVarsity, 2001.

Conradson, David. "Expressions of Charity and Action towards Justice: Faith-based Welfare Provision in Urban New Zealand." *Urban Studies* 45:10 (2008) 2117-2141.

Cordeiro, Wayne. *Sifted: Pursuing Growth through Trials, Challenges, and Disappointments.* Grand Rapids: Zondervan, 2012.

Crain, Liz. "Portland's North Williams Avenue." *Via Magazine*, July/August 2011. Online: http://www.viamagazine.com/destinations/portlands-north-williams-avenue.

Crot, Laurence. "'Scenographic' and 'Cosmetic' Planning: Globalization and Territorial Restructuring in Buenos Aires." *Journal of Urban Affairs* 28:3 (2006) 227–251.

Currid, Elizabeth. "How Art and Culture Happen in New York: Implications for Urban Economic Development." *Journal of the American Planning Association* 73:4 (2007) 454-467.

Davey, Andrew. *Urban Christianity and Global Order: Theological Resources for an Urban Future.* Peabody: Hendrickson, 2002.

————. *Crossover City:Resources for Urban Mission and Transformation.* New York: Mowbray, 2010.

Dear, Michael. *From Chicago to L.A.: Making Sense of Urban Theory.* Thousand Oaks: Sage, 2001.

de Gruchy, John W. *Christianity, Art and Transformation: Theological Aesthetics in the Struggle for Justice.* Cambridge: Cambridge University Press, 2008.

DeVerteuil, Geoffrey. "Reconsidering the Legacy of Urban Public Facility Location Theory in Human Geography." *Progress in Human Geography* 24: 1 (2000) 47-69.

Donegan, Mary, et al. "Which Indicators Explain Metropolitan Economic Performance Best?: Traditional or Creative Class." *Journal of the American Planning Association* 74:2 (2008) 180-195.

Durkeim, Emile. *The Division of Labor in Society.* Translated by G. Simpson. 1893. New York: The Free Press, 1964.

Edwards, Joel. *An Agenda for Change: A Global Call for Spiritual and Social Transformation.* Grand Rapids: Zondervan, 2008.

England, Kim and John Mercer. "The Canadian City in Continental Context." In *Canadian Cities in Transition*, edited by Trudi Bunting and Pierre Filion, 24-39. Toronto: Oxford University Press, 2006.

Ergun, Nilgun. "Gentrification in Istanbul." *Cities* 21:5 (2004) 391–405.

Estep, William. *Renaissance and Reformation.* Grand Rapids: Eerdmans, 1986.

Fischer, Claude. *The Urban Experience.* San Diego: Harcourt Brace Jovanovich, 1984.

Flanagan, William G. *Urban Sociology: Images and Structure.* Lanham: Rowman & Littlefield, 2010.

Florida, Richard. *The Rise of the Creative Class: And How It's Transforming Work, Leisure, Community and Everyday Life.* New York: Basic, 2004.

_____. *Cities and the Creative Class.* New York: Routledge, 2005.

_____. *Who's Your City?: How the Creative Economy is Making Where We Live the Most Important Decision of Your Life.* New York: Basic, 2008.

_____. "Detroit Shows Way to Beat Inner City Blues." *Financial Times*, April 9, 2013. Online: http://www.ft.com/intl/cms/s/0/7c1692b6-9c71-11e2-ba3c-00144feabdc0.html#axzz2QkzU3JeA.

Fogelson, Robert M. *Downtown: Its Rise and Fall, 1880-1950.* New Haven: Yale University Press, 2001.

Gallagher, John. *Reimagining Detroit: Opportunities for Redefining an American City.* Detroit: Wayne State University Press, 2010.

Germain, Annick and Damaris Rose. *Montréal: The Quest for a Metropolis.* West Sussex: John Wiley and Sons, 2000.

Gibson, Karen J. "Bleeding Albina: A History of Community Disinvestment, 1940-2000." *Transforming Anthropology* 15:1 (2007) 3-25.

Glaeser, Edward L. *Triumph of the City: How Our Greatest Invention Makes Us Richer, Smarter, Greener, Healthier, and Happier.* New York: Penguin, 2011.

_____ and Janet E. Kohlhase, "Cities, Regions and the Decline of Transport Costs," *Papers in Regional Science* 83 (2004) 197-228.

Goldberg, Michael A. and John Mercer. *The Myth of the North American City: Continentalism Challenged.* Vancouver: UBC Press, 1986.

Goodman, Earnest. "Where You Live Matters," *Missions Misunderstood*, January 27, 2011. Online: http://missionsmisunderstood.com/2011/01/27/where-you-live-matters/.

Goodyear, Sarah. "Bike Lane Backlash, Even in Portland." *The Atlantic Cities*, September 20, 2011. Online: http://www.theatlanticcities.com/neighborhoods/2011/09/portland-bike-lanes-open-racial-wounds/138/.

_____. "The Trendification of Brooklyn and the Perils of a Successful Urban Brand." *The Atlantic Cities*, August 16, 2012. Online: http://www.theatlanticcities.com/neighborhoods/2012/08/trendification-brooklyn-and-perils-successful-urban-brand/2973/.

_____. "The Surprising Diversity of the America Cycling Community." *The Atlantic Cities*, May 29, 2013. Online: http://www.theatlanticcities.com/commute/2013/05/surprising-diversity-american-cycling-community/5737/.

Gordon, Wayne. "Gentrification: The Good News and the Bad News." In *A Heart for the Community: New Models for Urban and Suburban Ministry*, edited by John Fuder and Noel Castellanos, 39-49. Chicago: Moody, 2009.

Greenfield, John. "Bike facilities don't have to be 'the white lanes of gentrification.'" *Grid Chicago*, May 10, 2012. Online: http://gridchicago.com/2012/bike-facilities-dont-have-to-be-the-white-lanes-of-gentrification/.

Greentstone, M., et al. "Identifying Agglomeration Spillovers: Evidence From Winners and Losers of Large Plant Openings." *Journal of Political Economy* 118 (2010) 536-598.

Grigg, Viv. *The Spirit of Christ and the Postmodern City*. Lexington: Emeth, 2009.

Grogan, Geoffrey W. *Isaiah*. In *The Expositor's Bible Commentary, Volume 6*, edited by Frank E. Gaebelein. Grand Rapids: Zondervan 1986.

Guinness, Os. *The Call: Finding and Fulfilling the Central Purpose of Your Life*. Nashville: Thomas Nelson, 2003.

Hackworth, Jason and Josephine Rekers. "Ethnic Packaging and Gentrification: The Case of Four Neighborhoods in Toronto." *Urban Affairs Review* 41:2 (2005) 211-236.

Hall, Peter. *Cities in Civilisation*. London: Orion, 2006.

Harper, Douglas. "Bohemian." *Online Etymology Dictionary*. Online: http://www.etymonline.com/index.php?term=bohemian&allowed_in_frame=0.

Harper, Stephen R. *They're Just Not That Into You: The Church's Struggle for Relevancy in the 21st Century*. Portland: Urban Loft, 2012.

Harris, Andrew. "From London to Mumbai and Back Again: Gentrification and Public Policy in Comparative Perspective." *Urban Studies* 45:12 (2008) 2407–2428.

Hays, Richard B. *The Moral Vision of the New Testament: Community, Cross, New CreationA Contemporary Introduction to New Testament Ethic*. New York: HarperOne, 2013.

He, Shenjing. "State-sponsored Gentrification Under Market Transition The Case of Shanghai." *Urban Affairs Review* 43:2 (2007) 171–198.

Helland, Roger and Leonard Hjalmarson. *Missional Spirituality: Embodying God's Love from the Inside Out*. Downers Grove: IVP, 2011.

Henley, Colby. commented on Sean Benesh, "Excerpt From View From the Urban Loft." *The Urban Loft*, December 21, 2011. Blog site no longer active.

Heying, Charles. *Brew to Bikes: Portland's Artisan Economy*. Portland: Ooligan, 2010.

Hiebert, Paul, "Critical Contextualization." *International Bulletin of Missionary Research* 11:3 (1987) 104-112.

_____ and Eloise Meneses. *Incarnational Ministry: Planting Churches in Band, Tribal, Peasant, and Urban Societies*. Grand Rapids: Baker, 1995.

Hiller, Harry H. *Urban Canada*. New York: Oxford University Press, 2009.

Hinton, Keith. *Growing Churches Singapore Style Ministry in an Urban Context*. Littleton: OMF, 1985.

Huckins, Jon: *Thin Places: Six Postures for Creating and Practicing Missional Community*. Kansas City: The House Studio, 2012.

Hunter, George G. III. *The Celtic Way of Evangelism: How Christianity Can Reach the West ... Again*. Nashville: Abingdon, 2010.

Igarta, Denver. "Livable Streets." Presentation at Portland State University, Portland, Oregon, April 11, 2012.

Jacobsen, Eric O. *Sidewalks in the Kingdom: New Urbanism and the Christian Faith*. Grand Rapids: Brazos, 2003.

Karner, Christian and Alan Aldridge. "Theorizing Religion in a Globalizing World." *International Journal of Politics and Culture and Society* 18:1/2 (2004) 5-32.

Keller, Timothy J. *Center Church: Doing Balanced, Gospel-Centered Ministry in Your City*. Grand Rapids: Zondervan, 2012.

Kim, Sukko and Robert A. Margo. "Historical Perspectives on US Economic Geography." Paper prepared for *Handbook of Regional and Urban Economics, Volume 4,* edited by J. Vernon Henderson and Jacques-Francois Thisse. Amsterdam: Elsevier, 2004.

King, Anthony D. *Re-presenting the City: Ethnicity, Capital and Culture in the 21st Century Metropolis*. New York: New York University Press, 1996.

King, Ross. *Kuala Lumpur and Putrajaya: Negotiating Urban Space in Malaysia*. Singapore: Asian Studies Association of Australia, 2008.

Kotkin, Joel. *The City: A Global History*. New York: Modern Library, 2005.

Lander, Christian. "Gentrification." *Stuff White People Like*, February 22, 2008. Online: http://stuffwhitepeoplelike.com/2008/02/22/73-gentrification.

Landry, Charles. *The Creative City: A Toolkit for Urban Innovators*. London: Earthscan, 2008.

Lees, Loretta, et al. *Gentrification*. New York: Routledge, 2007.

LeGates, Richard T. and Frederic Stout. *The City Reader*. New York: Routledge, 2011.

Ley, David. "Christian Faith and the Social Sciences in a Postmodern Age." In *Alive to God: Studies in Spirituality*, edited by J. I. Packer and Loren Wilkinson, 281-282. Grand Rapids: Eerdmans, 1992.

————. "The Inner City." In *Canadian Cities in Transition: Local through Global Perspectives, 3rd Ed.*, edited by Trudi Bunting and Pierre Filion. Don Mills: Oxford University Press, 2006.

————. "The Inner City." In *Canadian Cities in Transition: The Twenty-First Century, 2nd Ed.*, edited by Trudi Bunting and Pierre Filion, 274-302. Don Mills, Ontario: Oxford University Press, 2000.

Linthicum, Robert. *City of God City of Satan: A Biblical Theology of the Urban Church*. Grand Rapids: Zondervan, 1991.

Lloyd, Richard. *Neo-Bohemia: Art and Commerce in the Postindustrial City*. New York: Routledge, 2010.

Loving, Lisa. "Portland Gentrification: The North Williams Avenue That Was–1956." *The Scanner*, August 9, 2011. Online: http://theskanner.com/article/Portland-Gentrification-The-North-Williams-Avenue-That-Was--1956-2011-08-09.

Macdonald, Christopher. "The Vancouver Special Redux." *Canadian Architect*, July 1, 2004. Online: http://www.canadianarchitect.com/news/the-vancouver-special-redux/1000157154/.

Manning, Ivy. "Explore Portland's North William's Avenue." *Sunset Magazine.* Online: http://www.sunset.com/travel/northwest/portland-north-williams-00400000038096/.

———. "Go Green on Portland's North Williams." *Sunset Magazine.* Online: http://www.sunset.com/travel/northwest/portland-day-trip-00400000038083/.

Magnuson, Mike. *Bike Tribes: A Field Guide to North American Cyclists.* New York: Rodale, 2012.

Mapes, Jeff. *Pedaling Revolution: How Cyclists Are Changing American Cities.* Corvallis: Oregon State University Press, 2009.

Markusen, Ann. "Urban Development and the Politics of a Creative Class: Evidence from a Study of Artists." *Environment and Planning A* 38 (2006) 1921-1940.

Martel, Yann. *Life of Pi.* New York: Houghton Mifflin Harcourt, 2007.

Maus, Jonathan. "Meeting on Williams project turns into discussion of race, gentrification." *BikePortland,* July 21, 2011. Online: http://bikeportland.org/2011/07/21/racism-rears-its-head-on-williams-project-56633?utm_source=feedburner&utm_medium=feed&utm_campaign=Feed%3A+BikePortland+%28BikePortland.org%29.

———. "Williams project update: Media, meetings, money, and an end in sight?" *BikePortland,* February 16, 2012. Online: http://bikeportland.org/2012/02/16/williams-project-update-media-meetings-money-and-an-end-in-sight-67381#more-67381.

———. "Spotted: Portland's first 'street seats' - UPDATED." *BikePortland,* August 24, 2012. Online: http://bikeportland.org/2012/08/20/spotted-portlands-first-street-seats-76207.

McAlpine, William R. *Sacred Space for the Missional Church: Engaging Culture through the Built Environment.* Eugene: Wipf and Stock, 2011.

McCracken, Brett. *Hipster Christianity: When Church and Cool Collide.* Grand Rapids: Baker, 2010.

McLaren, Brian. *The Story we Find Ourselves In: Further Adventures of a New Kind of Christian.* San Francisco: Jossey-Bass, 2003.

Medearis, Carl. *Muslims, Christians, and Jesus: Gaining Understanding and Building Relationships.* Minneapolis: Bethany House, 2008.

Media.Ford.com. "Ford Motor Company Key Factor in Arab and Chaldean Migration to Metro Detroit." No pages. Online: http://media.ford.com/article_display.cfm?article_id=3462. Website no longer active.

Mian, Nadia. "'Prophets-for-Profits:' Redevelopment and the Altering Urban Religious Landscape." *Urban Studies* 45:10 (2008) 2143-2161.

Miller, Donald. *Blue Like Jazz: Nonreligious Thoughts on Christian Spirituality.* Nashville: Thomas Nelson, 2003.

Minear, Paul S. "Gratitude and Mission in the Epistle to the Romans." In *The Obedience of Faith: The Purposes of Paul in the Epistle to the Romans*, edited by Paul S. Minear, 106-110. Eugene: Wipf and Stock, 2003.

Mirk, Sarah. "It's Not About the Bikes." *Portland Mercury*, February 16, 2012. Online: http://www.portlandmercury.com/portland/its-not-about-the-bikes/Content?oid=5619639.

Morrill, Richard L. and John Symons, "Efficiency and Equity Aspects of Optimum Location." *Geographical Analysis* 9 (1977) 215-225.

Moses, Balan. *Brickfields: A Place, A Time, A Memory*. Kuala Lumpur: BN Communications, 2007.

Mumford, Lewis. *The City in History: Its Origins, Its Transformations, and Its Prospects*. Orlando: Mariner, 1968.

Murray, Alan T. and Rex Davis. "Equity in Regional Service Provision." *Journal of Regional Science* 41:4 (2001) 557-600.

Navas, Melissa. "North Williams traffic safety plan gives neighbors a chance to delve into deeper issues of race, gentrification." *Oregon Live*, August 11, 2011. Online: http://www.oregonlive.com/portland/index.ssf/2011/08/north_williams_traffic_safety.html.

Nelson, Gary V., et al. *Going Global: A Congregation's Introduction to Mission Beyond Our Borders*. St. Louis: Chalice, 2011.

Newbigin, Lesslie. *Foolishness to the Greeks: The Gospel and Western Culture*. Grand Rapids: Eerdmans, 1987

———. *Truth to Tell: The Gospel as Public Truth*. Grand Rapids: Eerdmans, 1991.

Newman, Peter, et al. *Resilient Cities: Responding to Peak Oil and Climate Change*. Washington, DC: Island, 2009.

Ogden, Greg. *Unfinished Business: Returning the Ministry to the People of God*. Grand Rapids: Zondervan, 2003.

Oldenburg, Ray. *The Great Good Place: Cafes, Coffee Shops, Community Centers, Beauty Parlors, General Stores, Bars, Hangouts, and How They Get You Through the Day*. New York: Paragon, 1998.

Ott, Craig and Harold Netland. *Globalizing Theology: Belief and Practice in an Era of World Christianity*. Grand Rapids: Baker Academic, 2006.

Pein, Corey. "The Other Portland," *Willamette Weekly*, October 12, 2011. Online: http://www.wweek.com/portland/article-18071-the_other_portland.html.

Penzo, Len. "21 Reasons Why Corner Lots Are For Suckers." *Len Penzo do Com*, September 22, 2010. Online: http://lenpenzo.com/blog/id1309-21-reasons-why-corner-lots-are-for-suckers.html.

Petrill, Michael J. "The fastest-gentrifying neighborhoods in the United States." *Thomas Fordham Institute*, June 11, 2012. Online: http://www.edexcellence.net/commentary/education-gadfly-daily/flypaper/2012/the-fastest-gentrifying-neighborhoods-in-the-united-states.html.

Phillips, E. Barbara, *City Lights: Urban-Suburban Life in the Global Society*. New York: Oxford University Press, 2009.

Recinos, H.J. "Racism and Drugs in the City: The Church's Call to Ministry." In *Envisioning the New City: A Reader on Urban Ministry*, edited by Eleanor Scott Meyers, 98-108. Louisville, KY: Westminster/John Knox, 1992.

Rhodes, Brandon. "Where Church Planters Fear to Tread." *Christianity Today*, November 10, 2011. Online: http://www.christianitytoday.com/thisisourcity/portland/plantersfeartrend.html.

Rimmer, Peter J., and Howard Dick. *The City in Southeast Asia: Patterns, Process and Policy*. Honolulu: University of Hawaii Press, 2009.

Robertson, Roland. "Globalization and the Future of 'Traditional Religion.'" In *God and Globalization: Religion and the Powers of the Common Life*, edited by Max Stackhouse and Peter Paris, 53-68. London: T &T Clark, 2000.

Rommelmann, Nancy. "There Goes the Neighborhood: Race, real estate and gentrification on my block." *Willamette Week*, July 4, 2007. Online: http://www.wweek.com/portland/article-7248-there_goes_the_neighborhood.html.

Rosado, Caleb. "Context Determines Content: Quantum Physics as a Framework for 'Wholeness' in Urban Transformation." *Urban Studies* 45:10 (2008) 2075-2076.

Rose, Joseph. "Portland's controversial North Williams bikeway (or whatever it's called) gets $1.47 million from ODOT." *Oregon Live*, March 21, 2013. Online: http://www.oregonlive.com/commuting/index.ssf/2013/03/portlands_controversial_north.html.

Roth, Louise Marie, and Jeffrey C. Kroth. "Risky Business: Assessing Risk Preference Explanations for Gender Differences in Religiosity." *American Sociological Review* 72:2 (2007) 205-220.

Sabri, Soheil, and Ahris Yakuup. "Multi-Criteria Expert Based Analysis for Ranking the Urban Gentrification Drivers in Developing Countries." In *Built Environment in Developing Countries*. Penang: USM, 2008.

Sardar, Ziauddin. *The Consumption of Kuala Lumpur*. London: Reaktion, 2000.

Scott, Aaron. "By the Grace of God," *Portland Monthly*, February 17, 2012. Online: http://www.portlandmonthlymag.com/news-and-profiles/culture/articles/african-american-churches-north-portland-march-2012.

Schreiter, Robert. *The New Catholicity: Globalization and Contextuality*. Maryknoll: Orbis, 1997.

Seguino, Stephanie. "Help or Hindrance? Religion's Impact on Gender Inequality in Attitudes and Outcomes." *World Development* 39:8 (2011) 1308-1321.

Sennett, Richard. *The Fall of Public Man: On the Social Psychology of Capitalism*. New York: Vintage, 1978.

Shaw, R. Daniel. "Beyond Contextualization: Toward a Twenty-first-Century Model for Enabling Mission." *International Bulletin of Missionary Research* 34:4 (2010) 208-215.

Shine, Kim North. "Art is in the air in Dearborn." *metromode*, May 26, 2011. Online: http://metromodemedia.com/devnews/0526dearbornarts0211.aspx.

Slater, Tom. "Gentrification of the City." In *The New Blackwell Companion to the City*, edited by Gary Bridge and Sophie Watson, 571-585. Malden: Blackwell, 2011.

Smith, Andrew. *Events and Urban Regeneration: The Strategic Use of Events to Revitalise Cities*. New York: Routledge, 2012.

Smith, Glenn. "Towards the Transformation of our Cities/Regions." In *Lausanne Occasional Paper No. 37*. Pattaya: Lausanne Committee for World Evangelization, 2004.

————. "Key Indicators of a Transformed City." Paper from Christian Direction website, http://www.direction.ca.

Smith, Neil. "Gentrification, the Frontier, and the Restructuring of Urban Space." In *Readings in Urban Theory*, edited by Susan S. Fainstein and Scott Campbell, 260–277. Malden: Blackwell, 2002.

————. "New Globalism, New Urbanism: Gentrification as Global Urban Strategy." *Antipode* 34:3 (2002) 427–450.

————. "A Short History of Gentrification." In *The Gentrification Debates*, edited by Japonica Brown-Saracino, 31-36. New York: Routledge, 2010.

————. "Building the Frontier Myth." In *The Gentrification Debates*, edited by Japonica Brown-Saracino, 113-117. New York: Routledge, 2010.

Smith, Rob. "This isn't the North Williams Avenue I remember." *Portland Business Journal*, April 3, 2013. Online: http://www.bizjournals.com/portland/blog/real-estate-daily/2013/04/this-isnt-the-north-williams-avenue-i.html.

Smith, Tom W., et al. *General Social Surveys, 1972-2012: Cumulative Codebook*. Chicago: University of Chicago, 2013.

Snyder, Tanya. "Cyclists of Color: Invisible No More." *DC Streets Blog*, May 29, 2013. Online: http://dc.streetsblog.org/2013/05/29/cyclists-of-color-invisible-no-more/.

Squires, Gregory D. "Partnership and the Pursuit of the Private City." In *Readings in Urban Theory*, edited by Susan S. Fainstein and Scott Campbell, 239–259. Malden: Blackwell, 2002.

Stafford, Tim. "This Samaritan Life: How to Live in a Culture that is Vaguely Suspicious of the Church." *Christianity Today* 52:2 (2008). Online: http://www.christianitytoday.com/ct/2008/february/21.47.html.

Stark, Rodney. *Cities of God: The Real Story of How Christianity Became an Urban Movement and Conquered Rome*. San Francisco: Harper San Francisco, 2006.

Stetzer, Ed. *Planting Missional Churches: Planting a Church That's Biblically Sound and Reaching People in Culture*. Nashville: Broadman & Holman, 2006.

Sullivan, Daniel M. Samuel C. Shaw. "Retail gentrification and race: The case of Alberta Street in Portland, Oregon." *Urban Affairs Review* 47:3 (2011) 403-422.

Taylor, Charles. "Defining Globalization." In *The Gospel and the Urban World*, edited by Glenn Smith, II. 9-15. Montréal: Christian Direction, 2007.

Taylor, Marylee C. and Stephen M. Merino. "Race, Religion, and Beliefs about Racial Inequality." *The Annals of the American Academy of Political and Social Science* 634 (2011) 60-77.

The Pew Forum on Religion and Public Life. *U.S. Religious Landscape Survey: Religious Affiliation: Diverse and Dynamic*. Washington, DC: Pew Research Center, 2008.

United Nations High Commissioner for Refugees. Global Trends Report: 800,000 new refugees in 2011, highest this century." Online: http://www.unhcr.org/4fd9e6266.html.

Unruh, Heidi Rolland. "Religious Elements of Church-Based Social Service Programs: Types, Variables and Integrative strategies." *Review of Religious Research* 45:4 (2004) 317-335.

Van Engen, Charles. "Constructing a theology of mission for the city." In *God So Loves the City: Seeking a Theology for Urban Mission*, edited by Charles Van Engen and Jude Tiersma, 241-269. Eugene: Wipf and Stock, 1994.

Visser, Gustav and Nico Kotze. "The State and New-build Gentrification in Central Cape Town, South Africa." *Urban Studies* 45:12 (2008) 2565-2593.

Von der Ruhr, Marc and Joseph P. Daniels. "The Relationship between Religious Affiliation, Region, Race, and Attitudes toward Globalization." *Faith and Economics* 42 (2003) 26-39.

Wagner, C. Peter. *Strategies for Church Growth*. Ventura: Regal Books, 1989.

Ward, Peter M. "Mexico City in an Era of Globalization and Demographic Downturn." In *World Cities Beyond the West: Globalization, Development and Inequality*, edited by Josef Gugler, 151–188. Cambridge: Cambridge University Press, 2004.

Warner, Sam Bass. *The Private City: Philadelphia in Three Periods of Its Growth*. Philadelphia: University of Pennsylvania Press, 1968.

Weber, Max. *Economy and Society: An Outline of Interpretive Sociology*, edited by Guenther Roth Claus Wittich. New York: Bedminster, 1968.

Weintraub, Jeff. "The Theory and Politics of the Public/Private Distinction." In *Public and Private in Thought and Practice*, edited by Jeff Weintraub and Kristan Kamur. Chicago: The Chicago University Press, 1997.

Wilson, William J. "From Institutional to Jobless Ghettos." In *The City Reader*, edited by Richard T. LeGates & Frederic Stout, 117-126. New York: Routledge, 2011.

Wikimedia Foundation Inc. "Alberta Street, Portland, Oregon." *Wikipedia*. Online: http://en.wikipedia.org/wiki/Alberta_Street,_Portland,_Oregon.

_____. "Location Theory." *Wikipedia*. Online: http://en.wikipedia.org/wiki/Location_theory.

_____. "Max Light Rail." *Wikipedia*. Online: http://en.wikipedia.org/wiki/Max_Light_Rail.

_____. "Metropolitan Area." *Wikipedia*. Online: http://en.wikipedia.org/wiki/Metropolitan_area.

_____. "Portland, Oregon." *Wikipedia*. Online: http://en.wikipedia.org/wiki/Portland,_Oregon.

_____. Portland Streetcar." *Wikipedia*. Online: http://en.wikipedia.org/wiki/Portland_Streetcar

Wong, King Wai. "A Heart for the Poor." *Asian Beacon*, August 2, 2013. Online: http://www.asianbeacon.org/a-heart-for-the-poor/.

Wordnet. "Gentrification." Online: http://wordnetweb.princeton.edu/perl/webwn?s=gentrification.

Wright, N.T. *The New Testament and the People of God: Christian Origins and the Question of God, Vol. 1*. Minneapolis: Fortress, 1992.

_____. "Jesus and the Identity of God." Online: http://ntwrightpage.com/wright_jig.htm.

Yeoh, Tricia. "Not Easy Housing Malaysians." *Penang Monthly*, August 24, 2012. Online: http://penangmonthly.com/not-easy-housing-malaysians/.

Zukin, Sharon. "Whose Culture? Whose City." In *The Urban Sociology Reader*, edited by Jan Lin and Christopher Mele, 281-289. New York: Routledge, 2012.

_____. "The Creation of a 'Loft Lifestyle.'" In *The Gentrification Debates*, edited by Japonica Brown-Saracino, 175-184. New York: Routledge, 2010.

_____. *Naked City The Death and Life of Authentic Urban Places*. New York: Oxford University Press, 2011.

About the Editor

Sean Benesh (DMin, Bakke Graduate University) lives in the Portland, Oregon and is the author of *The Urbanity of the Bible*, *The Bikeable Church*, *The Multi-Nucleated Church*, *View From the Urban Loft*, and *Metrospiritual*. He has been involved in urban ministry in the capacity of adjunct professor, researcher, church planter, and trainer of urban church planters. Currently Sean is the Developer of Urban Strategy and Training for TEAM (The Evangelical Alliance Mission) and Director of the PDX Loft.

Author Website: www.seanbenesh.com
Facebook Author Page: www.facebook.com/SeanAllenBenesh
Twitter: @mtbikerguy

About ULP

Urban Loft Publishers focuses on ideas, topics, themes, and conversations about all things urban. Renewing the city is the central theme and focus of what we publish. It is our intention to blend urban ministry, theology, urban planning, architecture, urbanism, stories, and the social sciences, as ways to drive the conversation. While we lean towards scholarly and academic works, we explore the fun and lighter sides of cities as well. We publish a wide variety of urban perspectives, from books by the experts *about* the city to personal stories and personal accounts of urbanites who *live* in the city.

www.theurbanloft.org
@the_urban_loft

Made in the USA
San Bernardino, CA
23 February 2014